The Salt Lake Temple

The Salt Lake Temple

SCOTT D. MARIANNO
AND
REID L. NEILSON

OXFORD
UNIVERSITY PRESS

Oxford University Press is a department of the University of Oxford.
It furthers the University's objective of excellence in research, scholarship,
and education by publishing worldwide. Oxford is a registered trade mark of
Oxford University Press in the UK and in certain other countries.

Published in the United States of America by Oxford University Press
198 Madison Avenue, New York, NY 10016, United States of America.

© Oxford University Press 2025

All rights reserved. No part of this publication may be reproduced, stored in a retrieval system,
transmitted, used for text and data mining, or used for training artificial intelligence, in any form or
by any means, without the prior permission in writing of Oxford University Press, or as expressly
permitted by law, by license or under terms agreed with the appropriate reprographics rights
organization. Inquiries concerning reproduction outside the scope of the above should be sent
to the Rights Department, Oxford University Press, at the address above.

You must not circulate this work in any other form
and you must impose this same condition on any acquirer.

CIP data is on file at the Library of Congress

ISBN 9780190881559

DOI: 10.1093/9780190881580.001.0001

Printed by Sheridan Books, Inc., United States of America

The manufacturer's authorized representative in the EU for product safety is
Oxford University Press España S.A., Parque Empresarial San Fernando de Henares,
Avenida de Castilla, 2 – 28830 Madrid (www.oup.es/en or product.safety@oup.com).
OUP España S.A. also acts as importer into Spain of products made by the manufacturer.

Contents

List of Illustrations	vii
Acknowledgments	ix
Introduction	1
1. Imagined Place	7
2. Center Place	25
3. Developing Place	47
4. Contested Place	65
5. Dedicated Place	88
6. Public Place	108
7. Administrative Place	124
8. Political Place	139
9. Commemorative Place	150
10. Media Place	165
Notes	187
Bibliography	213
Index	227

Illustrations

2.1	Salt Lake Temple groundbreaking, 1853.	26
2.2	Truman O. Angell architectural sketch, 1854.	34
3.1	Salt Lake Temple Block, 1863.	49
3.2	Little Cottonwood Canyon quarry, 1871.	53
3.3	Salt Lake Temple Block, 1875.	56
3.4	Salt Lake Temple, 1879.	57
4.1	William Ward drawing, 1855.	78
4.2	Salt Lake Temple, 1890.	82
4.3	World Room, Salt Lake Temple, 1911.	84
4.4	Salt Lake Temple capstone ceremony, 1892.	85
5.1	Salt Lake Temple dedication ticket, 1893.	96
5.2	Latter-day Saints traveling to Salt Lake Temple dedication, 1893.	97
6.1	Temple Block, 1910.	110
7.1	Council Room of the First Presidency and the Quorum of the Twelve Apostles, Salt Lake Temple, 1911.	131
7.2	Assembly Room, Salt Lake Temple, 1911.	132

Acknowledgments

Our careers as historians overlapped for many years at the Church History Library of The Church of Jesus Christ of Latter-day Saints in Salt Lake City, Utah. We began this history of the Salt Lake Temple while working there, across the street from Temple Square. We are grateful for the support of the Church Historian and Recorders as well as the Assistant Executive Directors of the Church History Department, including Elders Steven E. Snow, J. Devn Cornish, LeGrand R. Curtis Jr., and Kyle S. McKay. A number of our Church History Library colleagues helped prepare or review portions of this manuscript, especially Claire M. Haynie and Carson V. Teuscher. We are also grateful for the following religious historians and historic sites professionals who read the manuscript and provided helpful feedback: Richard E. Bennett, Elder LeGrand R. Curtis Jr., Keith A. Erekson, Matthew J. Grow, Jennifer L. Lund, Brandon J. Metcalf, Josh E. Probert, Jacob W. Olmstead, and Emily Utt. Outside editor Alison Palmer helped shape the book's content and improved our prose and Devery S. Anderson meticulously and expertly prepared the index for our book. But we are responsible for the volume's interpretation and any errors.

Our professional associates provided helpful guidance and access to primary source documents and secondary research along the way. The librarians, archivists, and professional staffs of the L. Tom Perry Special Collections, the Utah Valley Regional Family History Center and the Harold B. Lee Library at Brigham Young University, the Church History Library and the Family History Library at The Church of Jesus Christ of Latter-day Saints, the Special Collections and the J. Willard Marriott Library at the University of Utah, the Special Collections and Archives at Utah State University, and the Research Library and Collections at the Utah Historical Society are to be thanked for their remarkable assistance.

As we researched this material on the Salt Lake Temple, Scott was able to present our evolving ideas at a number of academic conferences and historical gatherings, including the annual regional meeting of the American Academy of Religion in Provo, Utah, in 2018; the annual meeting of the Mormon History Association in Salt Lake City in 2019; and the annual

X ACKNOWLEDGMENTS

meeting of the Mormon History Association in Rochester, New York, in 2023. We are grateful for the support of our colleagues and friends who have allowed us to share our working drafts in the various venues.

Together we previously edited and published *A Voice in the Wilderness: The 1888–1930 General Conference Sermons of Mormon Historian Andrew Jenson* with Oxford University Press (2018). We did this under the direction of then–executive editor Cynthia Read, who oversaw their religion book list for many years. She kindly recommended us for this current book project, for which we are very thankful. We are also grateful for the opportunity to work with the Oxford University Press team members, including Drew Anderla, Meredith Taylor, and Steve A. Wiggins. All of these publishing professionals have been delightful to work with and learn from during this project.

Finally, Scott dedicates this book to his mentors in the field of history: J. Spencer Fluhman, who introduced him to the world of Latter-day Saint history at Brigham Young University and to whom he owes his passion and love for the field; Philip L. Barlow, who adopted him in a graduate program at Utah State University and encouraged him to explore themes far and wide in his studies; and Reid L. Neilson, who mentored him as a young professional and welcomed him as a friend. Scott is also grateful for the continued support and encouragement of Kelli, his spouse, who bore the brunt of late nights of writing and a head continuously distracted by the ideas that naturally circulate during the research and writing process. Her grace and enthusiasm have fostered many other cheerleaders of his work.

Reid dedicates this book to Elder Clark G. Gilbert, the Commissioner of the Church Educational System, for facilitating his return to Brigham Young University in Provo. There he started a new chapter in his career as the Assistant Academic Vice President of Religious Scholarly Publications following his leadership service in the Washington DC North Mission. He is also grateful for his wife, Shelly, who continues to support him as a historian and who smiles at each new book project idea. And for his children Johnny, Kate, Ally, Whitney, and James who make being a dad a delight.

Introduction

Allie Pond was in her twenties when she entered the Salt Lake Temple in Utah alone. She remained there until the last temple workers had departed for the night and the building fell still. She had come to visit her grandfather, Lorenzo, who kept an office on the temple's upper floor. A diminutive build and long white beard rendered the stately man instantly recognizable. He was in his late eighties, but he moved unaided down the empty corridors of the temple, where he passed many midnight hours in contemplation and administrative work. His face displayed the maturing effects of time and hard experience.

Lorenzo Snow, the fifth prophet and president of The Church of Jesus Christ of Latter-day Saints (hereafter "the church"), personally knew Joseph Smith (1805–1844), the founding prophet and leader of the American-born restoration faith to which Snow had given much of his life. Yet the church, now nestled safely on the western edge of the Rocky Mountains, found itself far removed from upstate New York, where it had started nearly seventy years earlier. As Snow walked the quiet halls of the temple with his granddaughter, he brimmed with a lifetime of experience, heartache, and memories. Snow could have told his granddaughter in their private moment of the pivotal events in early Latter-day Saint history he had witnessed; however, he chose to share a single memory, stirred by his immediate location near the "celestial" room on the temple's second floor.

The ornate walls, trimmed in wood and furnished in a grand Victorian style, transported Snow back a few years, to a time he had come to the temple to pray. On that warm evening in early September 1898, Snow felt the weight of the entire church upon him. Only hours before, he had been walking the streets of Brigham City, fifty miles north of Salt Lake City, when a telegram notified him of the death of church president Wilford Woodruff (1807–1898), the leader who had finally seen the completion of the Salt Lake Temple after forty years of construction. Snow, as senior member of the Quorum of the Twelve Apostles, the second-highest governing body in the church, was the

The Salt Lake Temple. Scott D. Marianno and Reid L. Neilson, Oxford University Press.
© Oxford University Press 2025. DOI: 10.1093/9780190881580.003.0001

2 THE SALT LAKE TEMPLE

anticipated successor to Woodruff. Snow immediately returned to Salt Lake City and entered the temple. He ascended an interior staircase and retired to a circular room later referred to by Apostle James E. Talmage as the Holy of Holies, a special room "reserved for the higher ordinances in the Priesthood related to the exaltation of both living and dead."[1] While praying, he knelt near a stained-glass depiction of Joseph Smith's First Vision, a divine manifestation of God and Jesus Christ to the fourteen-year-old Smith in 1820, an event that sparked Smith's quest to reestablish Christ's church. "I have not sought this responsibility," Snow prayed, "but if it be Thy will, I now present myself before Thee for Thy guidance and instruction."[2] Snow would never publicly share the details of what followed this supplication in the same way he did with Allie that night. According to his granddaughter's own memory, the prophet-to-be received a vision.

As they walked the temple hallway together, Snow told his granddaughter that in response to his prayer in the temple, Jesus Christ had appeared to him. At the same spot in the temple corridor where he and Allie then stood, Christ had come in "such a glory of whiteness and brightness that he could hardly gaze upon Him." Snow described the resurrected Christ's "hands, feet, countenance and beautiful white robes" as well as his message. "He instructed me to go right ahead and reorganize the First Presidency of the Church at once and not wait," a move that departed from the indefinite pauses that occurred before the reorganization of the church's highest governing body after the death of each of the previous church presidents.[3]

The financial indebtedness of the church may have also been a motivating factor in the quick reorganization of the First Presidency. Furthermore, Woodruff had similarly expressed hopes that a new president would be installed without delay. Snow obeyed the instructions he received. Only two weeks after Woodruff's death, the Quorum of the Twelve Apostles approved Snow as church president in the Salt Lake Temple. He, in turn, selected George Q. Cannon and Joseph F. Smith as his counselors in the new First Presidency. At that same meeting, Snow disclosed to the church leaders present that in an answer to his prayer, the Lord had revealed "to him that the First Presidency should be organized, and who his counselors should be."[4] Apparently, he did not tell them of his vision of Jesus Christ in the Salt Lake Temple—the story instead became Allie's to tell.

Allie told others of her unique visit with her grandfather and reportedly wrote down her recollection shortly after their meeting occurred. However, no account of the vision directly from Allie (or Lorenzo) survives.[5] Instead,

INTRODUCTION   3

the primary account for the vision comes from Lorenzo Snow's son LeRoi C. Snow, who recorded his niece's memory of the event three decades after the vision had occurred.[6] Church leaders searched for documentary proof in the 1940s, after Allie's death, but turned up little beyond memories from some who had heard Allie's retellings of the vision. Still, there was little doubt in their minds that the vision had occurred.[7]

Although never canonized as official scripture, LeRoi Snow's published account planted his father's previously little-known vision within the collective memory of Latter-day Saints. To be sure, the vision did not acquire the same cultural and theological significance as Joseph Smith's First Vision of God and Christ in 1820; by the twentieth century, Latter-day Saints knew the heavens were open to them and that God, and Christ, could, if they so desired, selectively manifest themselves in sacred settings. However, in the decades that followed the vision, the church circulated LeRoi Snow's account of his father's temple experience in formal publications and videos.[8] Patrons who entered the Salt Lake Temple also made quiet and informal pilgrimages to the corridor near the celestial room to stand in the place where Jesus Christ was said to have appeared.

Determining the reality of Snow's vision in the Salt Lake Temple is beyond the scope of historical inquiry, but Latter-day Saints certainly believed Christ actually could—and even would—come and visit their temple. Indeed, one of the very purposes of building the Salt Lake Temple, according to the church's second president, Brigham Young (1801–1877), was to welcome divine presence—to give Christ a "place where he can lay his head."[9] Though Snow's vision was, in essence, personal, its subsequent devotional use by Latter-day Saints rendered it communal. Since Joseph Smith's initial First Vision, Latter-day Saints looked for confirmation of the continued appearance of God and Christ to their prophets. This narrative of Celestial presence was celebrated and shared, serving as evidence of the church's divine authority and authenticity.

This search for God's presence in a sacred space began early in the church's history and is fundamental to the Salt Lake Temple's identity. Joseph Smith sought to create a sacred place and the ideal religious society—called Zion—as early as 1831. As he gathered converts, observers feared the growth of a Latter-day Saint religious empire, a dangerous combination of church and state in a disestablished and pluralistic American society. Smith's own term for the ideal system that would govern a literal kingdom of God was "theodemocracy," a blending of God-fearing prophetic rule with the

4   THE SALT LAKE TEMPLE

democratic principles of antebellum America.[10] Smith's Nauvoo, Illinois, Council of Fifty, a private organization intent on establishing a new divine political kingdom on earth, even searched for a geographical location that would allow the church's merged religious and political hopes to fully blossom. Though Smith was murdered in 1844, before his religiopolitical project fully got off the ground,[11] the search for a protected place—a kingdom—was deeply rooted in the Latter-day Saint movement. Sacred space and political kingdom were closely linked in Latter-day Saint minds.

The centerpieces of Smith's utopian vision of Zion were temples, or houses of the Lord. They were at the center of three religious settlements planned by Smith, though only two of the temples—one in Kirtland, Ohio, and one in Nauvoo, Illinois—were actually built. The other was planned for Zion's "center place," in Independence, Missouri, but was never started.[12] The temples demarcated Latter-day Saint settlements from the secular world, giving form to Smith's aspiration to build a holy society. What began as a community meeting place transformed as Smith introduced new temple rituals like endowments and sealings toward the end of his life. Temple practice offered a significant revision to earlier scripture and church teachings on heaven and eternity. Initiates in the endowment ritual progressed through a ceremony that symbolically prepared them to enter the presence of God. They could then be sealed to their spouses in eternal marriage or adopted into expansive eternal, kinship networks.[13] In many respects, eternity as envisioned by early Latter-day Saints mirrored their physical, tight-knit communities and present sociality. They were, in other words, building earthly relationships to organize their heavens.

As the Latter-day Saint notion of temple expanded to include exclusive rituals, their temples became closed to initiates only. The rituals performed inside the temple enhance the sacredness of the space for participants. To protect the rituals' sanctity, the church, as a result, places clear boundaries around the temple, prohibiting unworthy church members and inquisitive outsiders from entering. Thus the estimated 5 million tourists who descend on Salt Lake City yearly to see the temple (unless they are initiated Latter-day Saints) remain outside its walls. Latter-day Saint temple rites, initially a strictly oral tradition, are highly liturgical, not unlike the Eastern Orthodox Christian tradition or elements of Catholicism, and the oaths and ceremonies are administered only within a dedicated temple. Unlike some of the popular shrines, temples, and holy spaces of Hinduism, Buddhism, Catholicism, and other world religions, the Salt Lake Temple and its surrounding square do not re-create for tourists the actual religious experience of devotees. While the exclusive nature of Latter-day Saint temple worship adds to the overall mystique of the Salt Lake Temple for the general public, the restrictions help differentiate sacred space from profane space for Latter-day Saints.

This is the story of a temple that sits prominently at the center of a complex and evolving religious ecosystem. Because the Salt Lake Temple cannot be understood apart from the people who built it and continue to use it, this book accounts for sacred space as "not merely discovered, or founded, or constructed" but as "claimed, owned, and operated by people advancing specific interests."[14] Religious intentions and experiences in sacred spaces can vary and change, as can the resulting power dynamics and meanings created in sacred space. These spaces are thus inherently dynamic.[15] The cultural significance and meaning of the Salt Lake Temple are dependent on human contexts, social and political forces, actual religious experience, and evolving beliefs and practices. Readers must dispense with the notion of a stone building as static, unchanging, and inanimate. This book positions the Salt Lake Temple not as a passive observer of the development and growth of the church but as a main player in that story. How did the Salt Lake Temple shape the religious system it protected? How did the temple serve as an agent for change within the church and as a powerful symbol of the collective image of the Latter-day Saints?

The following pages present a social and intellectual rather than an architectural history of the Salt Lake Temple. Useful histories have been published on the construction of the Salt Lake Temple, and more inevitably will be written with the renewed public interest in the temple since its closure in December 2019 for a major renovation.[16] While many of the existing histories of the temple end in April 1893, when the building was finished and dedicated,[17] this history proceeds chronologically to the present day. Each chapter also highlights a different function the temple performed for the people that interacted with the place, laying bare the abundant and multifaceted nature of sacred space. In some cases, the function and meaning derived from the temple span its existence; in others, the meaning ebbs and flows within the politics and culture of a particular time. The functional structure of the book is not comprehensive but merely a launching point for exploring the varied meanings of place for a growing and evolving religion.

With this broadened perspective, the Salt Lake Temple's cultural role and significance multiply. Beyond just a place that hosts temple ritual, the Salt Lake Temple is a repository for the Latter-day Saint people's hopes and

6   THE SALT LAKE TEMPLE

anxieties. The temple materialized from the church's long and contentious search for a literal kingdom and eventually provided belonging, protection, and eternal connectedness. Its construction was influenced by Joseph Smith's introduction of temples and sacred rituals, as well as Brigham Young's ceaseless desire to establish a permanent priesthood hierarchy, guarded and preserved by geography and politics.

The Salt Lake Temple also developed from the Latter-day Saints' quest to house the literal presence of God and to receive frequent divine revelations. More objectives developed over time, and the temple grew into a cultural symbol, an icon of an entire people, and the heartbeat of a now global faith. The Salt Lake Temple remains simultaneously a place of institutional pilgrimage, church administration, missionary proselytizing, and historic preservation—all connected to the church's public image. The religious expressions of the Latter-day Saint people are as much a part of the temple as the granite harvested from Utah's mountains.

Just weeks before the dedication of the Salt Lake Temple in April 1893, church president Wilford Woodruff invited the entire church to fast and repent in preparation for its opening. Forty years of "unceasing toil, undiminished patience and ungrudging expenditure of means" by Latter-day Saints had finally led to the temple's completion. The Salt Lake Temple would be, by Woodruff's declaration, the "Temple of Temples."[18] Latter-day Saints in 1893, who had collectively dedicated decades of time to building the temple, celebrated such a declaration. But even today, with over three hundred and fifty Latter-day Saint temples completed or announced worldwide, Woodruff's words still resonate for a global church membership of over 17 million people.[19] What follows is the story of how a wilderness temple project ultimately became the supreme sacred space and iconic symbol of the modern Latter-day Saint people.

1

Imagined Place

In the spring of 1846, thousands of Latter-day Saints abandoned their homes in Nauvoo, Illinois, to head to the Iowa frontier because of rising tensions with the surrounding citizens. William Clayton was one Latter-day Saint who found himself on the frontier, poorly provisioned and without Diantha, one of his plural wives.[1] She remained behind, too far along in her pregnancy to safely make the late winter journey out of the city. News soon reached Clayton that Diantha had given birth to a healthy son. Overwhelmed with relief and gratitude, he penned the now popular Latter-day Saint pioneer anthem, a few lines of which underscored the Saints' longing as refugees to find a place of safety:

> We'll find the place which God for us prepared,
> Far away in the West,
> Where none shall come to hurt or make afraid;
> There the Saints will be blessed.[2]

The search for place was the errand and pilgrimage of the early members of The Church of Jesus Christ of Latter-day Saints. Violent local opposition compelled them to abandon their settlements of Independence, Missouri; Kirtland, Ohio; and Nauvoo, Illinois. Like the Israelites of ancient times, their religious experience was largely one of displacement. Revelations from their prophet, Joseph Smith, had urged the Saints to construct temples, also called "houses of the Lord," in each of these locations, while later persecution sealed the temples' abandonment. The communal project of building sacred temples informed their quest for place. Smith, who was murdered in Carthage, Illinois, in June 1844, had left the Saints an inheritance of temple theology and ritual. During his life, he had received and distributed the divine authority to perform ordinances—religious rites conducted by priesthood authority that forge covenants between God and man—inside and outside the temple. The offering of ordinances had expanded significantly since the early days of the church, from baptism and the sacrament to a

The Salt Lake Temple. Scott D. Marianno and Reid L. Neilson, Oxford University Press.
© Oxford University Press 2025. DOI: 10.1093/9780190881580.003.0002

8 THE SALT LAKE TEMPLE

new and expansive system of teachings and rituals in the temple that promised to ensure the salvation of humankind. Smith had also inspired a select number of church members with his related vision of an earthly kingdom of God to unite and protect his followers. In order to build that kingdom, Smith initiated a new search for territory in the West before his death.[3]

As president of the Quorum of the Twelve Apostles, Brigham Young inherited the pieces of Smith's unfinished vision and began to search for a settlement site in the West. Young shared with church leaders a vision he had received in the Nauvoo Temple of the precise location for their new settlement. As recounted by Apostle George A. Smith in 1869, Joseph Smith appeared posthumously and "showed [Young] the mountain . . . immediately north of Salt Lake City, and there was an ensign [banner] fell upon that peak, and Joseph said, 'Build under the point where the colors fall and you will prosper and have peace.'"[4] According to another individual who heard Young's retelling of the vision, Smith showed Young the spot where a temple would be built. "The house of the Lord" would "be reared in the Tops of the Mountains & the Proud Banner of liberty wave over the valleys that are within the mountains," Young declared. "I know where the spot is & I [k]no[w] how to make the Flag."[5] Not just any spot would do for a new temple in the West. Young retained a specific place in mind that was designated as the sacred site for the temple.

As they continued to develop their unique temple theology, the Latter-day Saints poured into it their still emerging notions of ritual as well as their anxieties, hopes, and ambitions about finding permanence for their minority religion within an inhospitable religious and cultural landscape.

Zion and the Origins of Latter-day Saint Temples

The Book of Mormon, the foundational text of The Church of Jesus Christ of Latter-day Saints, signaled to Latter-day Saints their distinctiveness in America's religious landscape, but also stoked the millenarian imaginations of their leaders, specifically the notion of a dedicated sacred place for God's people. According to the Book of Mormon, the American continent would play a vital role in the events leading up to the millennial reign of Jesus Christ and thus be a promised land for the faithful. The book culminates in the final destruction of the Nephite people, its primary characters, but predicts the redemption of the descendants of the book's chief antagonists,

IMAGINED PLACE 9

the Lamanites, and the return of God's chosen people to a latter-day New Jerusalem. The Book of Mormon prophet Ether spoke of "a New Jerusalem upon [the Americas] . . . a holy city unto the Lord" that would "be built unto the house of Israel . . . like unto the Jerusalem of old" (Ether 13:4–8). The Ether prophecy appeared routinely in early church publications, suggesting that construction of a "holy city" captivated Joseph Smith early in his project of restoring the fullness of the gospel of Jesus Christ.[6] Smith was not content simply inhabiting an American landscape with a providential destiny. He worked to demarcate Latter-day Saint space from the secular by building a central temple.

The Book of Mormon was not the only inspiration for Smith's vision of a distinctive sacred space. Shortly after establishing the church in April 1830, Smith began his own revision of the Bible. In December of that year, inspired by his revision of Genesis, he significantly expanded the biblical text surrounding the prophet Enoch, narrating Enoch's efforts to construct "a City that was called the City of holiness even Zion." The expanded text also articulated the principles of a Zion-like society, in which a unified people eliminated poverty.[7] As Smith's utopian vision of Zion began to take shape, he began to develop a temple theology. In the same month, he dictated a revelation promising the swift return of Jesus Christ. "I am Jesus Christ, the Son of God," the December 1830 revelation declared, "wherefore, gird up your loins and I will suddenly come to my temple" (D&C 36:8). Smith soon issued Latter-day Saints their millennial errand of establishing Zion, with a temple at its center.

In July 1831, a revelation to Smith declared Independence in Jackson County, Missouri, on the outskirts of the American frontier, as the "center place" of Zion and the "spot" where a temple would be constructed (see D&C 57). The parallels between ancient Israel and Smith's growing band of believers became more pronounced over time in his revelations. In Missouri, a "New Jerusalem" would be "built unto the Lord," Smith said in a revelation that echoed Old Testament texts, "at the place of the temple . . . and a cloud shall rest upon it, which cloud shall be even the glory of the Lord" (D&C 84:4–5). Smith also instituted a law of consecration, which, through covenant, bound the Latter-day Saints in a communal economic arrangement that would eradicate poverty in the new Israel.

By 1833, church leaders had planned their "City of Zion," a sprawling 1.5-square-mile urban center, large enough to accommodate fifteen thousand people across twenty-six hundred lots.[8] As the distinctive centerpiece of the

10 THE SALT LAKE TEMPLE

city, twenty-four temples would fill two central blocks. Smith, with the assistance of a few of his trusted disciples, had creatively co-opted traditional American urban planning and imagined a space where commercial, agrarian, and social interests would all converge around a temple complex set aside for worship. The complex would also serve as an administrative center for Smith's developing conceptions of ecclesiastical authority, or priesthood.[9]

Establishing this independent Zion within the borders of the United States, however, proved a more challenging task than Smith had originally envisioned. The Saints never moved past laying the first temple cornerstone because persecutions in Jackson County throughout the latter half of 1833 forced them to abandon their communal Zion. However, the idea of orienting a Zion community around a temple left an imprint that influenced the planning of other Latter-day Saint settlements.

Though the plan to build temples in Missouri never came to fruition, Joseph Smith's vision of the House of the Lord eventually found physical form in Kirtland, Ohio. In December 1832, he delivered a revelation that intended to "establish a house" in Kirtland, "even a house of prayer . . . a house of learning, a house of glory, a house of order, a house of God" (D&C 88:119). The church Smith had started, however, was still new and impoverished, so no progress on the temple was made until a June 1833 revelation rebuked the Saints: "Ye have not considered the great commandment in all things, that I have given unto you concerning the building of mine house" (D&C 95:3). The slow progress in building the temple also may have been a result of church members' limited understanding about what the temple was for. Though Latter-day Saints were still intent on constructing a formal meeting place, up to that point no temple rituals had been revealed to them which might further justify building such a structure. Latter-day Saints understood temples to be residences for the presence of Deity, a notion they could discern from scripture, but they still lacked an understanding of the precise function their temples would serve. With the June 1833 revelation, Smith's followers were for the first time given an explicit reason for constructing a House of the Lord: the promise of a broad outpouring of spiritual gifts and experiences, an endowment of "power from on high" for those who were "chosen" (D&C 95:8).

This promised endowment of spiritual power set the wheels of temple construction in motion. Further construction details followed in a revelation (see D&C 95). Construction on the temple began in earnest in June 1833 and continued over the next three years, despite major financial challenges.

(The temple cost over forty thousand dollars—approximately two million in today's dollars.)[10] The finished temple in Kirtland, at two and a half stories, was made of plaster and rubble stone with a sandstone foundation; its exterior resembled that of some of the Protestant chapels that dotted the church's former New England home and the chapels in the surrounding Ohio communities, but Smith's still-developing temple theology, introduced and displayed in the temple's interior, brought distinctiveness to the structure. Reprising themes from the plan for the city of Zion in Missouri, the layout of the temple reinforced the centrality of priesthood authority; tiered pulpits on the lower level were designed to seat the presidencies of the Aaronic and Melchizedek Priesthoods. The remainder of the first-floor assembly hall consisted of pews.[11] The design reflected the multipurpose nature of Smith's original vision for the temple complex in Missouri as a sacred space that could serve both a religious and an administrative function.[12]

The House of the Lord in Kirtland gave Latter-day Saint spiritual power a new sacred home, one with particular implications for Latter-day Saints who had received the movement's priesthood, which the Saints believed was the authority and power of God. Joseph Smith had already distributed priesthood authority, allowing worthy men to be ordained to the priesthood beginning in 1831. (No specialized training or other credentials were required.) But he also centralized priesthood authority in 1833 when he organized a presidency of the high priesthood (later called the First Presidency), consisting of himself at the head with two counselors, and again in 1835 with the calling of twelve apostles, who were to help the First Presidency in administering the church. In establishing "the Holy Priesthood, after the Order of the Son of God," Smith told his apostles, "The order of the house of God has and ever will be the same, even after Christ comes. . . . [Y]ou need an endowment brethren in order that you may be prepared and able to overcome all things, and those that reject your testimony will be damned. [T]he sick will be healed the lame made to walk the deaf to hear and the blind to see through your instrumentality."[13] In other words, the endowment of power mentioned in this instruction was meant to help prepare men ordained to the priesthood to take the gospel to the world through evangelism. Charismatic expressions, such as healing, speaking in tongues, and prophesying, would also be inspired by the development of new temple space.

Before the temple was finished, Smith guided those ordained to the priesthood through a series of ordinances in the building's completed attic. These washings and anointings prepared the priesthood holders for the final

12   THE SALT LAKE TEMPLE

endowment of power that would come later (though not in Kirtland). The temple's spiritual outpouring reached its culmination at the temple's dedicatory services in March 1836, where attendees reported a Pentecostal-like abundance of spiritual gifts, including visions and speaking in tongues.[14]

Aside from the washings and anointings, no other formal ritual developed in association with the House of the Lord in Kirtland, but the temple became the site of heavenly visitations that pointed to future ritual developments. According to Smith and fellow church leader Oliver Cowdery, the pair were in the temple a week after its dedication when they saw Jesus Christ. "I have accepted of this house, and my name shall be here," Smith and Cowdery were told. "I will manifest myself to my people in mercy in this house" (D&C 110:7). Three other heavenly visitors, biblical figures Moses, Elias, and Elijah, also appeared in the temple to pass on important priesthood authority and messages. The ancient prophet Elijah conferred authority to Smith with the promise that he would "turn the hearts of the Fathers to the children, and the children to the fathers." In Nauvoo, Smith introduced new temple ordinances under the mission and authority he received from Elijah's visit.[15] Years passed before Smith and Cowdery's vision became widely known, but it became a source of authority for the later routinization of temple ritual started in Nauvoo. In the meantime, Smith's experiences in the House of the Lord emboldened his temple-building project.

Despite the heightened spirituality and miraculous experiences brought on by the movement's new sacred space, a tragic sense of loss soon formed a major part of the church's collective temple consciousness. By 1837, after a nationwide financial panic and the failure of a church-sponsored joint cooperative bank, rising opposition from within and without forced the church out of Kirtland. The temple was largely abandoned, and the church entered a brief period without any temples as the Saints gathered to Far West, Missouri, northeast of their former settlement in Independence. Still, they intended to build new temples.[16] Their stay in Missouri was brief, and persecutions, as well as the imprisonment of Smith and other leaders, forced another mass migration eastward, eventually to a marshy site along the Mississippi River, fifty miles north of Quincy, Illinois.

In December 1840, the Illinois General Assembly approved a charter to incorporate the city of Nauvoo, the Latter-day Saints' new settlement on the old town site of Commerce. The charter conferred liberal (though not unprecedented) power on church leaders to govern their new city and to create a city militia. Joseph Smith hoped such power would help create a refuge where all

Saints could safely gather. Emboldened by the city's new legal status, Smith received a revelation a month later that declared a temple was to be built in Nauvoo. Through the temple, Smith was told, God intended to "reveal unto [his] church things which have been kept hid from before the foundation of the world, things that pertain to the dispensation of the fullness of times" (D&C 124:41). Three months later, construction on the Nauvoo Temple commenced and church members were asked to donate their labor and resources as a tithe to expedite the project. Meanwhile, Latter-day Saints continued to gather to Nauvoo; the population expanded to over four thousand by 1842.[17]

Latter-day Saint women had contributed labor and material to the construction of the House of the Lord in Kirtland and attended meetings held therein, but they had not yet been invited to participate in temple rituals. Smith's temple theology, however, moved in new and creative directions in Nauvoo, with significant consequences for Latter-day Saint social relationships. The House of the Lord in Kirtland had functioned as both a community center and a worship site, the social space around which the community was oriented. As Smith expanded and introduced new rituals, however, the temple took on greater significance, becoming the center of the Latter-day Saint vision of the eternities and enhancing the role family and social connections played in salvation.

This new theology developed around sacred ordinances introduced outside the uncompleted temple. In 1840, Smith announced ordinances to be performed on behalf of those who had died, giving Latter-day Saints' deceased loved ones access to the ordinances necessary for salvation if they repented and accepted the gospel in the afterlife. As Smith explained, the ordinances recorded on earth would also be recorded and efficacious in heaven (D&C 127:7–8). At this time, Smith specifically spoke of baptism, declaring that Latter-day Saints could be baptized for "their friends who had departed this life."[18] Church members in Nauvoo began performing baptisms for their deceased friends and relatives in earnest in the nearby Mississippi River. Later, Smith halted these vicarious ordinances until they could be done in the temple.[19]

New ordinances also situated the Latter-day Saints within a sacred narrative with a distinctive past, present, and future.[20] Liturgy associated with a new ordinance that was eventually called the endowment used storytelling and ritual to move participants through a series of epochs, beginning with the creation of the world, transitioning into the Garden of Eden, and

14   THE SALT LAKE TEMPLE

culminating in their entrance into the Celestial realm, the highest degree of salvation obtainable. The process mirrored Joseph Smith's earlier teachings on a tiered system in heaven with the Celestial Kingdom housing individuals who obtained the full exalted glory available and would dwell in the presence of God for eternity (see D&C 76, D&C 137). The ceremony included ritual washings and anointings in preparation for a procession through successive stages in which participants learned about the laws of God and vocalized their consent to new covenants while learning symbolic truths that carried promises of spiritual power.

Smith transmitted the new ceremony orally to initiates beginning in May 1842 in the upper floor of his red brick store. He first revealed the endowment ordinance to a select group of nine men, instructing them in "the principles and order of the . . . Aaronic Priesthood, and so on to the highest order of Melchisedec Priesthood, setting forth the order pertaining to the Ancient of Days, and all those plans and principles by which any one is enabled to secure the fullness of those blessings which have been prepared for the Church of the first born, and come up and abide in the presence of the Eloheim in the eternal worlds."[21] Only months before, Smith had joined the fraternal Masonic lodge in Nauvoo. The performance of the endowment ceremony combined biblical imagery and symbols with some similarities (and also major differences) to Masonic rituals that recovered the "Ancient order of things" and offered the covenants necessary to receive exaltation in the afterlife.[22] Smith understood the freshly revealed endowment to be a pure restoration and expansion upon the rites of Freemasonry, which he believed charted roots back to antiquity but had become corrupted.[23] A year after the initial presentation of the endowment, Smith introduced women to the ordinance and the accompanying prayer circles.

However, Smith was not interested in offering only a small group the rites necessary for exaltation; rather, he intended to create eternal social and familial ties among all his people. Antebellum Americans worried over the perceived erosion of traditional family ties in their search for individual economic freedom and mobility.[24] Smith offered one theological solution: the spiritual linking of individuals through temple covenants to reduce the number of converted church members orphaned, without family ties.

One way this linking occurred was through ritual "sealings" of Latter-day Saints together in eternal relationships, including marriage relationships. In 1843, Joseph Smith recorded a revelation that explained the importance of the power of sealing. "All covenants, contracts, bonds, obligations, oaths, vows," the revelation explained, "that are not made and entered into and sealed by the Holy Spirit of promise, of him who is anointed . . . are of no efficacy, virtue, or force in and after the resurrection from the dead" (D&C 132:7). The same revelation spoke of a "new and everlasting covenant" of marriage that would seal Latter-day Saints under a covenant similar to that of biblical Israel, with the power, as a related Smith revelation promised, to initiate their entrance into the "highest" degree of the Celestial Kingdom (D&C 132:19, D&C 131:2). A new ritual ordinance solemnized such unions, and as the president of the church, only Smith could authorize the performance of such ordinances.

His 1843 revelation on marriage also put forward an ancient practice Smith may have been contemplating since the early days of the church's organization. He was told to follow the biblical patriarchs "Abraham, Isaac, and Jacob" and marry more than one wife in a restoration of an ancient law (D&C 132:1). Smith took to the practice slowly at first and kept his new marriages quiet so as to not draw the ire of followers and foes alike. However, he gradually introduced his closest associates in Nauvoo to the practice. Another belief also developed alongside the marriage ordinance: spiritual adoption, the notion of connecting or sealing the entire human family in a chain of belonging to build an expansive community in heaven. Through this developing system of teachings and rituals, which would eventually be performed within the completed Nauvoo Temple, Smith sought to create a network of kinship relations, bound together through priesthood power, that transcended the traditional lineal family order in an attempt to bring salvation to all Latter-day Saints.[25]

Joseph Smith's theological boldness and innovation in Nauvoo, however, gave rise to conflict between Latter-day Saints and other citizens of Illinois. His unfolding kingdom was met with disdain by his critics, who saw his amassing of authority in a singular community as a threat to American democracy. Any attempt to synthesize Smith's unfolding vision for the temple must end with an ellipsis rather than a period. Smith was murdered while jailed in Carthage, Illinois, in June 1844, before the Nauvoo Temple had been completed, and his death left his followers with the task of gathering together the threads of his developing temple ritual and theology. Brigham Young, as president of the Quorum of the Twelve Apostles, assumed control of church administration and oversaw the partial completion of the temple through 1846. Young rushed to implement Smith's project of administering the endowment and other ordinances to adult Latter-day Saints in Nauvoo.

16   THE SALT LAKE TEMPLE

By February 1846, when Latter-day Saints prepared to abandon the city because of persecution, over fifty-five hundred church members had received their endowment in the completed attic of the temple.[26] In addition, over eleven hundred marriage sealings had been performed. Young also began to introduce Smith's undeveloped ideas on spiritual adoption by performing formal adoptive sealings that united both biological and nonbiological individuals in "families."[27]

Complicating the forced exodus of Latter-day Saints out of Nauvoo, Young faced a series of internal challenges to his authority and that of the rest of the Quorum of the Twelve Apostles. One of Smith's early followers, Sidney Rigdon, a former member of the First Presidency, claimed guardianship over the church immediately after Smith's death. Rigdon's influence, however, was soon dispelled, and he was excommunicated. Young's most persistent threat came from James Strang, a recent convert who claimed to possess a letter from Smith appointing him as successor. Strang quickly peeled off followers in Nauvoo. The different claims on succession left the Quorum of the Twelve in a tenuous position as it moved to establish its authority to lead the church with the proper "keys" of the priesthood.[28]

The ordinances of the temple became a primary sign to the church body of the legitimacy of the Quorum of the Twelve Apostle's authority to continue to lead the church.[29] One of Young's arguments against those who challenged the quorum's authority centered on who maintained access to the temple rituals. At a pivotal meeting in August 1844, Young reminded the church that the apostleship was "ordained and anointed" by Joseph Smith himself "to bear off the keys of the Kingdom of God in all the world." At the head of the church "is the Apostleship," he asserted, and "if you let the Twelve remain and act in their place the keys of the Kingdom are with them, and they can manage the affairs of the Church and direct all things aright."[30] A month later, at Rigdon's ecclesiastical trial, Young affirmed that the temple was the place where Smith's vision for the entire church would unfold.[31]

By finishing the temple and introducing a large percentage of church members to temple ordinances, Young bound the community of believers together and deflected any rival claim from outside the Quorum of the Twelve Apostles to lead the church. As the Saints prepared to leave Nauvoo, they continued to construct the temple, and its completion carried practical and symbolic importance. The Nauvoo Temple was a monument to the legacy Smith had left behind and signaled that the religion had survived his martyrdom.

But more important, the temple wove together a covenant community bent on exodus westward.

For those like Sidney Rigdon and James Strang, the Nauvoo Temple was emblematic of Brigham Young's unauthorized authority and apostasy. Some restoration groups who rejected Young's leadership would later attempt to reconstruct forms of Joseph Smith's Nauvoo ritual in their own temple spaces.[32] The temple rituals introduced by Smith were radical and largely unsystematized, and the power associated with the temple inspired multiple individuals to claim authority over its administration. Young brought a semblance of order and precedent to Latter-day Saint temple space which also gave the body of the church confidence in his authority. As he prepared to lead this main body of Saints away from their sacred temple to a destination that was still largely unknown, he rallied them around their new covenants.

Temple Ritual and Latter-day Israel's Exodus

For the faithful Latter-day Saints who had braved the migrations from Ohio to Missouri, to Illinois, and now to the Iowa wilderness, their primary experiences with temples had always culminated in loss. Indeed, every sacred space for Latter-day Saints was scarred with emotional and physical violence. In their study of the contested Temple Mount in Jerusalem, Roger Friedland and Richard D. Hecht highlight how displacement and violence at a sacred site reinforce and shift meaning for a group that claims ownership over the space. For the Jews, the loss of their temple contributed to a unifying cultural narrative that reaches back into antiquity and informs the symbolic nature of the Mount in the present.[33]

The loss of their sacred space carried similar symbolic meaning for Latter-day Saints. At each juncture of communal success and loss, Latter-day Saints felt, as historian Philip L. Barlow suggests, that they were "recapitulating *living through* the stories of Israel and early Christianity—reestablishing the covenant, gathering the Lord's elect, separating Israel from the Gentiles, organizing the Church, preaching the gospel, building up the kingdom, living in sacred space and time."[34] During their Babylonian captivity, the Jews had anticipated an opportunity to one day restore their temple as "an abode of righteousness and a holy hill" (Jeremiah 31:23). For the Latter-day Saints, the parallels with ancient Israel were immediately present. They, too, had entered a period of exile.

18 THE SALT LAKE TEMPLE

Most Latter-day Saints, however, did not anticipate a swift and triumphant return to the existing temple in Nauvoo. Church leaders defended the temple from intruders after the bulk of Latter-day Saints had left the city, but they also intended to sell the building.[35] A new temple would be built elsewhere. Even before their departure from Nauvoo, church leaders alluded to the construction of this new temple in their imagined home in the West. At a general conference of the church in October 1845, Apostle Parley P. Pratt told the congregation, "Israel must be the head and not the tail. The Lord designs to lead us to a wider field of action, where there will be more room for the saints to grow and increase, and where there will be no one to say we crowd them, and where we can enjoy the pure principles of liberty and equal rights." There the Saints would "build a larger and better Temple in five years from this time than [they] now possess."[36] Apostle George A. Smith promised the Saints that demand to enter the new temple would be so high "they would be pulling the buttons off [his] coat to get into the temple to receive their blessings."[37]

Preparation for a mass exodus to the West the next spring consumed the city of Nauvoo from the fall of 1845 into early 1846 as the Saints gathered supplies and built wagons.[38] At the October 1845 general conference, concerned about an unprecedented refugee crisis in the Iowa wilderness, church leaders placed the Saints under a covenant to alleviate the poor who would soon gather on the plains. Formed in the Nauvoo Temple, the covenant exported Zion's principles of equality and communalism outside of Nauvoo's borders, extending the temple's reach.[39]

Though other sites for a new Latter-day settlement were explored, Brigham Young soon had his eyes on territory beyond the Rocky Mountains. "Upper California," as it was then called, was Mexican territory and would potentially afford the church the isolation and autonomy it needed to practice its religion undisturbed.[40] But Young's timeline for settling in the West soon faced challenges. Some three hundred hand-selected explorers (which quickly swelled to eighteen hundred men, women, and children) formed the initial "Camp of Israel" company and set out in February 1846 to prepare a place near the Rocky Mountains for thousands of other Latter-day Saints to gather in safety. It took over three months for the vanguard company to complete what should have been a six-week trek to the Missouri River. Extremely wet weather made otherwise passable roads a muddy bog, hindering the most able of the Saints and their cattle and wagons. Somewhat discouraged, Young revised his intentions to settle a company of church members in the

West that season and instead scouted a site suitable enough to house a large encampment of over twelve thousand refugees through the next winter.[41]

Social reformer Thomas L. Kane, in a sign of growing friendship with the Latter-day Saints, helped broker a deal with the federal government that permitted the church to winter on Pottawattamie lands to the east and more Indian lands to the west of the Missouri River. Because of his friendship with church leaders, Kane served as an outside observer of the somber yet resilient scene that unfolded on the western frontier. In July 1846, while attending a party held by encamped church members for the "Mormon Battalion," a group of five hundred men departing westward to assist the US government in the Mexican-American War, he heard a touching refrain: "The sun dipped behind the sharp sky line of the Omaha hills. Silence was then called, and a well cultivated mezzo-soprano voice, belonging to a young lady with fair face and dark eyes, gave with quartette accompaniment a little song . . . touching to all earthly wanderers. 'By the rivers of Babylon we sat down and wept. We wept when we remembered Zion.' "[42]

The psalmic lament was borrowed from captive Israel of the Old Testament and proved appropriate for the occasion. Brigham Young was organizing what he considered a modern-day Israel on the Great Plains, and the Saints' exile from their temple-centered Zion left many distressed, as it did biblical Israelites during their diaspora. Young would soon attempt to alleviate the suffering and give structure to the exiting Saints in his only canonized revelation. By the early winter of 1846, more than seven thousand church members camped in makeshift settlements scattered across Indian Territory, with headquarters at a site they termed Winter Quarters near the banks of the Missouri River. It was here that Young presented the "Word and Will of the Lord" in January 1847, which contained instructions concerning the "Camp of Israel," such as who would depart the next spring to locate a permanent settlement site for the entire church (D&C 136:1).

The camp would be organized into companies with captains and a president, who would give instructions as directed by the Quorum of the Twelve Apostles. According to Young's revelation, the camp would be guided by their "covenant" to "walk in the ordinances of the Lord" (D&C 136:4). Obedience to temple covenants was urged with the promise that the Saints would be preserved from their enemies like Israel of old. "I am he who led the children of Israel out of the land of Egypt; and my arm is stretched out in the last days, to save my people Israel," the revelation promised (D&C 136:22). The Saints increasingly identified their exodus with ancient Israel's flight from Egypt,

20 THE SALT LAKE TEMPLE

a comparison reinforced through their physical sacrifices and through their ordinances as they set out to cross an unforgiving frontier landscape.

Finding and Announcing the Temple Spot

In the wake of the hardship, disease, and death that had inflicted the dispersed encampments around Winter Quarters, a freshly chosen vanguard company of 143 men, 3 women, and 2 children, led by Brigham Young, departed westward in April 1847 to scout a new settlement site for the church. After some early disagreements and disobedience among the members of his company, Young encouraged them to remember their temple covenants.[43] The vanguard company moved quickly, traveling over a thousand miles in just over three months.

Some company members were filled with anticipation over what would result from their efforts to establish a new settlement. Vanguard member and Apostle Wilford Woodruff, like others, imagined the "journeys end whare we were to build up a stake of Zion." A "stake" symbolized church strength and growth but also represented a formal geographical structure presided over by church authorities, similar to a Catholic diocese. The exodus from Nauvoo dissolved all existing Latter-day Saint stakes, essentially collapsing the boundaries of the church organization. Stakes and temples symbolized stability, and the church would be without both for a season. Woodruff thus also dreamed of a temple that was "glorious" in appearance and "built of white & blue stone."[44] His vision reflected key components of Brigham Young's intentions to colonize the West: church settlement with a temple at the center. Yet even as the company trekked across the plains, they lacked a precise destination. After consulting available maps and reports of the western terrain (and later receiving firsthand accounts from famed mountain man Jim Bridger and others), church leaders anticipated settling beyond the Rocky Mountains somewhere in the Bear River Valley or near the Great Salt Lake.[45]

Sick with a burning fever and confined to a carriage in July 1847, Young gave instructions to an advance party to descend into the Salt Lake Valley without him. He told the group to find a site to settle and plant crops and then to scout the valley to document the terrain. On July 24, three days after the first scouts entered the valley, Young caught his first glimpse of the Salt Lake Valley from the back of Woodruff's carriage. As the pair overlooked

IMAGINED PLACE   21

the valley, Woodruff imagined a successful settlement surrounded by the "grandest and most sublime scenery probably that could be obtained on the globe." They meditated together and imagined the "House of God" that "would stand upon the top of the Mountains."[46] The weary Young, unable to scout the surrounding area himself, did not immediately declare a precise location for a new city.

Two days later, on July 26, Brigham Young's health had improved enough for him to take a walk with a few of the apostles to explore the area around their encampment in the valley. Woodruff later recalled that while on their walk Young made an unexpected and sudden stop. He took his cane, "stuck it down into the ground, and said, 'Here shall stand the Temple of our God.'" The surprise declaration "went through me like lightning," Woodruff remembered. Woodruff hastily located a sturdy piece of sagebrush and drove it into the ground to mark the place where Young's cane had left an impression in the dirt.[47] Later that day, Young's selected site for the temple was solidified further in his mind after he climbed a hill with a company of church leaders to better view the valley. The hill, which they named "Ensign Peak," matched the description of the peak Young had seen in a vision in Nauvoo years earlier.[48] Ensign Peak offered a visible reminder to the faithful who had followed Young to the Salt Lake Valley that their God had sanctioned the place as the starting point for their new settlement.

On July 28, Brigham Young took a small group of church leaders to the precise spot he had declared for the temple two days earlier. At the convergence "between two creeks" he waved his hand over the open landscape and said, "[H]ere is the forty acres for the Temple lot."[49] The select group of apostles determined to reconvene later that evening to vote and sanction Young's selected site. Scouting parties sent to explore the region were only just returning, and Young wanted their feedback on the site. At the evening council, Young expressed his belief that Joseph Smith had showed him the spot they then occupied. "I prayed that he would lead us directly to the best spot which he has done," Young declared. "I knew this spot as soon as I saw it."[50] According to an observer, Young oriented the priesthood leaders on the proposed settlement, informing the group they "were now standing on the south east corner of the Temple Block."[51] The council voted unanimously to build the settlement outward from the temple site and began to work on the details of their prospective city.

In the coming years, some Latter-day Saints would be anxious for Brigham Young, who did not deliver frequent revelations like his predecessor, Joseph

22 THE SALT LAKE TEMPLE

Smith, to present a formal revelation commanding Latter-day Saints to build a temple in the Great Basin, similar to revelations commissioning temples in both Kirtland and Nauvoo. At the cornerstone-laying ceremony for the Salt Lake Temple in 1853, Young remarked, "I scarcely ever say much about revelations, or visions, but suffice it to say, five years ago last July I was here, and saw in the Spirit the Temple not ten feet from where we have laid the Chief Cornerstone. I have not inquired what kind of a Temple we should build. Why? Because it was represented before me. I have never looked upon that ground, but the vision of it was there. I see it as plainly as if it was in reality before me."[52] Details of Young's vision from July 1847 are scarce, but he was confident that that vision, coupled with his initial vision in Nauvoo, were all the revelation needed for the church to be assured of the temple's divine origins. Young had told the vanguard company that all would be "entirely satisfied," even if their settlement and temple were laid out "on a barren rock," because they had been guided by the "direction of Joseph Smith" through revelation to choose the right spot.[53]

Outside of Young's declarations, the Saints found Old Testament significance for their wilderness settlement. They intended to raise a banner, or "ensign," above their settlement, and though no evidence suggests they formally did so, the notion was borrowed from an Isaiah prophecy about an "ensign" raised "for the nations" to signal the place where "the outcasts of Israel" would gather from the "four quarters of the earth" (Isaiah 11:12).[54] The physical features of the Salt Lake Valley also stoked the religious imaginations of church leaders; its walled mountains and valley streams seemed to offer the promised protection where ancient and new prophecy met and where a covenant community could gather in safety. Just days after the temple site had been selected, Apostle Orson Pratt delivered a sermon on the Temple Block, pointing the vanguard company to the prophecies of Isaiah, which seemed to allude "to us in our present position." Pratt added that "[t]he munition of rocks should be a defence unto" the gathering Saints, and "the Lord sware that their corn & wine should no more be given to their enemies, & that the house of God should be built upon the tops of the mountain."[55] While Young's visions helped justify the selection of the Great Basin as the stopping point for their westward trek, the repeated readings of biblical prophecy about "the Mountain of the Lord's house" being "established in the top of the mountains," along with similar Old Testament language, gave Latter-day Saints an ancient and sacred errand and underscored their chosen status as modern Israel.[56]

IMAGINED PLACE   23

A Prophet in the West

On August 2, 1847, Apostle Orson Pratt and Henry G. Sherwood began a survey of the land, laying out the city starting at the forty-acre Temple Block. The city was initially platted in 135 ten-acre blocks, starting at the southeast corner of the Temple Block and moving in all four cardinal directions. Its grid-like structure would allow anyone who resided in the city to know their precise location in relation to the temple, reinforcing the temple's symbolic role as the center of the new religious society. Brigham Young, Thomas Bullock, Orson Pratt, and others responsible for creating a plat for the city, however, made adjustments to the planned Temple Block after they realized it was too large, reducing the block from forty acres to ten.[57] The apostles in the vanguard company, following Young's example, selected lots for their families around the Temple Block.[58] As quickly as these first pioneers started to plan their settlement, some of the company prepared to return east to Winter Quarters. The next companies of pioneers were already en route to the Great Basin, and Young intended to get word back to them and those at Winter Quarters that they had found the place for their settlement. A series of departures east ensued, with Young, Heber C. Kimball, and other leaders among the last to leave on August 26.[59]

Before his departure, Young sent an epistle for Samuel Brannan to share as he left the Salt Lake Valley to rejoin a colony of church members he had brought by ship from New York to Yerba Buena (San Francisco) in California. The letter was one of the first communications from the vanguard company announcing the selected temple site.[60] News of a place for colonization, along with the intention to build another temple, spread by word of mouth as returning companies reached those along the trail still heading west. On September 3, for example, Young's company met an encampment of Latter-day Saints at Big Sandy Crossing in Wyoming. On that occasion, Apostle George A. Smith reported to the group of over 185 pioneers that the vanguard had "selected a beautiful place" for the temple where, with the "natural defences" of the mountains, the Saints could worship undisturbed.[61] When the eastbound companies arrived in Winter Quarters in succession throughout October, they enthusiastically shared descriptions of their planned settlement near the Great Salt Lake.

The return from the Salt Lake Valley also brought pressing leadership matters to the fore. Since the death of Joseph Smith in 1844, Brigham Young had functioned as the de facto head of the church as president of the Quorum

24 THE SALT LAKE TEMPLE

of the Twelve Apostles. Now he proposed to the Quorum (though two of its members, Parley P. Pratt and John Taylor, were absent, leading a large company west) that they reorganize by appointing a church president who would then select two counselors to compose a new First Presidency, distinct from the rest of the Quorum. After significant debate, the Quorum of the Twelve Apostles voted to sustain Young as president of the church on December 5, and Young selected two counselors, apostles Heber C. Kimball and Willard Richards, who had been helping him administer the church in the years since Smith's death.[62]

At a conference in a log tabernacle in Kanesville, Iowa, on December 27, 1847, one thousand Latter-day Saints grew silent as Apostle Orson Pratt introduced Brigham Young as the new church president.[63] A tumultuous period of three and a half years without a formal church president ended when the congregation unanimously voted to sustain Young and both of his counselors as the new First Presidency. The vote of confidence from the general membership was a relief to Young, who had survived multiple schisms to lead the church into a new era. And it would take Young's consolidated, authoritative leadership to help establish a successful frontier settlement in the Great Basin in the coming years. In a fitting celebration, the conference ended with a ritual shout originally performed at the March 1836 dedication of the House of the Lord in Kirtland: "Hosanna, Hosanna, Hosanna, to God & the Lamb Amen Amen & Amen."[64]

Less than a year after the jubilant occasion in Iowa, the Nauvoo Temple, a distinctive vestige of Joseph Smith's prophethood and religious vision, burned to the ground from suspected arson.[65] Only sorrowed walls of the hollowed-out structure remained. While the Saints mourned the loss of a building that had cost them much in the form of labor and resources, they had in a sense already moved on. Their attention was now directed to a new sacred spot at the heart of their planned community in the Salt Lake Valley. Another consecrated effort to build a temple marked a new beginning for the Latter-day Saints, who hoped that God's presence and protection would quickly fill their prospective kingdom in the West.

2

Center Place

President Brigham Young called for an assembly at the Temple Block on the morning of February 14, 1853. At least an inch of snow still blanketed parts of Salt Lake City, and the winter frost reached deep into the soil. A brass band greeted members of The Church of Jesus Christ of Latter-day Saints as they arrived, setting a festive mood and sending refrains echoing off the buildings around the temple site. To open the groundbreaking ceremony for the Salt Lake Temple, surveyor Jesse W. Fox, public works foreman Miles Romney, and architect Truman O. Angell staked out the foundation.[1] Though beset by the consequences of a harsh winter, the city still brimmed with excitement.

The demands of raising a pioneer settlement in the Salt Lake Valley initially deterred any focus on starting a new temple, perhaps in ways those who participated in the swift and consuming erection of the Nauvoo Temple could have never imagined. The pressing business of building homes and planting and harvesting crops, coupled with debilitating shortages of food and other supplies, made the temple an unreachable luxury for a season. The work of salvation first required survival in the desert wilderness. Young initially, and perhaps naively, thought the Saints could erect a temple along with the rest of their new settlement. He had provisioned for church architect William Weeks, the mastermind behind the construction of the Nauvoo Temple, to be one of the first to reach the Great Basin in 1847 to lay plans for a new temple. Weeks and his family arrived in the Salt Lake Valley in September 1847 but did not stay long. For unknown reasons, Weeks determined to vacate his position and leave the church altogether, heading to the Midwest with his family. With him he took the only proven architectural experience in the Salt Lake Valley. Despite anger and disappointment, Young remained firm in his decision to see a temple constructed in the selected spot. He appointed the untested Truman O. Angell as Weeks's replacement in 1850 but waited yet more years to begin construction.[2]

The groundbreaking therefore had all the festive trappings of a community holiday as it signaled the Saints had weathered the hardships of the early years of settlement building to begin temple efforts anew. Thousands

The Salt Lake Temple. Scott D. Marianno and Reid L. Neilson, Oxford University Press.
© Oxford University Press 2025. DOI: 10.1093/9780190881580.003.0003

Figure 2.1 Salt Lake Temple groundbreaking, 1853. Courtesy Church History Library.

gathered around the marked boundaries for the foundation (Figure 2.1). In the center, Brigham Young climbed atop a buggy to speak. The pain of the church's past exoduses inspired his remarks. "Seven years tomorrow [Young] left Nauvoo not knowing which track he should go," summarized First Presidency counselor Willard Richards in his report of the remarks for the local newspaper, the *Deseret News*. "Only as he had learned by dreams, and visions, and revelations, that there was a good place for the saints in the mountains. . . . [W]hen he arrived on the spot where he then was, he declared *that* the place for a Temple."[3] The Latter-day Saints had failed to retain possession of past temples, but Young declared, "I would just as well build a Temple that would Cost a million of Dollars if I knew we should be driven from it in a month by our enemies as though we should occupy it a Thousand years. It is all the same with me for when the Lord Commands us to do any thing we should do it just as freely without asking the whys & wharefore whether we have the privilege of enjoying it or not."[4]

Young was also aware that rallying support for another building project would strain a community already desperately short on labor and resources. Yet he persisted. "We want a Temple more than we want dwelling houses," he declared, so that the ordinances of the House of the Lord could be attended to.[5] His remarks at the groundbreaking touched on a challenging paradox inherent in the Saints' temple-building project. Only an understanding of the sacredness and divine import of the temple would motivate the impoverished refugees to give precious time and resources to completing the massive undertaking. Creating a shared sacred place from the dust proved a challenging spiritual and cultural undertaking.

Though Young did not deliver a new public revelation commissioning the Salt Lake Temple, as there had been for previous temples, the Saints believed in his authority as church president to select a site for the construction of a House of the Lord. They also viewed Joseph Smith's revelations that commanded them to build houses of the Lord as still binding (see D&C 84:5, D&C 88:119–20, D&C 97:5) and reason enough to build a new temple in the Great Basin. And most important Young used the Salt Lake Temple project to emphasize the priesthood as central to Latter-day Saint temple rituals and to the unfolding of a religious kingdom.

Following Young's remarks, the crowd followed him to the southeast corner of the temple site, where the ground had been picked and loosened. Young then shoveled and tossed the dirt from the site. As he did so, someone in the crowd tossed a silver dollar into the fresh hole as a sign of support for the new project.[6] The Temple Block soon became a bustling hub of activity and labor as church members rushed forward with their own tools to help ready the site for the foundation.[7] The community project was underway.

Cornerstones of the Priesthood

Almost two months after the groundbreaking, on the twenty-third anniversary of the church's organization, April 6, 1853, Brigham Young opened the church's semiannual general conference in the neighboring adobe tabernacle.[8] The sun had illuminated the temple site by ten o'clock in the morning, when four thousand Latter-day Saints moved from the tabernacle and crowded around the excavated area to witness the cornerstone-laying ceremony. By one estimate, the recent excavation of the temple site had taken about ten thousand cumulative days of labor, causing the *Deseret News* to ask, "How many days' work will it require to complete the excavation for the walls; erect the edifice, and finish the wall around the Temple Block, the stone being yet in the mountains, unquarried?"[9] But the weight of the

28 THE SALT LAKE TEMPLE

tasks still undone did not stifle the pageantry of the occasion. In a setting that resembled the 1841 cornerstone ceremony for the Nauvoo Temple, bands performed while local police and militia stood watch.[10] The entire proceedings, which included a discourse, prayer, and song after the laying of each cornerstone, took almost four hours to complete.[11]

Standing at the bottom of the sixteen-foot hole on the southeast corner of the site, the First Presidency—Brigham Young, Heber C. Kimball, and Willard Richards—along with John Smith, the church patriarch and Salt Lake Stake president, formally installed the first cornerstone.[12] Church clerk Thomas Bullock then read aloud Young's prepared remarks as the First Presidency stood atop the cornerstone. Young's written discourse reprised a theme from Sidney Rigdon's oration delivered at the dedication of the Kirtland Temple, in March 1836. Young suggested continuity between the church's current attempt to build a House of the Lord and previous temple-building efforts, both ancient and modern. All of these temples were consecrated offerings from God's chosen people to provide a place where Jesus Christ could dwell and visit.[13] "But what are we here for this day?" Young asked. "To celebrate the Birthday of our Religion! To lay the foundation of a Temple to the Most High God, so that when His Son, our Elder Brother, shall again appear, he may have a place where he can lay his head." The temple for Christ's return was intended to be a place where he could "not only spend a night or a day, but find a place of peace, that he may stay until he can say I am satisfied."[14] Young's sermon emphasized two intersecting tenets inspired by his understanding of the Bible and his memory of Joseph Smith's teachings: first, that temples offered an earthly abode for the divine; second, that Christ occupied a resurrected, material form. The temple would not simply be filled with God's presence but would also provide a literal place for an embodied Christ to come and go as he pleased prior to his formal Second Coming.[15] Such an abode would be located at the center of Latter-day Saint settlement as a reminder of community priorities.

Additionally, past temple cornerstone ceremonies, such as the one in Nauvoo, involved a ritual procession of select members of the priesthood. The cornerstones were laid in successive order by members of the priesthood hierarchy. Young, however, felt no fidelity toward the order exhibited in the Nauvoo cornerstone ceremony. Since Smith's death, he had spent considerable time defending the apostleship and warding off counterclaims to the Quorum of the Twelve Apostle's authority to administer the kingdom of God. And hundreds of Latter-day Saints had witnessed Young and other

CENTER PLACE   29

apostles officiating and supervising the performance of temple ordinances in the Nauvoo Temple before the exodus west. Temple work became a primary vehicle for reinforcing and crystallizing in the minds of Latter-day Saints the authority of the Quorum of the Twelve Apostles to lead the Church forward. Though Latter-day Saints in the Salt Lake Valley had accepted Young's authority to lead the church, he saw an opportunity at the cornerstone-laying ceremony to further instruct the membership in the proper order of the priesthood hierarchy and its relationship to administering temple ordinances. The ceremony on the Temple Block provided attendees with a visual representation of the order of authority in the church's priesthood hierarchy.

The Salt Lake Temple cornerstone-laying ceremony contained two notable alterations from the Nauvoo ceremony. While the First Presidency led both ceremonies with the placement of the southeast cornerstone, the southwest cornerstone in Nauvoo was laid by Nauvoo Stake President William Marks with the support of the presidency of the high priest quorum in Nauvoo.[16] Marks, like subsequent stake presidents, held ecclesiastical authority over a designated geographical region. The day-to-day affairs of the church in Nauvoo were under both his supervision and that of the high council appointed to support him. Smith and the rest of the First Presidency, however, retained significant control over general church business and gave direction to ecclesiastical leaders in Nauvoo.

The stake president, high priests quorum, and high council, however, did not immediately follow the First Presidency in laying cornerstones at the Salt Lake Temple ceremony. Instead, Young invited the Presiding Bishop, Edward Hunter, to lay the southwest cornerstone. He explained the reason for the change at general conference that afternoon in one of his most significant discourses on priesthood. The Presiding Bishop filled an office "pertaining to the temporal affairs of the kingdom," he clarified, and aided the First Presidency in caring for the needs of the church body. The Presiding Bishop, therefore, was the next "standing authority in the Kingdom of God" after the First Presidency and apostles.

Young, however, perhaps had another reason for superseding the stake president and high priests with the Presiding Bishop in the order of the cornerstone ceremony. One challenge to his authority after Smith's death came from Nauvoo Stake President Marks. Emma Smith, Joseph Smith's widow, supported Marks's succession to Smith's position as church president, though Marks himself ultimately backed Sidney Rigdon's claim to the presidency.[17]

30   THE SALT LAKE TEMPLE

Supporters of Marks cited a Joseph Smith revelation that positioned the stake high council, with the stake president at the head, as "equal in authority in the affairs of the church, in all their decisions," to the First Presidency and Quorum of the Twelve Apostles. The stake president would administer ecclesiastical affairs at home while the Quorum of the Twelve Apostles served as a "traveling high council" (D&C 107:36). But since that early revelation, the Quorum of the Twelve's authority in practice had expanded into a supervisory role over all the stakes of the church.

Young's second adjustment to the ceremony thus related to the first. After the Salt Lake stake president and high council laid the northwest cornerstone, the last cornerstone, in the northeast corner, was placed by the Quorum of the Twelve Apostles (rather than the Presiding Bishop, as had been done in Nauvoo). "When a man is ordained to be an apostle," Young later explained about the adjustment, "his priesthood is without beginning of days or end of life." "All the Priesthood, all the keys, all the blessings, all the gifts, all the endowments, and every thing preparitory to entering back into the presence of the Father and the son," he continued, "is ... circumscribed by or I might say incorporated within the circumference of the Apostleship."[18] Thus the ceremony led with the First Presidency, or the chief apostles, and ended with the Quorum of the Twelve, who held the authority to transact "every thing in the church of God on earth." As an illustration, Young told Latter-day Saints that he and First Presidency counselor Kimball had never been ordained as high priests but were told by Joseph Smith their ordinations as apostles granted them "all the keys that ever was, and that can be conferred upon mortal man," including a right to future heavenly visitations containing the conferral of new keys.[19] This is the "perfect order" of the priesthood, Young reiterated.

The leadership of the Quorum of the Twelve Apostles was more secure in 1853 than it was in 1844, after Joseph Smith's death. Yet Brigham Young felt the need to explain the order of the priesthood on the Temple Block to reassure the church that the authority to administer temple ritual resided in the apostleship. Indeed, as Young publicly announced after the first cornerstone was laid, the most pressing task for Latter-day Saints was to acquire "all those ordinances in the House of the Lord, which are necessary for you, after you have departed this life, to enable you to walk back to the presence of the Father, passing the angels who stand as sentinels; enabled to give them the key words, the signs and tokens pertaining to the Holy Priesthood, and gain your eternal exaltation in spite of earth and hell."[20]

CENTER PLACE   31

Most Latter-day Saints had experienced temple ritual only once, if at all, and thus possessed limited knowledge of the scope of the ritual. The cornerstone-laying ceremony allowed Young to expound upon the broader significance of the ritual and the interrelatedness of the temple project and his own priesthood authority. The ceremony visualized the priesthood as the foundation for the temple and positioned those holding the keys of priesthood authority as the gatekeepers for the ordinances that offered the path to salvation for Latter-day Saints.

Prototypes and Proto-Temples

Architectural drawings of the temple had been furnished by the time the first cornerstone was placed in 1853. Church architect Truman O. Angell and his assistant, William Ward, who had been trained in architecture in England, worked closely with Brigham Young on early renderings of the temple. Ward later reflected on this rough initial design: "Brigham Young drew upon a slate in the architect's office a sketch, and said to Truman O. Angell: 'There will be three towers on the east, representing the President and his two Counselors; also three similar towers on the west representing the Presiding Bishop and his two Counselors; the towers on the east the Melchisedek priesthood, those on the west the Aaronic priesthood. The center towers will be higher than those on the sides, and the west towers a little lower than those on the east end."[21] Young dictated dimensions and specified the height of the stories but apparently left the "style of the building" up to Angell. As a wood joiner on both the Kirtland and Nauvoo temples, Angell had limited architectural experience but possessed a general knowledge of building construction. He relied heavily on Ward's expertise in stone construction and drafting to prepare the early sketches and plans of the temple.[22]

Some debate surrounded which materials to use to execute Young's initial design. At the October 1853 general conference, First Presidency counselor Heber C. Kimball invited "a vote from the congregation concerning the temple, whether we shall have it built of the stone from Red Butte, or of adobies, or timber, or of the best quality of stone that can be found in the mountains." Kimball favored stone, and Latter-day Saints supported his motion in a vote but deferred to the First Presidency to "dictate where the stone and other materials shall be obtained."[23] Young, however, initially preferred thick adobe walls with a visible but thin stone exterior. He believed

32 THE SALT LAKE TEMPLE

that adobe mixed with stone would increase in strength and durability "in 500 years," as opposed to red sandstone or other stone types, which he predicted would degrade over time.[24] The prevalence of adobe also rendered it a popular choice for buildings and homes constructed during the early settlement period, including for the recently completed General Tithing Office on the Temple Block. But plans for the temple's composition would change in the ensuing years.

Though Brigham Young allowed for some flexibility in the temple's design, he impressed upon Truman Angell some necessary exterior characteristics. "I see it as plainly as if [the temple] was in reality before me," Young stated at general conference following the cornerstone ceremony. "I will say . . . that it will have six towers to begin with, instead of one."[25] Angell's early sketches in 1853–54 showed the six towers in near perfect symmetry on the east and west sides of the building. The rising towers affixed with battlements, turrets, and pinnacles resembled the Gothic and Romanesque style characteristic of medieval English cathedrals. Both Young and Ward had spent extensive time in England and were familiar with cathedrals there. The territorial library offered a few design books, including one by Scottish architect Peter Nicholson, which seemed to influence Angell's incorporation of the medieval crenellated design.[26]

The Romanesque style similarly captivated architects in the United States by the middle of the nineteenth century. Even evangelical Protestants, who had long decried the centralized authority conveyed by medieval high church architecture, embraced a neo-Gothic style as a means of asserting their own authority during a chaotic era of industrialization, urbanization, and political disunion. Those advancing the militaristic features of the neo-Gothic style largely conceived of Protestantism, and Christianity more broadly, as a refuge and spiritual fortress arming congregants against the advancing ills of urban life.[27]

Latter-day Saints harbored their own concerns about American life, informed by their contingent status as religious refugees in the American West. The temple's design became their own unique expression of this discourse, asserting religious authority and power through architecture to guard against the popular impulses of an American society whose religious intolerance had so far wrested from them their previous sacred strongholds. Architectural drafts by Angell and Ward imagined the temple as a castle or fortress reflecting the repeated sentiments of church leaders that the Saints' new wilderness home would provide a refuge from worldly influence and persecution. The physical safety afforded by their relative isolation in the mountains was to be inscribed by the granite stones of their temple fortress. Church leaders promised the temple would guarantee temporal security and divine protection for all who gathered in the Salt Lake Valley.[28]

The Saints also internalized their own history and felt the commencement of a temple would actually provoke more persecution, requiring a defensive posture. Apostle Ezra T. Benson believed the new effort to build a temple displeased Satan. Temple work in "Kirtland, Missouri, and Illinois" stirred "up the devil," he asserted. "Will it not be so in the City of the Great Salt Lake?"[29] Similarly, Ann Secrist, writing to her missionary husband Jacob, then in Germany, predicted, "When the Lord begins to have a house reared to his name, the devil will begin to work."[30]

Church members believed the anticipated increase in Satanic threats stemmed from worldly wickedness, which signaled the imminence of the Second Coming and demanded the construction of a temple. Apostle Parley P. Pratt, for example, viewed laying the Salt Lake Temple cornerstones as preparatory to the return of Jesus Christ, who would subdue the enemies of the Saints and usher in a "universal empire in heaven and on earth, as sure as innocent blood was ever shed on Mount Calvary, or the official seal broken on the door of the tomb of the Son of God." Their new "Temple amid the mountains" served as "one advancing step in the progress of the necessary preparations for these mighty revolutions."[31] As church members heard sermons on the importance of the Salt Lake Temple's construction, many discerned a causal relationship between the temple's development and the end times events that were seemingly unfolding around them.

By August 1854, the exterior design of the temple was settled enough that Truman Angell felt comfortable giving *Deseret News* readers a brief description of the dimensions and exterior of the anticipated temple. "The whole structure," Angell wrote, "is designed to symbolize the great architectural work above."[32] Like the Nauvoo Temple, the future Salt Lake City Temple was to feature cosmic symbols—suns, moons, and stars—etched on the façade, emphasizing the building's orientation toward the heavenly realm (Figure 2.2). Apostle Pratt reported feeling the presence of "Joseph Smith, and his associate spirits" hovering just above "the brink" of the temple foundation at the cornerstone ceremony. According to Pratt, the eyes of the departed were centered on the temple site because the Saints were the only ones "preparing a sanctuary for the holy conversation and ministrations pertaining to . . . exaltation."[33] Like other church leaders, Pratt suggested the

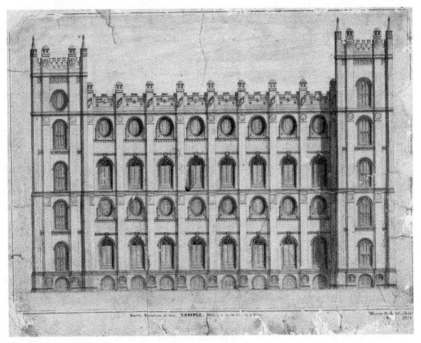

Figure 2.2 Truman O. Angell architectural sketch, 1854. Courtesy Church History Library.

new temple would function as the main conduit between heaven and earth. To Apostle George A. Smith, the temple design evidenced to the world the "Mormon *Order* of Architecture," in which "every stone has its moral lesson, and all point to the celestial world."[34]

As Latter-day Saints experienced temple rituals themselves, they would also, in theory, understand the urgent and sacred purpose of a permanent temple and invest more labor and resources into its construction. Church leaders searched for a temporary solution to initiate the thousands of convert-immigrants arriving in the Salt Lake Valley into temple ordinances. The performance of ordinances without a dedicated temple space had precedent. Joseph Smith first introduced the endowment in the upper room of his red brick store in Nauvoo.[35] The makeshift arrangement included the creation of a series of partitions through which initiates passed as they proceeded through the endowment. When the Nauvoo Temple neared completion, the administration of the endowment again included the use of temporary compartments.[36] In at least once instance, the endowment was also administered atop Ensign Peak, overlooking the Salt Lake Valley. In July

CENTER PLACE   35

1849, Addison Pratt, who was departing on a mission to the Society Islands, received special permission from Brigham Young to proceed through the endowment in case he died while on his mission.[37] Pratt's wilderness endowment reinforced the Saints' desperate need for a dedicated, temporary site in which to perform and streamline temple ordinances for the living. But with the pressing demands of constructing a new city, the pioneer settlers mostly tabled temple ordinances until such a space could be built.

In 1852, adaptations were made to the Council House, Utah Territory's first public building, to facilitate the performance of temple ordinances. The Council House occupied a dual role in the early territory: the first floor housed the work of the territorial legislature, and the second floor, among other purposes, served as a worship space for church members to perform temple rituals, including marriage sealings. Sealings were also performed in Brigham Young's office and in the homes of church members throughout the territory. Though it was a temporary, limited, and multipurpose space, the Council House enabled church leaders to administer over two thousand endowments from 1851 to 1854.[38] Eventually, however, federal officials who were not Latter-day Saints were appointed to territorial positions and required use of the Council House; their civic business further exacerbated space constraints in the building.[39]

In spring 1854, architect Truman Angell continued his slow and painstaking work on the Salt Lake Temple but also began working on a plan to accommodate sustained demand for the administration of the endowment. He sketched an architectural design specifically tailored for the endowment ceremony: a building that would be called the Endowment House. The two-story adobe building, located on the northwest corner of the Temple Block, was finished in May 1855, and at the building's dedication, Brigham Young called it The House of the Lord.[40] For the next three decades, the Endowment House helped alleviate the lack of a temple in the Salt Lake Valley by hosting more than twenty-five hundred marriages annually and over fifty-four thousand endowments. The addition of a baptismal font allowed the Saints to resume performing baptisms for their deceased ancestors. (Over 134,000 were performed.)[41]

The Endowment House was never intended to replace the temple, but Latter-day Saints considered the site sacred because it housed the holy ordinances of the temple. Its presence on the Temple Block ensured that prospective initiates, even as they dispersed and settled throughout the Salt Lake Valley and further south, would have to travel to a central place to participate

36   THE SALT LAKE TEMPLE

in temple ritual. The Endowment House also brought routine to the administration of temple ordinances, with priesthood leadership headquartered in close physical proximity, ensuring the church's highest leaders could control both access to and the administration of ordinances performed inside the building. The "Temple Pro Tempore," as Angell imagined the Endowment House, modeled how a completed House of the Lord could function in the rhythm of Latter-day Saint religious life.[42] The simple adobe structure lacked the adornment of later temples, but its simplicity reinforced that it was the interior layout, symbolic furnishings, and rituals within that made a space sacred for Latter-day Saints.

A Sacred Infrastructure

The temple construction project moved in tandem with the church's Public Works Department, which supported the developing infrastructure in the Salt Lake Valley beginning in 1850. The Public Works Department quickly became the largest employer in Utah Territory, retaining on average between two hundred and five hundred workers throughout the 1850s to support a centrally planned public infrastructure, including the construction of roads, mills, and public buildings.[43] In the early territorial period, there was little distinction between civic and community construction projects and religious ones. All public works projects, including the temple, were supervised by the superintendent of public works Daniel H. Wells, a respected civic and church leader. Church interests drove the development of the territorial infrastructure. The Public Works Department established its headquarters on the northeast corner of the Temple Block and supported a carpenter shop, stone-cutting shop, and blacksmith shop.[44]

Temple development also depended on the successful implementation of two major religious tenets: the notion of a literal gathering of Latter-day Saints in one location and the principle of tithing (the donation of 10 percent of one's increase to the church). Both supplied the church with needed labor and resources to build the infrastructure for a new religious kingdom. The church would need to recruit skilled laborers to bolster its colonizing aims. At a special general conference only six months before the temple groundbreaking, Brigham Young had assigned over one hundred missionaries to serve missions to Europe, Africa, Asia, and the Pacific Isles—the largest missionary force ever called at one conference in the church's three-decade

CENTER PLACE 37

history.[45] The announcement signaled that Young had no intention of slowing the church's evangelizing effort, but the departure of one hundred missionaries before the winter season also temporarily taxed the church's available labor supply.

In theory, however, the missionaries would reap a new supply of converts with skills that could assist in building the kingdom. The missionaries could also encourage others to immigrate by advertising the Saints' new settlement in the West and the planned temple at its center; for example, news of the groundbreaking and cornerstone laying for the temple was sounded abroad to these and other missionaries through newspapers and correspondence. George Q. Cannon, then serving a mission in the Sandwich Islands, heard about the cornerstone ceremony in June 1853 from his sisters Mary Alice and Anne, who wrote to him that the conference "was the best conference they ever attended."[46] The British Mission periodical, the *Millennial Star*, featured the proceedings of the cornerstone ceremony in early July. "The Saints in the country have been very anxious to know when a Temple would be commenced in the vallies of Ephraim," the editors wrote. "We will say— *A Temple shall be built, which shall be holy to the Lord.* A temple to which the upright of many nations shall flow, and receive washings, anointings, and exaltations for themselves and their dead."[47] Latter-day Saint converts abroad were kept apprised of developments on the temple because they were expected to gather to the place where saving ordinances would be performed.

The call for Latter-day Saints to gather to the Salt Lake Valley was based on both practicalities and religious principles. In desperate need of skilled workers, church leaders called on European craftsmen to bring their skills to support the church's developing civilization. Over time the notices, written in epistles and published in church-owned newspapers, became more specific about local needs.[48] Church leaders asked for mechanics, artisans, and machinery as much as they searched for general laborers. However, the church had always sounded a broad message for all to gather in one spot. Since September 1830, Latter-day Saints had been under a divine commandment to gather together the Lord's "elect . . . unto one place upon the face of the earth" (see D&C 29:7–8). Bringing church members to one region allowed leaders to watch over the church, enforce conformity to religious standards and doctrine, and pool resources to build up their colony. Once Latter-day Saints reached the Great Basin, the First Presidency invited them "to unite" a portion of "their gold, their silver, and their cattle, with ours" into a pool called the Perpetual Emigrating Fund, which was used to offset

38 THE SALT LAKE TEMPLE

impoverished Saints' cost of migrating west. Those who received an advance from the Perpetual Emigrating Fund were expected to repay their debt after establishing themselves in the Great Basin. Many, however, never repaid the debt, taxing the church's ability to support new immigrants traveling to the valley.[49]

Over the pulpit, in epistles, and through local newspapers, church leaders also encouraged Latter-day Saints to tithe consistently to support the Public Works Department so construction on the temple could proceed. Tithing could be paid in the form of cash, property, labor, livestock, or other in-kind donations.[50] "Who will bring to the Tithing Office some of the first cutting of their hay?" one midsummer newspaper notice asked. "The teams are not able to do more than half work for want of hay to feed on."[51] Another notice asked, "What did you do with your surplus grain? Did you bring it into the Lord's Store House, and say to your Trustee in Trust, feed this grain to the laborer, and cause it to help build a house in the 'Tops of the mountains'. . . or, did you hoard up your wheat in your houses, and let the laborer starve."[52] Frustrated by inconsistent tithe paying, the First Presidency encouraged the "elders and officers, and especially the bishops, to instruct the saints, that the paying of their tithing" would help them "secure a future residence in the heaven they are seeking after." In order to gain a "celestial heaven," the church needed "a terrestrial temple, builded to the name of Israel's God." "From henceforth," the First Presidency declared, "the living may not expect the blessings of the Temple unless they help build it. Your tithing we value not, only as it affects your salvation and the salvation of the dead."[53] Temporal and spiritual initiatives in early territorial Utah were thus nearly indistinguishable.

Brigham Young was also increasingly aware of a labor paradox that hampered the construction of the temple and public works initiatives. The more laborers immigrated to the Salt Lake Valley, the greater the strain on the General Tithing Office and the Bishop's Storehouse; the funds and goods of both these entities were used to support the poor and to pay public works laborers. In a cash-strapped economy, church leaders relied on agriculture yields and the surplus donation of goods and livestock to feed and supply their workforce by members who were hardly settled themselves in the valley. Young was intent on building a self-sufficient society in the Great Basin and frequently emphasized self-reliance and home industry as means of keeping Latter-day Saints beyond the influence of the East and its costly exports. In the early 1850s, Young made a concentrated effort to establish sugar, iron, cotton, wool, paper, and pottery industries to aid the

CENTER PLACE 39

development of territorial infrastructure and to further reinforce Latter-day Saint autonomy.[54]

While the church's fledgling home industries struggled initially, the Public Works Department finished buildings on and around the Temple Block. In addition to the Council House (completed by 1850) and the Endowment House (1855), workers built a large adobe meetinghouse known eventually as the Old Tabernacle, a two-story Social Hall, the General Tithing Office, and the Bishop's Storehouse (for surplus goods and in-kind donations)—all by 1852.[55] In addition, the church sought to enclose the Temple Block with an adobe wall, which was seen as a necessary step in delimiting and protecting the ground for the temple preparatory to its construction. In 1851 a trench was dug for the wall's foundation and teams of oxen began carting stones to the Temple Block. Though church leaders hoped to enclose the Temple Block in time to prepare for the groundbreaking and cornerstone-laying ceremonies, work on the wall dragged on for at least another four years.[56] The lack of lime for mortar to build the wall's water table slowed construction considerably.[57] By April 1855, the nearly completed wall approached fifteen feet in height, and iron gates were hung "so as to entirely close up the square during the night."[58] The wall acted as an extra layer of security against unauthorized visitors and livestock and as a symbolic border that became an extension of the temple itself, demarcating the sacred from the profane.

The expansion of construction projects around the Temple Block required laborers to invent and refine transportation methods for moving heavy stone and other raw materials. To ease the task of carting quarried stone for the Temple Block wall, for example, the Saints took steps to construct a wooden rail track in May 1851 that would run from Red Butte Canyon to the east down to the Temple Block.[59] The railroad was surveyed and partially graded, but an insufficient labor force slowed progress, and by 1852 the plan was scrapped.[60] Sandstone for the wall and temple foundation were then hauled along the same road by wagon. At one point, twenty ox teams were employed to bring stone from the quarry to the Temple Block at an average of two loads per team per day.[61] The method was time- and labor-intensive and prompted pleas for available church members to donate their livestock and labor to expedite the hauling of materials.[62]

Changes to the temple design also inspired innovations in transportation and infrastructure. In early 1855, Brigham Young finalized a decision to change the temple's material composition. "Beautifully variegated" granite (quartz monzonite) had been discovered in the Cottonwood canyons south of Salt Lake City and proved more suitable and durable than adobe for the temple exterior.[63] By the time the decision was made to use granite, the foundation was nearly eight feet high and sixteen feet thick at its base and approximately eight to ten feet wide at its top. This footing extended three feet beyond the structure's planned walls and culminated with a flagging course that ensured the footing would be level for the basement course atop it. The footing and basement walls comprised the below-grade foundation for the temple. In two years, nearly 15 million pounds—over 100,000 cubic feet—of sandstone had been quarried and hauled by teamsters from Red Butte Canyon for the foundation, which was a third more than the amount of stone that was reportedly used to construct the entire Nauvoo Temple.[64] After the foundation footing was finished in July 1855, workers began the arduous task of building the inverted arches, buttresses, and basement walls to complete the foundation.[65] Even with the experience acquired from hauling a large amount of stone for the temple's foundation, the switch to a granite quarry twenty miles from the Temple Block only intensified the challenge of moving stones at a consistent pace for temple construction.

With the announcement of a new quarry in Big Cottonwood Canyon, over fifteen miles to the south of the temple construction site, church leaders commissioned a canal to ship granite to the Temple Block. The initial survey intended the canal to run from the mouth of Big Cottonwood Canyon to a point within Salt Lake City limits.[66] Under the supervision of the Big Cottonwood Canal Company, labor on the waterway took high priority as work on the Temple Block eased for a season. Ecclesiastical wards from Salt Lake City provided labor for the canal, which had progressed enough by 1856 to irrigate lots on the south and east ends of the city.[67] The canal underscored the interconnectedness of public works and temple construction. The superintendent Daniel H. Wells and church architect Truman O. Angell coordinated the timely completion of civic and religious projects. The ambitious scope and pace of building throughout the 1850s especially taxed Angell, who bore the burden of not only designing buildings but also organizing and inspecting the quality of construction.

Work on the temple eventually slowed and then stopped in 1856, at the same time Angell's health suffered. Stress from long hours spent supervising building construction of all kinds, including the temple, eventually overwhelmed him, leading him to petition Brigham Young for "temporary relief" from his role as temple architect.[68] Concerned about Angell's welfare, Young devised a mission for him that would take him out of the Great Basin,

CENTER PLACE   41

to Europe, for over a year. The reasons for the new assignment were two-fold: Young hoped Angell would get some needed rest and would also return home having seen many examples of the grand historic architecture of Europe. His mission was to study "the works of the ancients and marvel to see what they have done" and "comprehend the architectural designs of men in various ages."[69] Angell, whose architectural skill was learned on the job, somehow failed to be impressed by the buildings he observed in Britain and France. He returned home neither rested nor determined to radically change his architectural designs. But in the year since he had departed, much had changed in the territory. As he began to draw a master plan for quarrying granite for the temple, he found the Latter-day Saint population far more committed to the public works and temple projects he supervised.[70]

Rebellion and Reformation

The newfound enthusiasm for the temple's construction that Truman O. Angell noted was due in part to the trials that the Latter-day Saints faced as the outside world they had tried so hard to shut out began to encroach on their settlement. With a few exceptions, Young's isolated settlement in the Great Basin enjoyed relative peace in the early years of its existence. The homogeneous colony, however, was not a sovereign theocracy, despite the best efforts of Latter-day Saint leaders. After the United States—through war and the Treaty of Guadalupe Hidalgo in 1848—had wrested the region from Mexican control, church leaders petitioned the US government for statehood in an ambitious proposal that would have gifted them an outsized portion of the American West. The State of Deseret (the proposed name for their settlement) imagined a Latter-day Saint empire within the shifting borders of the United States. But not surprisingly, politicians and government officials were unwilling to place the newly opened West in the full control of an exiled religious minority. Instead, the Compromise of 1850 carved out the smaller Utah Territory for white settlement, creating a complicated power dynamic. Young still held ultimate authority in the eyes on the territory's residents, who were also his religious adherents, but the US president Millard Fillmore, with the approval of the Senate, retained power to appoint territorial government officials. In an act of goodwill, Fillmore initially selected Young as the territory's governor and superintendent of Indian affairs. Other federal appointees to Utah, however, were outsiders, who lasted only a few months

42   THE SALT LAKE TEMPLE

in the territory before returning to Congress with scathing reports of a theocratic kingdom gone rogue.[71]

The reports were exaggerated, but with the Latter-day Saints' combination of civic and religious authority, they had again seemingly transgressed principles viewed as foundational to the American republic. For raising a functional territory from the dust, Brigham Young's religious influence proved a blessing at first. He could urge support of public works from the pulpit more effectively than he could within the halls of the legislature. Though federal officials grew weary of Young's sweeping gubernatorial power, their failure to act immediately against him gave the Saints room to shape their colony to their liking in the early territorial years. During this time, the territory's most pressing issue was not federal meddling but conflict with dispossessed Native Americans, as well as drought, low crop yields, and scarce resources.

Young began to associate these and other challenges with a declining commitment among the Latter-day Saints to live the principles taught by the church. Over fifteen thousand European emigrants had descended on the Great Basin since 1849,[72] and though the influx in labor was welcomed, not all immigrants remained faithful participants in the communal religious project.[73] Making matters worse, by 1855 the Perpetual Emigrating Fund was heavily in debt, severe drought and insect plagues had depleted the crop reserves in tithing storehouses, and donations flagged. The church's immigration system and public works became strained.[74] In their rush to grow industry and infrastructure, church leaders had overextended scarce resources. In March 1856, Daniel H. Wells called for a suspension of public works: "We have work enough to do, but we have not provisions to give the laborer. It is unpleasant to stop the public works, not only because it retards improvement, but because those who have been laboring on the works look to that quarter for their subsistence. Many who have labored there are without breadstuff or anything to eat."[75] Wells's bleak account coincided with a public announcement from Young that work on the temple would be suspended for a year until church members could prepare themselves "more fully for that work."[76] Still relatively uninhibited by federal interference, the church turned inward, fearful that spiritual and community priorities in their "great nation ... composed of Saints" were slipping.[77]

In their own veritable promised land, the crisis conjured parallels to Old Testament–style punishments invoked by a vengeful God. Calls for reform soon echoed in meeting halls around the territory. The Mormon Reformation (1856–57), as it became known, recentered the minds of Latter-day Saints on the imminence of Christ's millennial return. The religious revival was initially carried out by home missionaries appointed to preach repentance and catechize families on church doctrine and proper moral conduct. In March 1856, Brigham Young called on church leaders to deliver "sermons like peals of thunder" to stir the public.[78] The Reformation refocused the Latter-day Saint population back on Young's communal goals. Many were rebaptized to signify their repentance and commitment to sacrifice for the church's sake. The Reformation also brought in more tithing donations and prompted more plural marriages, both markers in the community of true orthodoxy. Since Joseph Smith's limited introduction of plural marriage in the early 1840s, the practice had expanded to involve nearly half of all households in Utah Territory by 1857.[79] Entering plural marriage was not required for fellowship in the church, but those who did were seen as living a higher form of the Latter-day Saint marriage covenant.

Cleansing the inner vessel had dangerous excesses as well. The impassioned rhetoric of church leaders at times sparked violence and fear.[80] The Reformation also drew stronger borders around the Latter-day Saint empire, which encouraged more apostates and critics and did nothing to resolve the growing chasm between church administration and federally appointed officials in Utah Territory. Building a physical kingdom required steadying the spiritual kingdom, but larger threats to a cohesive Latter-day Saint space were the unintended consequence.

The cause of tension between Latter-day Saints and federal officials was based in ideology and power in the open West. Church leaders repeatedly invoked the political doctrine of popular sovereignty—which became increasingly central to fomenting sectional tensions in the United States during this period—asserting their political autonomy and right to select officials who would reflect the popular ideals of the territory. Congress, however, was concerned that "the Mormons are quite as hostile to the republicanism of government as they are to the usual forms of Christianity. . . . They desire a kingly government, in order to make their patriarchal institutions more homogenous."[81] The Republican platform targeted the Saints during the 1856 election season, castigating the "twin relics of barbarism"—polygamy and slavery—as pressing threats to the Union.[82] Plural marriage and politics in Utah Territory grabbed national newspaper headlines, suggesting that the brief period when the Latter-day Saints had managed to remain free from the public spotlight, in the shadows of the Rocky Mountains, was over. Latter-day Saint expansion into the West tested federal policy and the strength of

44   THE SALT LAKE TEMPLE

Young's religious kingdom.[83] Both empires could not survive together as they were currently arranged.

After his cabinet had received competing status reports from the Latter-day Saints and from sitting territorial officials, newly elected president James Buchanan determined to replace Brigham Young as governor. Buchanan was prepared to install new federal appointees by force if necessary. His eventual choice for Young's successor was Alfred Cumming, who supervised Indian affairs but possessed little administrative experience. In May 1857, with Buchanan's approval, the US Army began planning an expedition to Utah Territory with twenty-five hundred soldiers to escort the new governor and establish a permanent garrison in the territory. By the end of June, news of the pending invasion had reached Utah Territory. Young marshaled the reconstituted Nauvoo Legion (a Latter-day Saint militia that had originally formed in Illinois) and intended to use guerrilla tactics to slow the army's advance.[84]

Even as the Saints stared down military conflict, work started again on the temple in spring 1857, though laborers were diverted to support defensive efforts. Stone was chiseled for the temple's basement, and the first block was placed in June.[85] At an August meeting on the Temple Block, Brigham Young explained his reason for continuing with construction: "With me it is the kingdom of God, or nothing; with us it must be the kingdom of God, or nothing. I shall not go in for anything half-way. We must have the kingdom of God, or nothing. We are not to be overthrown." Even if, with the army approaching, all the buildings in the city were going to burn "next season," Young encouraged the Saints to continue "making improvements." He was apparently addressing some who had been critical of such an "extravagant . . . and deep" foundation for the temple.[86] Given their history of forced migrations, Latter-day Saints were understandably concerned about pouring resources into another temple that would potentially be lost because of their enemies. Yet earlier that year, Young had promised at general conference, "If this people will do as they are told, will live their religion, walk humbly before their God, and deal justly with each other, we will make you one promise, in the name of Israel's God, that you will never be driven from the mountains."[87] His tone on the subject was unwavering throughout 1857.

Though work continued on the temple, Young was less confident about defending the city against the coming army and began considering evacuation routes.[88] The meddling tactics of the Nauvoo Legion as well as early winter storms had delayed the army's progress enough to prevent its arrival in the Salt Lake Valley before winter, giving Young a few months to determine a course of action. As commissioned exploration parties searched for a new settlement site, Thomas L. Kane, a longtime friend of the church and a provisional diplomat of President Buchanan's, entered Utah Territory in February 1858 to negotiate an end to the standoff on vague terms supplied by Buchanan.[89] Kane assured Young the army meant no harm to the Latter-day Saint residents or their property. Still, as a precautionary measure, Young convened a "council of war" on March 18, 1858, and mulled over his idea of taking at least five hundred families from Salt Lake City "into the desert," to let the army "destroy themselves" with no support or supplies from the Latter-day Saints.[90] He announced the decision to the public three days later on the Temple Block.[91] Reassurances from both Kane and Cumming did little to sway Young from his chosen course.

Salt Lake City stood ready to burn in June 1858. A few hundred Latter-day Saints remained in the city, prepared to torch ten years of progress rather than allow the city to be occupied by federal troops. On the heels of a devastating famine in 1857, the resulting move south proved a significant economic disruption to the Latter-day Saint colony. Around thirty thousand residents in the vicinity of Salt Lake City answered the call to move to Provo (forty-five miles to the south of Salt Lake City) and possibly farther south to resettle.[92] For the next two months, a stream of wagons loaded with foodstuffs and valuables flowed out of the city, disrupting the planting season and taxing the city's impoverished residents. Only days after Brigham Young's public order to evacuate, workers at the Temple Block cached the blocks for the basement story and buried the foundation in dirt.[93] The ox teams hauling stone for the temple's basement were reassigned to carry supplies south.[94] The centerpiece of the Latter-day Saint community would appear to the incoming army as a plowed field, marked only by the surrounding adobe wall.

Moving away from the decade-long focal point of Latter-day Saint social, cultural, and religious life carried less measurable, but nonetheless significant, consequences for church morale. The migration south was characterized by disorganization and communication challenges, and it soon became clear that the army did not intend to occupy the city and that the evacuation would be temporary. The army arrived at the end of June and was greeted by the silence of a deserted city. They passed through quickly to establish a garrison nearly fifty miles south of Salt Lake that they named Camp Floyd.[95]

46   THE SALT LAKE TEMPLE

Both the obedient exodus from the city and the slow return of thousands of Latter-day Saints over the summer of 1858 displayed Brigham Young's power and reach in the territory.[96] But beneath the surface, cracks started to form in Latter-day Saint ranks as some bristled at Young's decision to initiate the costly move south. Bishops reported rising apostasy in their ranks, and some of the disillusioned Saints defected to seemingly more hospitable settlements in California.[97] For a people who measured the blessings of providence in crop yields and consecrated public works, the setbacks in these areas—incurred by the hasty departure out of the city—tested the resiliency of the church. The crisis of war may have been averted in the summer of 1858, but it was replaced by a brief crisis of morale.

The fiery rhetoric of the recent Reformation had chastised, purified, and reenlisted church members in building the kingdom of God on earth, but for their obedience, the faithful anticipated progress and prosperity, not more poverty and conflict. The Reformation had reestablished the central importance of public works and the temple to the church's spiritual future. However, the willingness of church leaders to quickly abandon a place of such divine import in the face of impending military conflict threatened to sow discord in the Latter-day Saint movement, particularly among those who bore the economic burden of Brigham Young's orders to relocate. Though apocalypse may have been stayed for a season, reestablishing the church's center place from a temple foundation that had visually disappeared into the dust offered a new challenge.

3

Developing Place

Under the watchful eye of Colonel Albert Sidney Johnston's forces, members of The Church of Jesus Christ of Latter-day Saints uneasily returned to their daily lives. They spent the remainder of 1858 and 1859 restocking depleted tithing storehouses, returning machinery and equipment used by the Public Works Department to the Temple Block, and planting and harvesting crops. Though the evacuation south had hurt the local economy, the economic devastation was short lived. Latter-day Saints quickly entered into trade relations with the army and profited from the army's surplus goods. In 1860, the army garrison of approximately four thousand troops was reduced to just fifteen hundred, and in 1861 the outbreak of the Civil War forced the remaining troops back east. The swift departure of the army left the Latter-day Saints an economic windfall of discounted property and goods, much of which went to restart public works.[1]

By the fall of 1859, digging could be heard from within the walls of the Temple Block as workers excavated the buried foundation and the stone layers, or courses, of the temple's basement walls. In early December, the top of the temple's walls could be seen and inspected resulting in a work stoppage when Truman O. Angell recorded measurements that the foundation was out of level by two inches.[2] Blame fell initially on mason foreman Alonzo H. Raleigh, who had ignored Angell's suggested leveling technique in favor of his own.[3] The discovery proved a costly setback, though it likely saved the structure from crumbling under its own weight later. It would take two more years to fully uncover the foundation and begin repairing the flawed courses of stone.

Work on the Salt Lake Temple did not move at a persistent hum over the construction's forty-year time frame but was instead a project of fits and starts. No one cause, but rather a number of factors in Utah Territory affected the relatively slow rise of the temple walls. Though transportation and technology innovations often improved the speed and efficiency of construction work during this time, economic troubles, war, labor shortages, and shifting ecclesiastical priorities, including the construction of new public buildings

The Salt Lake Temple. Scott D. Marianno and Reid L. Neilson, Oxford University Press.
© Oxford University Press 2025. DOI: 10.1093/9780190881580.003.0004

48　THE SALT LAKE TEMPLE

and temples outside of Salt Lake City, slowed progress on the Salt Lake Temple.

Restarting from the Foundation

Granite blocks littered the Temple Block in June 1862 when Brigham Young ordered First Presidency counselor Daniel H. Wells, who also served as superintendent of public works, to tear down the existing basement walls and remove entirely the underlying sandstone flagging and gravel, to produce a level foundation.[4] Additional repairs were made to portions of the foundation footing. Young's instruction reflected a thoroughness and attention to detail that superseded the desire for a short construction timeline. He railed against the stone masons who contributed to the structural weakness in the foundation by using "pieces of timber as big as [a] coat sleeve to prop up the temple." He was "ashamed of such men," who were "dishonest as the devil" and "slothful" in their hasty work that made the foundation unlevel.[5] Young's comments likely referred to wooden rollers used by the masons to move stones for the foundation that they then neglected to remove when they secured the stones with mortar. Poor mortar at the joints compromised the integrity of the wooden rollers and shims and likely caused some of the dramatic settling observed in the foundation.[6]

Young called for reform among the workmen, inviting them to recommit to quality workmanship. "I could not ask my Father in Heaven to accept a piece of sham work like it," he said in July 1865.[7] Young anticipated "hundreds" of temples "built and dedicated to the Lord," but he predicted the temple in Salt Lake City would "be known as the first Temple built in the mountains by the Latter-day Saints." And he was "willing to wait a few years for it" because a high quality of construction would ensure the building would "endure through the Millennium . . . as a proud monument of the faith, perseverance and industry of the Saints of God in the mountains."[8] Workmen completed the majority of the foundation repairs by the onset of winter 1862.

Over the previous two years, laborers had continued to haul stone to the Temple Block.[9] Hauling the stone required the coordinated work of teamsters along a public road that had been improved for the purpose of moving granite from a new quarry established in Little Cottonwood Canyon. Though other innovations had been implemented to move the stone quicker, many eventually failed.[10] Segments of the canal, for example, which had been dug to float quarried stone to the Temple Block, failed to retain water, causing Young to declare in May 1862 that the canal was defective.[11] Despite challenges in transporting rock from the quarries, granite continued to pile up at the temple site, while no progress was made in assembling the temple walls (Figure 3.1).

The temple's construction was also slowed because it competed with other building projects in the territory that had resumed in the 1860s. The temple was one of several pressing priorities for the Public Works Department, including a theater in Salt Lake City and a larger venue capable of seating thousands for general conference. Plans had been made as early as 1861 to build a tabernacle west of the temple for such a purpose, and it opened in time for the October 1867 general conference.

Overwhelmed by the work of these several projects, Truman Angell resigned his position as church architect in the fall of 1861 to retreat to his farm and recuperate from persistent illness. William H. Folsom, a former carpenter on the Nauvoo Temple and a building contractor, assumed Angell's role for a time. Without Angell's supervision, however, work on the temple

Figure 3.1 Salt Lake Temple Block, 1863. Courtesy Church History Library.

50   THE SALT LAKE TEMPLE

lacked the same direction and focus. Additionally, public works laborers found themselves divided between work on the Tabernacle and work on the temple. The divided priorities also led to labor and material shortages. The need for teamsters to transport stone to the Temple Block became so intense, for example, that in 1864, Young elected to reduce the number of wagon teams sent east to aid immigration to the Salt Lake Valley so they could be reallocated to temple construction.[12]

The urgency to build the temple that had been felt in the 1850s yielded in the 1860s to an understanding that the temple's construction would require time, patience, and careful work. Privately, Brigham Young nurtured reservations that the temple would not be completed in his lifetime. The Civil War fueled speculation among the Latter-day Saints (and Protestants more broadly) that the end times were near. In 1862, while on a stroll of the Temple Block, Young himself shared his opinion with Apostle Wilford Woodruff and others that the temple would likely remain unfinished. Anticipating the second coming of Jesus Christ, Young predicted a return to Zion in Jackson County in seven years to complete a temple there. "There will not be any Temple finished until the One is finished in Jackson County Missouri," he said, admonishing those within earshot to "keep this a secret."[13] But Young continued to believe the Salt Lake Temple would play a millennial role for the church. As the 1860s progressed and the war ended, a return to Jackson County appeared less imminent, and the Salt Lake Temple again took on more urgency.

Maintaining a reliable labor force and an orderly workflow during a time of disruptive hardships and settlement proved the most challenging tasks for those overseeing public works. Fortuitously, Truman Angell returned to his position as church architect in 1867 to complete the interior work on the Tabernacle and to reorganize work on the temple.[14] Folsom, distracted by the new theater and tabernacle, apparently had given little attention to Angell's prior organization of the stonework on the temple. His instruments and charts in disarray, Angell worked quickly to restore order. In his absence, the foundation had been leveled and masonry work had resumed on the temple walls, but the stonecutters and masons lacked firm direction on the Temple Block. The temple walls were barely visible at ground level in 1867. Angell quickly set to revising his earlier stone charts and a corresponding master plan for the temple walls to guide stonecutting and stone placement. Each course of stone received a letter, and each stone within the course a number with corresponding dimensions so that the granite brought to the

Temple Block could be organized, labeled, and finished according to its destination within the temple walls.[15]

With better prospects for future progress on the temple, Brigham Young again rallied church members around the temple at the April 1867 general conference.[16] "We do not calculate that that building will fall down," he noted, since necessary improvements had been made to the foundation. But the "rock does not come as we want it," he reported. Though church members were sending their grain, crops, and livestock to the tithing storehouses, such goods "did not bring the rock here to the temple."[17] Young needed church members to donate their labor, wagons, and livestock to haul rock from the quarries. Hauling assignments were given to the ecclesiastical wards as far north as Box Elder County and as far south as Utah County, and bishops were encouraged to send teamsters to the quarry before the end of the fall season.[18]

Sustained progress, however, still proved elusive, in part because of the transcontinental railroad. Just as construction on the temple hit its stride, Young entered into a federal contract to grade a portion of the railroad in and near Utah Territory. Brigham Young worried that Utah's insular economy might not withstand the cultural and economic disruption effected by the railroad, but he felt the benefits outweighed the risks. Latter-day Saints would be better connected to eastern markets and could dispel prejudices against them as more people crossed through their territory. The railroad would also give Latter-day Saints the opportunity to show national loyalty while bringing seemingly lucrative rail contracts to their cash-starved economy.[19] And the improved national infrastructure would ease the immigration of church converts and provide better transportation for missionaries heading east.

The push to complete the railroad taxed the territory's labor supply. In August 1868, Young suspended work on the temple, instructing the masons and stonecutters to return to their homes for the remainder of the season.[20] The labor shortage that forced the stoppage, however, was of Young's own creation. Throughout summer 1868, he advertised the need for up to five thousand men from around Utah Territory to fill railroad contracts. Many answered the call, motivated by the promise of stable and quality wages. Young himself oversaw the filling of the contracts with the Union Pacific and Central Pacific railroads.[21] Latter-day Saint laborers graded significant portions of the transcontinental railroad through Echo and Weber canyons and from the Utah-Nevada border.[22] It was not until after the two rail lines

52 THE SALT LAKE TEMPLE

were joined on May 10, 1869, at Promontory Summit, north of the Great Salt Lake, that significant progress on the temple resumed.

Unfortunately, Brigham Young's alliance with the major railroad companies failed to bring substantial cash investment into the Utah economy. Both the Union and Central Pacific railroads delayed paying Latter-day Saints wages for their work, and later settlements on outstanding debts proved insufficient, forcing the church to pay uncompensated subcontractors in goods from its own tithing storehouses.[23]

Experienced Latter-day Saint railroad laborers, however, could now set their sights on quickly laying track linking Ogden to Salt Lake City for Brigham Young's newly established Utah Central Railroad. Then a rail spur could be laid further southward to the quarry in Little Cottonwood Canyon. In January 1870, Young drove in the final spike connecting Salt Lake City and Ogden with a mallet inscribed "Holiness to the Lord," the same inscription that would eventually grace the façade of the Salt Lake Temple and a symbolic reminder of the lack of distance between sacred and secular construction projects in most of Utah Territory: both railroad and temple contributed to an unfolding Kingdom of God.[24] Young, to his credit, had anticipated since the temple's groundbreaking that stone would eventually be carted by rail car to the Temple Block.[25] Now, just under two decades later, the time-intensive hauling by teamsters was replaced by the swift movement of rail cars whisking stone to the Temple Block.

From Quarry to Temple Block

The granite stone taken from the quarry in Little Cottonwood Canyon had emerged over the course of millennia. The granite chosen for the temple—a durable igneous stone formed from a mixture of quartz, feldspar, and mica—was sheared from the canyon walls as forceful glaciation exploited its natural fissures, weakening and embrittling the stone. When the fissures cracked, stones often forty or fifty feet tall dislodged and cascaded down the canyon's walls, breaking apart when they hit the ground in the lower reaches of the canyon.[26] The boulders "could not be sawn into blocks like ordinary building stone"; instead, quarrymen armed with hammers and drills split the boulders by driving wedges into predrilled holes. Once the boulder was reduced to roughly the size prescribed by Truman Angell's chart, another stonecutter would chisel it into the precise size and shape (Figure 3.2).[27] As

Figure 3.2 Little Cottonwood Canyon quarry, 1871. Courtesy Church History Library.

the supply of usable boulders in one spot was exhausted, the quarrymen moved up the canyon in search of more rock.

The development of a reliable quarry gave rise to small towns nearby in the 1870s. The first, Granite City, served as the main camp for the quarrymen. However, a superior supply of granite was eventually located up the canyon, and the camp moved closer to where the stonecutting occurred. A new canyon boomtown named Wasatch formed and grew rapidly from thirteen residents in 1874 to over three hundred in 1883. Rails continued to be laid to connect Wasatch to the rail spur, completed in 1873, that ran to Sandy and then northward to Salt Lake City, supported in part by mining companies operating in Little Cottonwood Canyon. Brigham Young celebrated the completion of that line by accompanying a train loaded with granite on its trip to Salt Lake City.[28] Wagons and teamsters again bridged the distance between the new quarry at Wasatch and the rail spur.[29] With better transportation, the growing town of Wasatch hosted church leaders and other prominent Salt Lake City residents who constructed summer homes near the creeks flowing through the canyon, where they could glimpse the difficult work of the quarrymen.[30]

Wasatch boasted a diverse and transient group of rail workers, quarrymen, and miners. Most of the workers in the quarry were young, single Latter-day Saint men from Western Europe who hoped to use their wages to repay their debt to the Perpetual Emigrating Fund or to send money to distant family members for their immigration. Church converts from around the world with any level of ability in stonework were encouraged to join the Saints in the Salt Lake Valley.[31] Demographic trends in church immigration generally corresponded with that of the laborers, most of whom came from England, Wales, Denmark, Sweden, Italy, Scotland, and across regions of the United States. Though strong ethnic pride sometimes stirred debates and contention among the quarrymen, they largely experienced a measure of camaraderie because of their shared work.[32] In addition to those drilling and splitting the rock, a few blacksmiths worked in the camp to sharpen and repair tools. Young boys, too inexperienced to hammer and drill, moved through the work site picking up dull or broken drills and wedges and taking them to the blacksmith shop for sharpening. The remaining work at the quarry site was performed by unskilled laborers assigned by local wards to donate work as a form of tithing.[33] In some cases, quarry work was familial and intergenerational: fathers, sons, and brothers worked together to support the construction of the temple, and mothers and daughters staffed the camp kitchens. On occasion laborers met their future wives in the quarry camp.[34]

The laborers' daily work schedule was arduous. The camp bell roused the workers from their bedrolls at 6:00 a.m., and after a simple meal the men would grab their tools and walk to their stations in the quarry.[35] During an hour break at midday workers received another meal, consisting of donated supplies brought to the camp each week—sides of beef and local produce, fresh or preserved depending on the season—in addition to mutton from local sheep herds.[36] The men would return to their labors until evening, when the cooks again mobilized to prepare an evening meal. The camp then filled its time with leisure activities like games of checkers or mock court trials.[37] At the conclusion of work on Saturday, those who lived nearby returned to their homes to visit family. Others remained at the camp, walking the short distance to the Granite Ward to worship in sacrament meeting and participate in Sunday School.[38]

The quarry was supervised by a hardscrabble Scotsman, James Campbell Livingston. Livingston had joined the church in his native land in 1849 and emigrated four years later, arriving in Salt Lake City in 1853. He soon began working at the quarry at Red Butte, obtaining stone for the Temple Block wall and the temple's foundation and excelled at his work. With Brigham Young's blessing, Livingston started directing the new quarry in Little Cottonwood Canyon sometime in the 1860s. The transient nature of wage labor required him to maintain the morale of a diverse and underpaid workforce while also navigating occasional labor shortages. Despite the challenges, he earned the respect and trust of church leaders as a skilled laborer and administrator who could efficiently manage the complex operation in Little Cottonwood Canyon, and he served in his supervisory role until the quarry work was interrupted by the railroad contracts. While working on a contract near Promontory, Livingston lost his arm in a blasting accident, but in 1870 he returned to his position as supervisor of the quarry until the need for granite diminished in 1892.[39]

Before the railroad provided more efficient transport, contracted teamsters hauled the stone from the quarry to the Temple Block. John Sharp, who assisted Wells in managing the Public Works Department, oversaw the teamsters' work. To help with hauling stone to Salt Lake City, church wards were issued load quotas that ward members were to fulfill throughout the season, and they were also asked to bring equipment and livestock to relieve the church-owned livestock corralled at the mouth of Little Cottonwood Canyon.[40] The trek from the quarry to the Temple Block could take three to four days, which resulted in dozens of wagons scattered along the road into Salt Lake City at any given time. The railroad dispensed with the need for such complex labor arrangements. By 1877, three to four cartloads of stone were departing the quarry each day.[41]

Once the freighted granite reached the Temple Block, it was unloaded, positioned, and labeled based on each stone's planned course within the temple walls. Fifty to eighty stonecutters then set to work reducing the stone to its precise shape according to a drawn chalk outline on the stone so that masons could place and mortar the stone within the walls with little adjustment needed. Stonecutters could take up to one month to finish shaping some stones.[42] According to T. P. Thomas, who supervised the masonry work on the block, the expertise of the fine stonecutters enabled the masons to position the stones with no need for alterations "in the least particle." In 1874, Thomas calculated that his masons had laid over thirty-eight thousand cubic feet of stone, raising the walls sixteen feet from the first floor by the close of the season (Figure 3.3).[43] After the stones were positioned in the temple walls, stonecutters worked on the exterior-facing stones to ensure they presented a smooth, uniform look.[44]

Just as the rail lines made work at the quarry more efficient, technological improvements and innovation made construction at the temple site easier. For example, to expedite the process of lifting stones off the ground and onto the temple walls, Truman Angell devised a derrick system that could hoist the heavy granite blocks to their assigned position.[45] Though this system was originally hand powered, by 1876 a steam engine inside the walls was able to power, one at a time, four different derricks, each located at one of the corners of the temple. Using the derricks, workers were able to lay the stone courses in segments.

Figure 3.3 Salt Lake Temple Block, 1875. Courtesy Church History Library.

As the temple walls moved higher, other methods were used to more efficiently place the granite blocks. In 1878, Angell advocated and received approval for the construction of internal trestles so that workmen could climb up and aid the derricks in properly placing the stones. In this derrick-and-trestle system, a steel tramway moved blocks from outside the temple to a platform inside the temple walls. A derrick then hoisted the blocks up to another platform positioned at the current wall height, from which another tramway moved the stones to their respective destinations in the walls. A derrick, along with masons, then secured the stone in its final position (Figure 3.4).[46] This process for placing stone was elaborate and attracted regular crowds to the temple site, who hoped to catch a glimpse of the large stones being lifted into place.[47]

This system, Truman Angell calculated, saved the church thousands of dollars in wages by cutting down the time it took to place the stones.

Figure 3.4 Salt Lake Temple, 1879. Courtesy Church History Library.

58   THE SALT LAKE TEMPLE

The wood trestles were later repurposed and used to frame the interior floors and walls of the temple.[48] The benefits, however, came at a cost. As the temple walls rose, so too did the risk of injury or death, mostly from falls. With novice workers and donated labor as a form of tithing, accidents, though surprisingly rare, occurred, despite some safety protocols in place. For example, in 1881, William Pullen died while managing a derrick on the southwest corner of the temple after a gust of wind blew the derrick into him, pushing him away from the wall and causing him to fall to the temple's basement, over sixty feet below.[49] Another death occurred in January 1890 when Robert Ford slipped from a circular window and fell thirty feet, hitting exposed timbers as he fell.[50]

Inexperienced workers not only created safety concerns but also made consistent progress difficult. The workflow and technological innovations established by Truman Angell were intended to improve labor conditions and offset labor shortages to accelerate the speed of construction. Despite the improvements, public works struggled to maintain a labor pool with the skills needed to finish temple construction. To address the shortage, in 1876 the First Presidency sent a circular to the priesthood quorums in wards throughout the territory asking for "finished stonecutters" capable of perfecting the exterior walls of the temple, a task that required more technical skill than did working on the hidden interior walls. The work was to be done during the winter months as a donated service.[51]

The demand for skilled workers for the temple's construction was a persistent problem that was exacerbated as the church's control over the territorial economy weakened. With the entrance of the railroad into the territory, the home enterprises that the church encouraged competed more directly with imports from eastern markets. In addition, emerging industries like the mines in Little Cottonwood Canyon pulled Latter-day Saints away from church-owned manufacturing, agriculture, and public works projects with the promise of cash wages. With a labor market starved for cash, public works projects, including the temple, relied on in-kind payments from the tithing storehouses. Into the 1880s, for example, the church continued to compensate its workers predominantly with goods taken in by the General Tithing Office. As a result, the quarrymen were significantly limited in the goods they could purchase for their families. In May 1880, John C. Livingston and his fellow quarrymen wrote a letter to church leaders pleading for an increase in their meager salaries.[52] But the church's legal situation grew more precarious in the 1880s, which did little to relieve the cash shortage in the territory and also sapped the tithing storehouses of surpluses as membership donations flagged for a time. Work on the temple in all its forms thus remained a sacrifice for many as they attempted to follow prophetic command to build in difficult circumstances.

Recognizing the need to support the workers on the temple, local ward women's organizations, known as Relief Societies, supplemented the men's payment with donated food and clothing that was generally homegrown or handmade, including wool and cotton trousers and shirts, socks, quilts, fruit, and vegetables.[53] The charitable labor of female volunteers reprised a tradition from Nauvoo, where the first Relief Society was organized to support the construction of the Nauvoo Temple.

As technological innovations like the railroad introduced outside influences to Utah Territory and significantly disrupted its economy, Brigham Young's response was to rally the community to greater obedience and unity. For Young, the loss of economic control portended the loss of spiritual control in the territory. Calling for financial and physical support for the temple from all Latter-day Saints became one avenue for shoring up community allegiance to distinctive church ideals. To ensure broad participation in temple construction, including from church members who lived far from the Temple Block or canyon quarry, Young made a radical departure from prior church temple-building efforts. Even with a tepid economy, Young determined that church members should build more than one House of the Lord.

Expanding the Temple Network

Temples physically represented the theological aspirations of the Latter-day Saints and their efforts to find kinship and create eternal connections with one another—connections that were formalized through ordinance and ritual. But the Salt Lake Temple's slow development left some promises and religious expectations unfulfilled. The temporary Endowment House satisfied the demand for living ordinances for a time; over the course of thirty-four years, close to sixty-nine thousand marriage sealings and over fifty-four thousand endowments for the living were performed there. The Endowment House became a significant stopping point for all new immigrants entering the Salt Lake Valley who wished to progress through Latter-day Saint ritual.

60 THE SALT LAKE TEMPLE

The ordinance work done at the Endowment House, however, did not satisfy all of the expectations of Brigham Young and other church leaders. Endowment House ritual, for instance, did not include ordinances that would later be performed in temples, including the sealing of parents to children and endowments for the dead. These potential expansions to temple ritual were occasionally spoken of by Young and other church leaders. In an 1873 discourse, for instance, Young promised that children would one day be sealed to their parents, living or dead, in temples: "To connect the chain of the priesthood from father Adam until now, by sealing children to their parents, being sealed for our forefathers, etc., they cannot be done without a Temple. . . . Neither will children be sealed to their living parents in any place other than a Temple."[54] In addition, apostle and later church president Wilford Woodruff, who found himself drawn to genealogy and temple work more than some of his fellow apostles, imagined a time when "all the ordinances of the gospel of Christ" would be available to "all the dead who have died without the gospel," though it would "take 1,000 years with Jesus Christ at the head" before their vicarious work would be completed.[55] Though baptisms on behalf of those who had died had been consistently performed by the Latter-day Saints, other vicarious ordinances, including endowments for the dead, had not. These expansions in vicarious work were pushed to a future day when Latter-day Saints would again possess a dedicated temple. Given the slow timeline of temple construction, however, the notion of vicarious work for the dead predictably lapsed in the ensuing years.[56]

Nearly seventy years old in 1870, Young grew fearful he would not see the day when Latter-day Saints again crowded a dedicated temple to partake of all temple ordinances for themselves and their dead. The aging church president, slowed by arthritis, made annual winter trips in the 1870s three hundred miles south of Salt Lake City to the warmer southern settlement of St. George, where the red-rock desert landscape enjoyed a mild winter climate. Young had frequently mused about the possibility of building other temples outside of Salt Lake City, and his new winter home seemed an ideal place to commence just such a project. On January 31, 1871, he asked Apostle Erastus Snow, then president of the Southern Mission, about the feasibility of constructing a temple in the city. The proposal was met with excitement and approval.[57] If Young harbored any reservations about commencing a new costly temple in the wake of the chronic delays plaguing the construction of the Salt Lake Temple, he did not express them.

In actuality, St. George held advantages that enabled the church to avoid the challenges associated with the Salt Lake Temple construction. The region's moderate winter climate meant fewer weather-related construction delays. St. George did not shoulder as many competing priorities like the Salt Lake Valley did with its massive public works enterprise. The city was geographically isolated from other major settlements, protecting the temple from prying federal authorities who were beginning to more actively oppose the Saints' plural marriages, which were solemnized through sealing ordinances. At such an advantageous location, St. George appeared to be the best place to begin a new era of temple work.

Church leaders broke ground on the St. George temple on November 9, 1871. To expedite construction, the best of the public works talent was sent there. This included Truman Angell, who was responsible for the new temple's design, and Miles Romney, who served as superintendent of construction. After experiencing some challenges in excavating the ground for the foundation, the first cornerstone was finally placed in March 1873. Only two years later the stone walls had reached their maximum height. By 1876, work on the interior of the temple moved forward at a rapid pace. Visitors to the city stood in awe at the white-plastered temple, towering in stark relief against the lava rock and red sediment that formed the mountains surrounding the settlement.[58] If the slow crawl of the Salt Lake Temple began to wear on the emotions of the Latter-day Saints, the swift raising of the St. George Temple stirred renewed excitement for temple worship.

On New Year's Day 1877, over two thousand people converged on the mostly finished temple to attend the dedication of the baptistery, the upper assembly hall, and a sealing room. After the dedicatory prayers, Brigham Young, who had been confined to a chair and carried throughout the temple for the service due to a debilitating bout of rheumatism, spoke next. His forceful sermon urged the Saints to recommit to work on behalf of the dead. "Do you have any feelings for those who have died without hearing the gospel?" he asked. "The spirit was awakened in the people in the North [Salt Lake City] when we gave the word that we should do no more work in the Endowment House they Came to us Crying and pleading to be baptized for their dead," he continued. "What Els[e] Could they do? They Can Come here and do the work for their dead."

Young urged the Saints to avoid the influence of outsiders and to rally around their new temple by reawakening their duty to bring about the "salvation of the human family." At the end of his sermon, Young struck his

62 THE SALT LAKE TEMPLE

hickory cane on the pulpit and promised to never be "satisfied until the devil is whiped and driven from off the face of the Earth."[59] As the Latter-day Saints witnessed the dedication of a temple for the first time since Nauvoo, Young ignited a spiritual fire.

With expanded options for temple work—including temple sealings to children and vicarious endowments—the temple experience for Latter-day Saints underwent a critical shift. After being initiated into temple work individually, Latter-day Saints were encouraged to return and experience the ordinances again on behalf of their deceased ancestors.[60] Brigham Young had lamented publicly as early as 1851 that those who had received an endowment in Nauvoo still "know but very little about the endowments" because "there was no time to learn them and what little they did learn" they had now "forgotten."[61] Latter-day Saints could now reexperience temple ordinances as they performed them vicariously for family, increasing their exposure to the language and narratives of temple ritual and the time they spent in their sacred spaces.[62]

Anticipating a massive increase in temple work, Young sought standardization in the process of administering temple ordinances for the living and the dead. This included the complex task of writing down the scripts of all the ordinance ceremonies, including the endowment ceremony, whose text had been only an oral tradition to this point. Apostle Wilford Woodruff, with the aid of others, spent weeks after the opening of the St. George Temple carefully recording and revising the language of the ordinances under Young's supervision. By mid-April 1877, when Young was preparing to head north to Salt Lake City, the procedures and language of temple work had been standardized to his satisfaction.[63]

With new vicarious ordinance opportunities, Latter-day Saints flocked to the temple. Some even traveled from the north to enter the first full-scale dedicated temple since Nauvoo. In just one day, January 9, under the supervision of church leaders still in St. George after the dedication, 224 baptisms for the dead were recorded. (The temple would reach over thirty thousand by year's end.) The first endowments for the dead were completed on January 11, and over 112 were completed by the end of the month. The chance to redeem the dead increasingly recaptured the imagination of Latter-day Saints, leading to the performance of tens of thousands of endowments and sealings for the dead before century's end.[64]

With the temple as its central project, St. George had become a test site for Brigham Young's effort to rejuvenate spiritual commitment, including economic cooperation, throughout Utah Territory. In his twilight years, Young grew anxious that the moral principles of the church's Zion in the West were slipping. Allegedly influenced by outsiders to the territory, church members were yielding to individualistic economic enterprises, sin, and complacency in their religious endeavors. Attempts to fortify the Saints' faith had so far brought only mixed results. In 1874, following an economic panic, Young had attempted to return church members to a cooperative economic arrangement he called the United Order. Church leaders attempted to establish this new order in St. George, but though the city's residents proved adept at donating and building the temple, they were less successful in living out the true aims of the United Order, which sought to foster economic self-sufficiency, personal righteousness, and community unity. Young lamented in both private and public that many were reticent to enter the communal order and to share their labor, wages, and goods for the benefit of others.[65]

The short-lived United Order, however, did bring into focus a plan Young set in motion over the final years of his life. With large corporate industries like mining and rail service at Zion's doorstep, he initiated a retrenchment to center Latter-day Saints on their own spiritual and temporal communities. At the same time, he advocated for the settlement of outposts throughout the American West. His colonizing push was not just an attempt to preserve the local merchant and farming industries of the territorial economy but also an effort to protect the religious identity of his flock. Young hoped to create spiritual enclaves where the church's distinctive temporal and spiritual ideals could be lived out unfettered by outside interference.

Brigham Young's desire to better minister to the Latter-day Saints led to a churchwide reorganization in the final year of his life. Though Salt Lake City had originally been imagined as the center stake of the church, now each county in the territory, if possible, was to have its own stake and a stake presidency comprised of local residents. The reorganization released many of the apostles from their dual role as apostles and stake presidents and led to the creation of new stakes, bringing the total number to twenty. After the reorganization, church members' behavior was still under the observation of priesthood leaders, but the administrative burden shifted away from church headquarters in Salt Lake City.[66]

Young's reorganization was in harmony with his other initiatives: establishing the United Order and temple building. These reforms were intended to work together to create communities centered on covenants. On his return trip from St. George to Salt Lake City, Young detoured to Sanpete

64 THE SALT LAKE TEMPLE

County, where on April 25, 1877, he selected a site on a small hill in Manti for another temple.[67] Less than a month later, on May 18, he repeated the process north of Salt Lake City, in Cache Valley, choosing another temple site at a scenic overlook near the heart of Logan.[68] The selected sites divided the Latter-day Saints' attention on the Salt Lake Temple among three other temples and eventually brought most of those living in the territory within one day's travel to a temple.

When Brigham Young selected the spot for the Salt Lake Temple shortly after reaching the valley in July 1847, he hoped he would live to preside at its dedication. However, he never saw the temple higher than its second floor. By the end of summer 1877, his health had deteriorated, and he passed away at the age of seventy-six on August 29. At the time of his death, the leader who had guided the church through a leadership crisis, a wholesale exodus from the United States, and the colonization of the Great Basin was as celebrated for his more recent reforms. "The great desire of President Young in the last year of his life," Wilford Woodruff remarked at his funeral, "was that before he passed away he might erect Temples to the name of the Lord, in that way and manner that men bearing the holy priesthood in the flesh could enter into those temples and perform their missions for the redemption of the dead."[69] Apostle Erastus Snow counted it a "great joy" that before his death, Young had been able to "complete one Temple" and set "in order . . . the priesthood and the ordinances for the redemption of the dead, as well as for the exaltation of the living."[70] The great charge left to Latter-day Saints in the wake of Young's death was to recommit themselves to the community project of temple building.

Latter-day Saints had long imagined temples at the center of their communities. After decades without a functioning temple, the completion of the St. George Temple in 1877 put such a notion back into practice. But while temples became more closely tethered to the religious and cultural lives of Latter-day Saints, they also became sites of opposition from the US government. As church members celebrated the spiritual benefits offered by their new temples, federal officials focused more seriously on completely terminating any House of the Lord operated by the church.

4

Contested Place

Thirty-six miles south of Salt Lake City, Elizabeth Brown stood before a gathering of women of The Church of Jesus Christ of Latter-day Saints at a small meetinghouse in the Utah County community of Pleasant Grove. News had spread quickly out of Salt Lake City: Latter-day Saint leaders were in trouble. In the winter of 1884–85, federal marshals descended on the territory to root out and prosecute high-profile polygamists. In the midst of this threat, Brown, who had served as Relief Society president for the Pleasant Grove congregation since 1868, attempted to rally the spirits of her sisters. "This is a blessed day in which we live," she declared. "The same power that delivered Ancient Israel is over us today, and the Lord is just as able to deliver us and he will protect his chosen people." She had previously condemned the federal officers, calling them "peddlers who have an object in prying into our family affairs."[1] Brown urged members to be faithful to the purpose and mission of the Relief Society to engender God's protection.

Local ward relief societies were organized beginning in 1867, drawing on the tradition of the first Relief Society, founded in Nauvoo, Illinois, in 1842. In the Utah Territory, the societies became a significant political and economic force through which Latter-day Saint women effectively engaged in public debate and politically mobilized, defending plural marriage while also supporting women's rights and women's suffrage, a cause gaining steam in the East. (Women in the Utah Territory won the right to vote in 1870.)[2] Church leaders expected Relief Societies to promote the production of home goods in order to foster self-sufficiency among the Latter-day Saints and to decrease members' reliance on outside markets. Latter-day Saint women also led a retrenchment movement to "annihilate degenerating habits and customs" and to support the poor.[3] By 1870, over one hundred Relief Societies were operating throughout the territory.[4]

Church president Brigham Young and subsequent church leaders relied on Relief Societies to assist with community initiatives and building projects, including the four temples being constructed in the Utah Territory. Over the span of twenty-four years, Brown's Pleasant Grove Relief Society had

The Salt Lake Temple. Scott D. Marianno and Reid L. Neilson, Oxford University Press.
© Oxford University Press 2025. DOI: 10.1093/9780190881580.003.0005

66   THE SALT LAKE TEMPLE

donated $135 in cash to aid in constructing the Salt Lake Temple and an additional $443 in goods. They were not alone in their charitable efforts.[5] Relief Society leaders for the Salt Lake Stake commissioned members as God's "handmaidens . . . called to be co-laborers with our brethren in building up the kingdom of God upon the earth, in assisting to build Temples, wherein we can receive blessings for time and eternity."[6] Relief Societies across the territory donated shoes, socks, shirts, hats, quilts, and other homespun goods earmarked for the Salt Lake Temple fund. Societies also offered their surplus wheat and produce to benefit temple construction. Children's primary organizations, which were all led by women, held fairs and activities to raise temple funds. The sacrifices and labor of thousands of Latter-day Saint women and children, combined with the donations of countless others, sustained temple construction in an era when cash was scarce and many lived modestly.

As the 1880s progressed, however, the financial donations of those who contributed to the temple were threatened along with polygamist church leaders. Antipolygamy legislation permitted federal officials to confiscate the church's property, including its temples, sparking a battle over the core practices of the religion. The two key identity markers of the Saints—polygamy and the temple—were placed in contest with one another. Federal officials would not let them have both. In challenging plural marriage, critics of the church were contesting the legitimacy of the Saints' empire in the American West; the practice was viewed as an outgrowth of a theocratic misuse of power and politics by a deviant hierarchy. The church, as a result, appeared wholly undemocratic to the American public. To lawmakers and reformers in the East, the Temple Block in particular represented how the church failed to measure up to Protestant conceptions of a legitimate American faith.[7]

Latter-day Saints, however, refused to see as valid the public indictment of their system of marriage and kingdom-building aspirations. Plural marriage held economic advantages by bringing disadvantaged women into financially stable households. The practice also facilitated a demographic surge in children born into Latter-day Saint households.[8] But beyond its suggested practical advantages, Latter-day Saints defended the practice as a commandment from God through their prophet, which placed any questions about its continuance squarely in the realm of a fight over the constitutional protection of religious liberty.[9] By the 1870s, the number of participants in plural marriage had shrunk from about half of all households in Utah Territory to only one-quarter.[10] The practice, however, was still a critical component of church teachings on eternal marriage and exaltation. If the federal government could legally force a discontinuance of Latter-day Saint marriage practices, then it could also significantly regulate other aspects of church religious practice and worship, so church leaders reasoned. Public outcries against such interference in the Latter-day Saint system of salvation came from all corners of the church, including the Relief Society. Self-rule within their own Zion society hung in the balance as distinctive temples continued to rise from the Great Basin floor.

At its core, the church's kingdom in the West worked because of the Latter-day Saints' devotion to the central vision of their priesthood leaders, to whom they granted significant power. Individuals were sincerely dedicated to the idea of a Zion society, evidenced in part by the material sacrifices they made to build ornate worship spaces for temple ordinances. And it was these sacrifices—nearly forty years of physical labor and tithing donations by lay Latter-day Saints—that weighed on the mind of church president Wilford Woodruff as the federal antipolygamy campaign reached a climax.

For Temporal Salvation: Temples and the Manifesto on Polygamy

Brigham Young had so far mostly avoided direct federal intervention in the territory over the practice of plural marriage. Lawmakers had railed against polygamy in the halls of Congress but were hesitant to spend more financial and military resources after the Utah War. The antipolygamy legislation passed in the 1860s had few real provisions for enforcement and did little to slow the practice.[11] The Civil War and the subsequent work of Reconstruction also consumed legislative priorities and distracted Congress for a number of years from implementing a solution to the polygamy problem.

Latter-day Saints, too, were anxious to settle the polygamy question after enduring decades of public debate and threats of prosecution. Hoping to achieve protections for their religious practice, church leaders determined to test the courts. In 1874, with the support of church leaders, polygamist George Reynolds yielded himself to federal authorities and was placed on trial for violating the 1862 Morrill Anti-Bigamy Act. After Reynolds was found guilty, the verdict was immediately appealed on grounds of religious freedom. The test case backfired, however, when the US Supreme Court

68   THE SALT LAKE TEMPLE

in 1879 did the opposite of what church leaders had expected: the justices upheld the conviction, affirming the constitutionality of antipolygamy legislation under the First Amendment, which they asserted safeguarded religious belief but offered no protection for religious practice.[12]

The *Reynolds* decision gave Congress precedent to impose harsher legislation against polygamists and inspired reformers who decried plural marriage as barbaric, exploitative, and antirepublican. A wave of national attention swept over the Utah Territory in the 1880s, and Latter-day Saints dug in. For a time, church leaders feared they would meet the same legal fate as Reynolds, who had been imprisoned. Wilford Woodruff, then an apostle and president of the St. George Temple, briefly left the territory in 1880 to visit Latter-day Saint settlements in Arizona.[13] While on his journey, in late January 1880, near the Little Colorado River, Woodruff awoke "about midnight" when "the Lord . . . opened the vision of [his] mind" to the "will of God." In his vision, Woodruff was told of pending apocalyptic devastation. "I have decreed plagues to go forth and lay waste mine enemies and not many years hence they shall not be left to pollute mine heritage," the Lord told Woodruff. The revelation condemned "the presidents of the United States, the Supreme Court, the cabinet, the Senate and House of Congress of the United States, the Governors of the States and Territories, the judges and officers," and anyone else who persecuted the Saints. To bring about the destruction of the church's enemies, the revelation instructed the Saints to repent and stay close "to the ordinances of [God's temple]" or risk being severed from them.[14] For the Saints, temples were thus both the target of and the solution to their persecution.

Woodruff returned from the south in time for the April 1880 general conference and shared his revelation with the Quorum of the Twelve Apostles. According to the provisions of the revelation, less than a year later church leaders gathered in prayer to condemn the church's enemies. The prayer—read by John Taylor, who after Young's death had been sustained as church president in October 1880—asked God to "protect thy Church, thy Kingdom and thy people from the Power of the wicked" so that they might continue in "building the Temples of our God and redeeming Our dead."[15]

Latter-day Saints viewed external persecution as endemic to the mortal experience of God's chosen people, so church leaders naturally expected their temples to be threatened in the final scenes before Christ's return. Believing they were marching steadily toward the Millennium, the Saints anticipated that "the rage of the arch-enemy of mankind [would increase]" and his emissaries" would "grow more relentless and cruel, more brutal and inhuman in their efforts ... as the number of temples" grew.[16]

The First Presidency sounded a constant refrain during this period for the church membership to fulfill their religious obligation to perform temple work. For example, an 1886 epistle to the church urged the "thousands of Israel" to attend the temples "to minister the ordinances of salvation for their ancestors and departed friends."[17] Large numbers of church members obediently traveled to the Logan Temple (completed in 1884) to the north and to the temples in Manti (completed in 1888) and St. George (completed in 1877) to the south to perform ordinance work for themselves and their dead.

The growing emphasis on temples and vicarious ordinance work for the dead did not result in a corresponding de-emphasis on plural marriage. Instead, church leaders appeared uncompromising on this religious practice, hoping their obedience to the doctrine would bring about the church's deliverance. Angus M. Cannon, who maintained considerable authority and influence as president of the church's largest stake in Salt Lake City, declared to church members in 1881, "We are not called upon to make exceptions to the rules God had established." He denounced those who taught that a man "would attain to the same exaltation with one wife, as with more."[18] He reiterated this message four years later, in 1885: "It seems to be the aim of certain parties who do not comprehend our position as a people, to have us renounce the principle of the Celestial law of Marriage." It was "God who revealed it," and only God would deliver the church "from the power of the wicked," Cannon maintained.[19]

Federal authorities, however, were prepared for a fight that would eventually transform the Salt Lake City Temple Block into a hunting ground to capture polygamist church leaders. More comprehensive antipolygamy legislation in 1882 created a new prosecutable offense—"unlawful cohabitation"—which carried a sentence of up to six months in prison and a three-hundred-dollar fine. In addition, the law disenfranchised polygamists and permitted federal courts to exclude jurors who supported polygamy.[20] The law inspired a polygamist manhunt in Utah Territory. Convictions for unlawful cohabitation spiked as each arrested polygamist was indicted and brought to trial. The "Raid," as these frequent arrests became known, forced church leaders into hiding and out of Salt Lake City (generally to the north or south). While federal marshals searched mostly for the leaders, polygamists in the pews, with fewer options for concealment, bore the brunt of the Raid.[21] The Raid reached even the Salt Lake Temple's workforce, including James

70 THE SALT LAKE TEMPLE

Moyle, foreman of the stonecutters on the Temple Block.[22] Meanwhile, the First Presidency vanished from their usual place of public administration near the temple.[23]

With church leaders "underground," moving along an intricate network of homes and hideouts, church business slowed to a crawl. In their absence, Apostle Franklin D. Richards became the public face of the church; he had decided not to cohabitate with his plural wives and maintained strong connections with judicial officials in Weber County, where he used to serve as a probate judge.[24] He administered the church from the Historian's Office southeast of the Temple Block. Late in 1887, Richards and his secretary, John M. Whitaker, began to move church records and materials from the Historian's Office in case federal marshals raided or assumed control of church property.[25] The Edmunds-Tucker Act passed by Congress earlier that year authorized the disincorporation of the church, the confiscation of church property, and other punitive provisions for the persistence of polygamy.[26] To prevent federal officials from confiscating some of the church's property, leaders dispersed corporate property and documents into private hands and into newly created nonprofit ecclesiastical corporations, managed by loyal local leaders.[27] In November 1887, however, Frank Dyer, the Democrat-appointed federal marshal in Utah Territory, briefly confiscated the Temple Block and a number of other church properties.[28]

Political pressure continued to mount against the church, shifting the balance of power in Utah Territory. By 1890, just over half of the territory's nearly 208,000 residents were Latter-day Saints. The church-supported People's Party lost key municipal elections in 1889 and 1890, further weakening the alliance the church had previously enjoyed with local civic and judicial officials.[29] Additional pressure from the federal government forced church president Wilford Woodruff to make certain concessions. In June 1890, he confidentially ordered church leaders to stop performing new plural marriages within the borders of the United States.[30] But this measure was unknown to the public and failed to satisfy the church's critics. The next month a newly appointed receiver, Henry W. Lawrence, officially replaced Dyer, who was accused by Republicans of being too soft on the church. Woodruff feared that Lawrence, an excommunicated Latter-day Saint who had frequently protested Young's political and financial control over the territory in the past, would not stop short of the church's complete destruction.[31]

The final frontier for the antipolygamy campaign seemed to be not just the Temple Block but the Salt Lake Temple itself. Rumors swirled in August 1890 that Lawrence would soon take control of Latter-day Saint temples. Despite legal protections for properties used for religious worship, Woodruff had long worried something like this would happen.[32] First Presidency counselor George Q. Cannon wrote in early September, "The effort seems to be to prove a connection between the Church and the temples, so as to get some claim upon them, and to show that they are used for illegal purposes."[33] On September 24, Woodruff met with select church leaders to weigh a response to the rumors. The next day, Woodruff wrote in his journal, "I have arived at a point in the History of my life whare I am under the necessity of acting for the Temporal Salvation of the Church. The United State Government has taken a Stand & passed Laws to destroy the Latter day Saints upon the Subjet of poligamy or Patriarchal order of Marriage. And after Praying to the Lord & feeling inspired by his spirit I have issued ... [a] Proclamation which is sustained by My Councillors and the 12 Apostles."[34]

Woodruff drafted this proclamation, known as "the Manifesto," and invited church leaders to provide input. The Manifesto declared Woodruff's commitment to encourage church members to obey federal laws on polygamy, marking the culmination of a slow move away from the defiance sounded in his January 1880 revelation. Church leaders had already been discouraging preaching on the doctrine of plural marriage for a few years.[35] The First Presidency ordered the demolition of the Endowment House in the fall of 1889 to prevent new plural marriages from being solemnized in Salt Lake City.[36] By all appearances, Woodruff had started to prepare for the end of plural marriage well before the Manifesto.

Wilford Woodruff later offered insight into his decision to issue a public manifesto, emphasizing the importance of protecting temple work. "I have had some revelations of late and very important ones to me," he declared at a conference in Cache County in 1891. "The Lord has told me by revelation that there are many members of the Church throughout Zion who are sorely tried in their hearts because of that manifesto. ... The question is this: Which is the wisest course for the Latter-day Saints to pursue—to continue to attempt to practice plural marriage ... at the cost of the confiscation and loss of all the Temples, and the stopping of all the ordinances therein, both for the living and the dead." Woodruff said that he saw "in vision" what would happen to the church and its temples if plural marriage persisted: "All ordinances would be stopped throughout the land of Zion. Confusion would reign throughout Israel and many men would be made prisoners."[37] The temples occupied Woodruff's mind as he weighed the future of the church against its present circumstances.

72 THE SALT LAKE TEMPLE

The Manifesto marked the beginning of the end of plural marriage, but it was not the conclusion itself.[38] When Woodruff first issued the Manifesto, he gave no counsel to existing Latter-day Saints in plural marriages, and many did not know if they should continue living in their polygamist families. No prescriptions were offered on how Latter-day Saints should treat future plural marriages, and Latter-day Saints were uncertain if the church would fully disavow its controversial doctrine. Instead, the Manifesto amounted to a statement intended to alleviate the firestorm of public controversy over plural marriage, which it did. Indicted polygamists were ultimately pardoned, and church property was returned.

In the end, it was the church community and culture that bore the final costs of the antipolygamy crusade. The Manifesto commenced a slow evolution away from a religious practice formative to Latter-day Saint notions of eternity and salvation that structured much of their community and family life. Polygamy also helped Latter-day Saints stake out their separateness from the world, fostering a vital sense of peculiarity. Plural marriage, however, composed just a piece of the church's unique doctrine on heaven and families. The temple formed another critical piece; its ordinances and rituals had developed in tandem with church teachings on marriage since the 1840s. All marriages, plural or not, required a sealing ordinance to be efficacious for eternity, and such ordinances would be confined to the church's new temples. The temple guarded one important marker of Latter-day Saint identity and purpose in the wake of the Manifesto.

The Salt Lake Temple's anticipated completion thus sat at a pivotal juncture for the church. If the antipolygamy crusade left the Latter-day Saint community reeling, the Salt Lake Temple, the church's central and most elaborate project, offered a rallying point with a rich cosmology capable of reminding Latter-day Saints of their distinctive peoplehood. And by 1890 its walls had finally reached a height where its granite symbols became visible to all who passed by.

A Granite Sermon: Temple Symbolism

The ornateness of the Romanesque and Gothic styles chosen for the Salt Lake Temple catered to the potential for a tableau of symbolism on its exterior. And while nineteenth-century Protestant-born Latter-day Saints remained skeptical of the historical iconography found within the Roman

CONTESTED PLACE 73

Catholic tradition, for example, their own architecture was not devoid of symbols. Common Christian and Masonic symbols appeared on buildings and headstones throughout Utah Territory. The overt symbolism employed to instruct participants in Latter-day Saint temple liturgy left church culture symbol rich. Certain aspects of Latter-day Saint temple worship were confined strictly to within the temple, but other symbols could serve as a reminder of the centrality of priesthood and temple within the church's whole system of religion. The symbolism on the exterior of the Salt Lake Temple served to mark the richness and doctrinal import of the hidden and guarded ritual on the interior. And both would pique the curiosity of uninitiated visitors to Salt Lake City for years to come.

The Salt Lake Temple's exterior wall design followed that of the earlier Nauvoo Temple, which was the first Latter-day Saint temple to have extensive symbols carved into the exterior stone. (Symbols played a far less visible role on the pioneer temples in St. George, Manti, and Logan.) The symbols on the Salt Lake Temple were intended to reflect the spiritual truths and cosmology learned within the temple. Though neither Truman Angell nor Brigham Young ever publicly explained the full meaning behind all of the symbols, they appeared to be inspired by church doctrine and scripture, the Nauvoo Temple, and traditional Christian iconography.

Young used material symbols to clarify to Latter-day Saints the connection between temple worship and the priesthood. At the temple cornerstone ceremony in April 1853, Young's sermon showed Latter-day Saints "the order of the Priesthood," which was "circumscribed by, or . . . incorporated within the circumference of, the Apostleship."[39] The hierarchical order of the priesthood was underscored by the Salt Lake Temple's towers and spires. Assistant architect William Ward recalled Young's instructions to build "three towers on the east, representing the President and his two counselors; also three similar towers on the west representing the Presiding Bishop and his two Counselors; the towers on the east the Melchisedek priesthood, those on the west the Aaronic priesthood. The centers towers will be higher than those on the sides, and the west towers a little lower than those on the east end."[40] Additionally, Angell claimed the twelve pinnacles on the east and west towers represented, respectively, the Quorum of the Twelve and the twelve members of the stake high councils.[41] This iconography for Young's conception of priesthood was a material marker of church leaders' authority over the religious society in the Great Basin. But the combination of priesthood symbolism with cosmological symbols, which also featured prominently

74 THE SALT LAKE TEMPLE

on the temple walls, also pointed to temple worship's central focus on the eternities.

In recounting the details of the temple's design in 1854, Truman Angell said the temple would "symbolize the great architectural work above."[42] Earth stones, moon stones, sun stones, and star stones were successively chiseled into the temple walls. The sun, moon, and stars were used in Latter-day Saint scripture to symbolize the church's tiered heavenly glories—the Celestial, Terrestrial, and Telestial kingdoms, respectively—but they do not ascend in corresponding order on the temple walls. Fifty earth stones, the largest of the astronomical stones, were placed even with the basement floor, representing the universal destiny of the church;[43] early in Angell's design, these stones were more ornamented, representing different areas of the globe, but executing the design in granite proved too challenging.[44] Directly above the earth stones and just below the second string course of stone, a series of moon stones, weighing twenty-eight hundred pounds each, depicted the different moon phases for the year 1878.[45] The east side of the temple showed the lunar phases for the month of April, likely to commemorate the organization of the church on April 6, 1830.[46] The sunstones were placed just below the buttresses on the upper portion of the temple. These, like the Nauvoo Temple's sunstones, were to be animated with a face, but again the ornate design was later abandoned. Instead, each of the sunstones was a simple circle with fifty-two pointed rays. Two cloud stones were carved on the top of the east central towers to symbolize heavenly revelation descending to earth. The light emitting from the clouds represented "the Gospel light piercing the dark clouds of superstition and error."[47] Other astronomical symbols were quietly left out of the final design, including large Saturn stones, which were to adorn columns on the north and south sides of the temple near the battlements.[48]

The constellation Ursa Major, or the Big Dipper, was carved in bas-relief on the west central tower. Angell intended the constellation, which in the night sky points to the North Star, to serve as a reminder "that the lost may find themselves by the Priesthood."[49] Star stones were selectively placed under the battlements on the east towers only, marking the preeminence of the Melchizedek Priesthood, which the east towers were meant to represent. In addition, stars were carved into the keystones above many of the temple's windows. The stonework above the doors featured inverted stars like those seen on the Nauvoo Temple. The inverted star, called the Star of the Morning by Latter-day Saints, commemorated Christ's role as the Morning Star (see 2 Peter 1:19; Rev. 22:16).[50]

Though Brigham Young said he had seen the Salt Lake Temple "plainly" in vision "as if it was in reality before him," the only major component of the design he shared with the public related to the system of towers.[51] It is possible that his vision included the ornate symbols that eventually appeared on the temple's exterior. It is more likely, however, that Young, Truman Angell, and William Ward consulted Latter-day Saint scripture, including the Old Testament and the church's Pearl of Great Price, a volume of Joseph Smith revelations and scripture originally compiled by Apostle Franklin D. Richards in 1851, for help in selecting the iconography for the temple's exterior.

A portion of the Pearl of Great Price features an expanded narrative of the Old Testament prophet Abraham that, among other things, lays out the order of the heavens with commentary on the state of and eternal nature of time and the cosmos. Additionally, the book offers some commentary on priesthood and ritual.[52] The Salt Lake Temple's iconography similarly oriented the Latter-day Saint cosmos around priesthood and ritual in the temple and mapped out through astronomical symbols a figurative representation of eternal time.

As the temple's design was taking shape, Brigham Young discoursed frequently on themes from the Pearl of Great Price (finally canonized in 1880), including time, eternity, and the progression of eternal spirits, or "intelligences." In April 1853, he encouraged Latter-day Saints to contemplate "the heavenly bodies, and their times and seasons," including the "worlds" described by "Enoch of old" in the Book of Moses which was also included in the Pearl of Great Price.[53] By 1854, when Angell and Ward had finalized the temple's design, the books that composed the Pearl of Great Price had become common reading thanks to their compilation into a pamphlet in 1851; although the Pearl of Great Price's influence on temple symbolism can only be surmised, Young found the pamphlet important enough to include a copy in a hollowed-out "record stone" placed in the southeast corner of the temple foundation in 1857.[54]

Other exterior temple symbols seemed to be inspired by ancient Christian symbolism and Freemasonry, which had intersected with Latter-day Saint temple worship since Joseph Smith's introduction of the temple rites in Nauvoo. Smith himself was a Freemason during the same period he

76 THE SALT LAKE TEMPLE

introduced a close circle of adherents to the temple endowment ceremony, a ceremony he believed had ancient origins.[55] Symbols and gestures shared between the Masons and Latter-day Saints graced the exterior of the Salt Lake Temple. On both the east and west central towers, above the lower windows, clasped hands surrounded by rays of light were carved into the stone. The clasped hands reflected "the bond of brotherhood and the free offering of the right hand of fellowship."[56] Just above that stone was a scroll stone featuring the scriptural declaration "I am Alpha and Omega," a title given to Jesus Christ (Rev. 1:8, 22:13). Above the second window, on both central towers, the Christian symbol of the All-Seeing Eye was carved with a veil drawn around it.

The aesthetic of the Salt Lake Temple's exterior performed a number of functions for the religious community. The iconography visually affirmed the preeminence of priesthood authority within the religion. Importantly, too, the symbols bound that priesthood to the purpose of the rituals that took place inside the temple. The complexity of the temple exterior also visually reinforced the temple's heavenly origins.

The physical temple performed another basic function: it communicated a sense of permanence to a religious society that had been threatened repeatedly in the nineteenth century. At the same time church leaders were reeling from the federal government's challenge to their authority and practices, the Salt Lake Temple's distinctive exterior was completed. The Salt Lake Temple, a structure born, in part, out of the collective trauma of the Latter-day Saints, acquired increased cultural significance as a monument to the church's survival. Largely the exterior remained tied to Truman Angell and Brigham Young's original purpose to reflect the heavens above in the design. The temple's architectural plans, however, did not remain static over the long course of its construction. Design modernization in the 1880s as the walls neared completion attempted to remain true to Young's intent for the temple to stand through Jesus Christ's millennial return as a functional space for temple work.

New Visions for Design: The Salt Lake Temple in the 1880s

For decades, Brigham Young had been available for consultation when questions about the temple's construction arose. Truman Angell and Young had formed a close partnership, and Angell had latitude to make minor adjustments to the architectural plans without Young's approval. Young's death in 1877 ended this arrangement and disrupted the channels that had generally kept church authorities apprised of temple construction. Over three years passed before the First Presidency was reorganized in October 1880, with John Taylor as the new church president.[57] Taylor stepped into Young's role as the final authority on the temple's construction, but he lacked the same conceptualization of the temple's details. Taylor's limited knowledge of the project was exacerbated by the nature of church administration during this period. He wanted to see the temple finished, as the rest of the Quorum of the Twelve Apostles did, but he spent the final years of his administration (from 1885 until his death in 1887) away from the Temple Block, hiding from government officials who sought to prosecute him for plural marriage. To manage the temple's construction, he thus had to rely on observations from public works employees and general authorities who visited the Temple Block.

After Young's death, church leaders searched for a definitive source that captured his vision for the temple. Church leaders feared major revisions to the temple's design would contradict God's will for the temple, which had been revealed only to Young. In the 1880s, when questions arose about the temple's design, church authorities possessed no architectural drawings from Angell to consult. The latest drawings remained at the Church Architect's Office on the Temple Block and circulated only among those directly involved in the construction. For those not involved in the temple workflow, the prototype for the design became William Ward's perspective drawing of the temple, which had been commissioned in 1855 and was based on Angell's 1854 description.[58] Angell had Ward's perspective drawing photographed and turned into a daguerreotype for his 1856 architectural mission to Europe and then had an engraving made and marketed to Latter-day Saints in the United States and Europe (Figure 4.1).[59] The original drawing hung in Young's office until his death. The engraving became the most recognized rendering of the building and was viewed as the closest depiction of Young's original vision. Though Ward's drawing contained no technical specifications to guide construction, church leaders still consulted it, comparing it to the temple's exterior as it was being finished.

Much of the innovation on the temple's design was instigated by Truman Angell, but in 1881 he confessed to President John Taylor that he lacked the "health and strength" and emotional well-being to continue managing the work on the Temple Block. He also felt unappreciated by church leaders. "My

Figure 4.1 William Ward drawing, 1855. Photographed by C. R. Savage. Courtesy Church History Library.

plans are for the best," he wrote to Taylor, "for the good of the work hereafter, and I feel insulted as I never did before." Angell felt his innovations were saving money, but "the Church has it, and not me," he told Taylor. "I have not been selfish, and will go down to my grave a pauper."[60] To offset his flagging spirits and physical strength, Angell invited his son Truman O. Angell Jr. to take over much of the planning for the remaining stone courses. Angell Jr. had apprenticed under his father and had recently been invited by the First Presidency to work on designs for the Logan Temple. During his time in Logan, however, Angell Jr. was accused of making adjustments to the temple's exterior without consulting his superiors.[61] Church leaders were thus concerned not just with the father's slow retreat from the day-to-day management of the temple project but also with the son's increased involvement in the temple's design.

In early spring 1886, workers on the Temple Block notified Apostle Richards that they feared Angell Jr. was making unauthorized changes to the original plan for the west towers. The "Freeze course on the tower" was being "placed six courses or seven feet lower" than depicted in the "accompanying

CONTESTED PLACE   79

engraving," presumably the engraving made from Ward's original drawing.[62] In addition, workers had been ordered to omit a row of windows on the west towers, which disrupted their symmetry with the east towers. The solid wall, according to Richards, gave "that part of the building a very odd appearance."[63] When Richards asked Angell Sr. about the changes, Angell made no mention of his son authoring any changes to the temple's exterior and defended his right as church architect "to alter and amend at his pleasure," as he had "during President Young's administration, and since during President Taylor's presidency." Richards asked Angell what authority he was consulting in approving windowless west towers, when windows could be clearly seen in the engraving. Angell claimed "the whole matter" of designing the temple "was original with him and had been subject to his amendments and improvements all the way through." He dismissed the existence of a definitive and divine blueprint of the temple. Instead, he said he felt inspired to make the changes to "preserve the harmony of the building in its parts, as relating to the order of the two priesthoods. The Aaronic, in the West, being subject to the Melchisedek in the East; and therefore the Western part of the Temple should derive its light from the Eastern part." Additionally, there were no rooms in the west towers that required natural light. According to Angell, Young had apparently been informed of the changes to the west towers before his death.[64]

Richards found this answer unsatisfactory and ordered work on the temple to stop until the design amendments could be considered further. Angell furnished Richards and other members of the Quorum of the Twelve Apostles with more recent architectural drawings of the temple for them to consult.[65] In May 1886, Angell and his son met with Taylor at the Salt Lake City home of Frank Armstrong, one of Taylor's many hideouts. Others in attendance included George Q. Cannon; John D. T. McAllister, president of the St. George Temple; assistant architect William Folsom; and Frank Y. Taylor.[66] After the meeting, President Taylor felt confident enough in Angell's changes to permit the resumption of stone laying on the temple.[67]

In these meetings participants reconsidered the practicality of the Salt Lake Temple's design based on Latter-day Saints' experiences at the St. George and Logan temples. Though church leaders considered the original design given to Brigham Young a revelation from God, some practicalities of administering temple work had evolved significantly since the 1850s. Angell Jr., for example, wrote to John Taylor to recommend altering the internal floor plan of the Salt Lake Temple based on designs he implemented for the

80 THE SALT LAKE TEMPLE

Logan Temple. The redesign included reducing the number of large meeting halls from two to one to give space for larger endowment rooms on the main floor. Angell Jr. felt his new rendering reflected the "experience and progression" in temple work that had occurred over the previous three decades. His proposal would allow "three hundred persons" to "go through in one day with convenience, while the first plan would only accommodate less than half that number clumsily." Additionally, Angell Jr. reduced the number of entrances to the basement floor from four to one, connected by an exterior corridor that led to an annex.[68]

The original pattern was based on the Nauvoo Temple's design, but Angell Jr. felt justified in making changes because of a conversation he had had with Brigham Young, who reportedly told the young architect "that it was not required that Temples should be alike, neither in their interior or exterior design and construction."[69] Angell Sr., however, lobbied Taylor to disregard the proposal. "It seems to me," he wrote, "to alter the plans now would make a bad thing of the house; but I should think the plans as approved all along till now better continue."[70] Taylor favored the redesign but felt loyalty to Young, his predecessor, and thought it best to proceed cautiously on a new interior design. He encouraged Angell Sr. to remain fully involved as the "architect of the temple" and to have "whatever plans are submitted to be drawn out under your supervision and with your approval" to guard against a wholesale redesign by Angell Jr.[71]

At John Taylor's encouragement, Truman Angell Sr. kept a close watch over his son as new plans were made. Health problems, however, precluded both Taylor, still in hiding, and Angell Sr. from being extensively involved in temple construction. On July 25, 1887, Taylor passed away in Kaysville, north of Salt Lake City.[72] Wilford Woodruff, as president of the Quorum of the Twelve, immediately took on the role of approving plans for the temple. After Taylor's death and with his own father ill, Angell Jr. felt the timing was right to make another change he had been contemplating for years: spires made of granite. Though specifications for the spires had not been settled when Angell Sr. released his description of the temple in 1854,[73] in the ensuing years he determined to build the spires of wood, even though they would not match the granite exterior. His son favored uniform granite spires but had tabled his proposal because of stiff opposition from his father and Taylor. Woodruff favored the proposed granite spires, but Angell Sr. protested, criticizing his son's plans as too expensive and time-consuming to execute.[74]

Eventually overruled by Wilford Woodruff, Truman Angell Sr.'s unheeded petition for wood spires served as one of his final acts as church architect. He died five days later at the age of seventy-seven. Announcing his death, the *Deseret Evening News* celebrated Angell as the "unassuming" architect of the temple, which would "perpetuate his memory" for future generations.[75] For one who possessed no professional qualifications as an architect, Angell achieved remarkable success in his role. He seemed to be one of the few Latter-day Saint architects determined to remain faithful to Brigham Young's vision for the temple and to the ambitious aims of Latter-day Saint temple work in general. This dedication came at an immense personal physical, emotional, and financial sacrifice. Despite the accolades from his admirers, Angell died impoverished.

The temple design questions of the 1880s highlighted larger issues of authenticity and original authorship. These issues came to the fore as church members prepared for the capstone ceremony in April 1892.[76] The increased focus on and enthusiasm for the temple during this time stirred public discussion about who designed the building. An interview with former assistant architect William Ward clarified for the public that the framework for the design was original to Brigham Young but had been executed by Truman Angell, who sought to "make it different to any other known building."[77] The temple's prolonged construction schedule forced church leaders to ask difficult questions: what were the revealed, functional, and dispensable elements of the temple's design? In the end, however, a design was achieved that the entire church felt eager to celebrate.

Capping Thirty-Nine Years: Celebrating the Conclusion of Temple Construction

In the final push to complete the temple, a Young was at the helm once again. Church leaders wanted to move away from Truman O. Angell Jr.'s leadership, though they retained him as an assistant for a time. As the new church architect, leaders appointed Brigham Young's son Don Carlos, and his appointment was approved in February 1888. Don Carlos Young had studied engineering at a university in New York and brought an unprecedented level of professional training to the temple project.[78] As a Young, church leaders believed, he would remain true to his father's vision for the temple and see it to completion.[79]

Don Carlos Young became the most influential architect of the temple's interior. Though church leaders had approved a new arrangement for the interior at the request of Angell Jr., Young wasted no time after his appointment in revising those plans, adjusting the layouts of both the basement and second floors as well as the assembly hall. Work on the towers continued, and in August 1889 workers placed the final tile on the roof before installing a tin covering (Figure 4.2).[80] Young, excited about the prospect of an enclosed temple, knew that concerted work could now be done through the winter season.[81] His hopes were temporarily dashed, however, when delays in placing the window glass prevented the temple from being completely weatherproofed. The windows would not be fixed in place until after the 1891 work season. Even though portions of the interior were exposed to the elements, Young ordered plasterers to continue their work on the interior walls. He also started finalizing the plans for heat, electricity, ventilation, and hydraulic passenger elevator service.[82] By the 1892 work season, the temple was ready for interior decorating and painting.

The First Presidency understood that fully furnishing the temple's interior would require skilled craftsmen and painters. In particular, the plans for the endowment rooms, including the Garden Room, the World Room, and the Terrestrial Room, called for detailed murals reflecting scenes from the

Figure 4.2 Salt Lake Temple, 1890. Courtesy Church History Library.

endowment to enhance the ceremony's presentation. Qualified artisans were in short supply, however, and the church lacked the capital to outsource the work to renowned professionals. Nonetheless, there was artistic interest and talent among the Latter-day Saints themselves.

Around 1890, three aspiring painters, John Hafen, Lorus Pratt, and John Fairbanks, proposed to the First Presidency that they study abroad in Paris for one year as art missionaries for the church. After they refined their techniques, they would return and paint the interior murals for the temple. Church leaders agreed and committed to cover over two thousand dollars of their expenses. The three artists (later joined by Edwin Evans) departed for Europe in June 1890.[83] Hafen returned from his study at the Académie Julian in Paris the next year, while Fairbanks, Pratt, and Evans remained an extra year. Hafen began painting in the temple in 1891, but the remaining painters did not commence their work until they completed arrangements with the First Presidency in January 1892. Hafen, Evans, and Fairbanks, with some assistance from Pratt and a local art instructor, Dan Weggeland, painted an original mural for the Garden Room.[84] One newspaper account suggested that the mural, depicting the Garden of Eden, presented such "vividly real-istic scenes" of "forest scenery, streams, mountains, and wild beasts" that "the spectator is almost convinced that he is standing in the midst of the creation wilds."[85] Weggeland, Fairbanks, and Evans combined their work for a mural in the World Room (Figure 4.3).[86]

The murals created by the art missionaries epitomize the collective work that went into finishing the Salt Lake Temple, which relied on the talents and training of many church members. The work that had occurred on the Salt Lake Temple since its inception was truly a churchwide effort. Through contributions ranging from skilled labor to financial donations, individual Latter-day Saints responded to the call to build a House of the Lord and turned the wheels of construction forward. Accordingly, church leaders anticipated a large public ceremony to celebrate the completion of the exterior work on the temple.

In Nauvoo in May 1845, church members had gathered a year before the dedication of the building to fix the capstone atop the temple.[87] A similar ceremony was envisioned for the Salt Lake Temple as early as 1891, but church leaders determined to wait another year, until construction on the towers was finished.[88] They scheduled the ceremony for April 6, 1892, thirty-nine years after the first cornerstone of the Salt Lake Temple was laid and sixty-two years after The Church of Jesus Christ of Latter-day Saints was

Figure 4.3 World Room, Salt Lake Temple, 1911. Courtesy J. Willard Marriott Library.

organized. The ceremony would be the largest official gathering in the history of the church to that point.

On April 6, close to fifty thousand people (exceeding the approximate population of Salt Lake City) descended on the Temple Block for a program that had apparently been finalized only the day before.[89] The celebration carried all the trappings of a patriotic holiday, with large US flags prominently placed on the south side of the temple and bunting adorning the stages. A portion of the attendees crowded the Tabernacle to hear President Woodruff speak before the ceremony. Woodruff felt confident there was never a "scene on the face of this earth that will attract the attention of the God of heaven and the heavenly host" more than the present one. He hoped the ceremonies would reach "into the presence of God" so that Joseph Smith, Brigham Young, Heber C. Kimball, and others would "rejoice thereof" that Latter-day Saints were redeeming their progenitors through temple work.

After his remarks, priesthood leaders participated in a processional to the southwest corner of the temple, where they sat on a stand according to their place in the church's hierarchy, with the First Presidency at the head. Before thousands of Latter-day Saints, Joseph F. Smith offered a prayer, which alluded to the Saints' recent precarious situation. He thanked God for preserving the church "through the years that have passed" to "this present time," when the Saints again lived "under ... favorable circumstances." Don Carlos Young, atop a platform near the capstone, then shouted to the audience that the capstone was ready to be placed on top of the central eastern tower.[90] At the push of a button by Woodruff, a device powered by an electrical current released the capstone, and it was fixed into place (Figure 4.4). The audience erupted into the traditional "Hosanna Shout," led by Apostle Lorenzo Snow.[91] A form of the ritual shout had been introduced by Joseph Smith at the dedication of the House of the Lord in Kirtland, Ohio, in 1836.[92] The version led by Snow, however, included the use of handkerchiefs for the first time. A multicolored array of handkerchiefs waved in the air as the crowd exclaimed in unison three times, "Hosanna, hosanna, hosanna, to God and the Lamb, Amen, Amen, and Amen." Moved by the collective show of faith

Figure 4.4 Salt Lake Temple capstone ceremony, 1892. Courtesy Church History Library.

86   THE SALT LAKE TEMPLE

and devotion, Woodruff later wrote that April 6, 1892, was "the greatest day the Latter-day Saints ever saw in [the] mountains."[93]

Apostle Francis M. Lyman read a resolution inviting the assembled to "pledge themselves, collectively and individually to furnish as fast as it may be needed, all the money that may be required to complete the temple," with an anticipated dedication date of April 6, 1893.[94] Six months earlier, church leaders had privately decided to make a final fundraising push. A goal of $150,000 was set, and rather than just petition a few wealthy donors, they determined "all should have the opportunity of contributing according to their means and their faith towards the completion of the building."[95] Those within earshot of Lyman's words collectively assented to the resolution.

As the crowds dispersed from the downtown block, some remained and ascended the scaffolding to view the capstone firsthand. Those who lingered on the block until the end of the day witnessed another ceremonial display when a twelve-foot-tall copper angel finished in gold leaf was affixed to the capstone on the east central tower. The statue was a departure from the initial temple design by Truman Angell Sr., which featured a recumbent flying angel styled as a weathervane, like the one placed on the original Nauvoo Temple. By the 1890s, however, weathervanes had fallen out of vogue in American architecture, and many late-Victorian civic and religious buildings featured upright sculptures at their highest points. The tall, heavy statue tested the engineering capabilities of Don Carlos Young, who had to determine how to secure such a statue to the temple's capstone. Cyrus E. Dallin, a local sculptor trained in Boston and Paris, who was then finishing busts of the church leaders, was consulted.[96] Dallin was eventually persuaded to build a model for the statue, though he was not a Latter-day Saint and expressed some hesitation about adequately representing a religious figure he did not believe in. By September 1891, Dallin had created a bronze model of what Geoge Q. Cannon initially described as "an angel" with a "trumpet in hand."[97]

The model was sent east to Ohio, where W. H. Mullins and Company finished the statue in time for Woodruff to inspect it just days before the April general conference.[98] The identity and significance of the bronze statute were unclear to some Latter-day Saints. Dallin asserted that church leaders had always intended for him to sculpt the Book of Mormon figure Moroni, who appeared to Joseph Smith in 1823 as an angel,[99] but even the commemorative pamphlet at the capstone ceremony identified the sculpture as the New Testament "Angel Gabriel."[100] Throughout the twentieth century, however, the statue that became known as the Angel Moroni increased in cultural importance, particularly after another Moroni statue was placed on the newly completed Los Angeles California Temple in 1956. Its placement on the Salt Lake Temple figuratively bridged two eras of Latter-day Saint history: a past era of ritual innovation and isolation and a future era when the church would have to account for its religious practices to the American public.

Along with its signs of national patriotism, the capstone ceremony reinforced to the church at large the institutional reasoning behind capitulating to the US government's antipolygamy crusade. The temples were the church's supreme sacred space and required protection, as did the associated doctrine and practices introduced and enhanced by church presidents Joseph Smith, Brigham Young, John Taylor, and Wilford Woodruff. The church's temples were to guard innovative doctrine and practice—prophetic revelation, temple ordinances, vicarious work for the dead, and eternal progression—that united the Latter-day Saint community.[101] Though the contest over plural marriage had shaken the faith of some adherents, the Angel Moroni reminded the church that its unique prophetic foundation had survived, despite the collective trauma of the previous decades. The figure of Moroni, however, with its trumpet raised eastward, also looked outside the Latter-day Saint kingdom. When the Angel Moroni first visited Joseph Smith in September 1823, he told the teenager, "The time [is] at hand for the gospel, in all its fulness to be preached in power, unto all nations that a people might be prepared for the millennial reign."[102] If the previous decades of Latter-day Saint history were characterized by insular kingdom building, the decades ahead would be ones of engagement and reconciliation as the church fashioned its spiritual kingdom for a new century as a growing American religious minority.

5

Dedicated Place

"Offer up to the Most High . . . heartfelt and solemn thanksgivings for His goodness and mercy . . . and the deliverance that He has wrought out," a First Presidency circular urged on the heels of the jubilant capstone ceremony. President Wilford Woodruff and his counselors saw divine assistance in the now "spoiled" schemes of the "adversary" and felt the church had made a providential "escape from his power."[1] The nearly completed temple became the focus of their gratitude. The circular appointed Sunday, May 1, 1892, to be a day of fasting, which would launch fundraising efforts to complete the Salt Lake Temple. The First Presidency encouraged members of The Church of Jesus Christ of Latter-day Saints "throughout the world" to gather together to worship on that Sunday "in fasting and prayer."[2] At the conclusion of their fast meetings, church members brought their temple donations to the ward clerks to have them recorded.

Donations poured in, some directly to Woodruff's office, from church members inside and outside of Utah Territory. For example, a ledger for the church's Sunday School for Deaf Mutes, affiliated with the Utah School for the Deaf in Salt Lake City, collected over nine dollars, averaging thirty cents per pupil, on the May fast day. The children, according to a letter sent to the First Presidency, paid "their mite for the Temple . . . so that the Lord may remember them when it is completed."[3] Similar donations were recorded in many of the ecclesiastical units of the church.

The cost to complete the building, however, continued to rise. Total expenditure on the temple, with volunteer labor, in-kind donations, and the extraction of local natural resources, was hard to estimate but likely reached $3.5 million.[4] The church now required cash on hand to purchase goods to furnish the temple. Church leaders welcomed any donation small or great but targeted specific members of Salt Lake City's upper class for major cash donations—anywhere from five hundred to five thousand dollars. Some Latter-day Saints gave 8 to 10 percent of their entire net worth to help complete the temple.[5]

The Salt Lake Temple. Scott D. Marianno and Reid L. Neilson, Oxford University Press.
© Oxford University Press 2025. DOI: 10.1093/9780190881580.003.0006

Pleas for more donations continued into 1893 as the church's financial situation remained dire. In just the first six months of 1893, according the Presiding Bishops' Office, over $210,000 was donated to the temple fund. However, the expenses required to finish the temple during that same period nearly exceeded that amount. And with some accounts related to the temple still unpaid, the church found itself tens of thousands of dollars in debt, despite the generosity of its membership.[6] The First Presidency, however, had a particular design aesthetic in mind for a House of the Lord and refused to cut corners despite a tight budget. Latter-day Saints were to conceive of the importance and sacredness of their temple space with the assistance of an elegant, high-class design of Gilded Age beauty. The intent of the design, as with the exterior, was to underscore the temple's connection to the heavens above and the special and chosen status of those who participated in the ritual.

In its final stages of construction, the Salt Lake Temple remained a communal project at a critical juncture in the church's development. With some Latter-day Saints anxious that their status as God's chosen people had eroded in the wake of the antipolygamy crusade, church leaders used the completion of the Salt Lake Temple to bind the community back together and to remind the church that if God elected to accept his temple, he would also accept the people who built it.

Elegance and Grandeur: Finishing and Furnishing the Temple

The funds were needed to complete two principal tasks: the construction of a Temple Annex and the interior furnishing of the temple. The Annex, located one hundred feet to the north of the temple and connected to it by a corridor, served as the building's main entrance and contained an assembly hall, office, storage space, and a fireproof repository for records. A spacious Byzantine-style building built of stone from the same quarry used for the Manti Temple, the Annex was designed by church architect Don Carlos Young. Construction on the Annex started in May 1892 and over a year later was not yet finished.[7]

The other central task—decorating the temple—fell mainly to the Temple Furnishing Committee. Members of the committee had been called to their assignment by the First Presidency only four months before the temple's scheduled dedication.[8] Many had business experience, some with the textile

90 THE SALT LAKE TEMPLE

industry. Some of the members came from the same elite social circle in Salt Lake City and understood the refined design tastes of the wealthy upper class.[9] Some, like Henry W. Naisbitt and Thomas G. Webber, were longtime employees of Zion's Cooperative Mercantile Institution (ZCMI)—a department store founded by Brigham Young in 1868—and knew how to efficiently import fine furnishings from eastern manufacturers. The committee also included Priscilla P. Jennings, the wife of William Jennings, a wealthy merchant of the American West who resided in the Devereaux House, a Victorian mansion three blocks west of the Temple Block. Priscilla Jennings was joined by Lillie Staines, the wife of William C. Staines, another wealthy businessman. Caroline E. Dye, a successful merchant of fine hats in Salt Lake City, also served on the committee.[10]

Women also joined in the effort to furnish the interior of the temple by creating handmade objects. Textile work—sewing, embroidery, crocheting, and so on—evidenced the commitment of Latter-day Saint women to finishing the Salt Lake Temple and placed them within a cultural tradition of building temples from the inside; women had performed similar textile labor for the temples in Kirtland and Nauvoo and for subsequent temples in Utah Territory. Though men primarily constructed the Salt Lake Temple's exterior and interior structure, Latter-day Saint women created the internal material objects that rendered the building a distinctive temple space.[11] For example, in 1893, just weeks before the temple's dedication, Relief Societies in Salt Lake City donated altar covers, decorative furniture covers, and other homespun objects for use in the temple.[12] As volunteers, women created the material context for the performance of ordinances in the Salt Lake Temple, including the endowment and sealings.

The interior ultimately projected elegance and grandeur. The decorations did not convey excess or gaudiness, like some of the homes of the European aristocracy or the new millionaire class in the United States, but tapped into an aesthetic that resembled the tastes of society's elite. The Furnishing Committee strove to create a design inspired by the eccentric style common during the Industrial Revolution and Gilded Age that captured the refined sensibilities of the upper class. Such a design predictably came with a high price tag. To pay for the furnishings, church leaders took out a loan in early 1893 for twenty thousand dollars at 8 percent interest over ten years.[13] Despite the church's mounting debt, the interior of the Salt Lake Temple intentionally projected wealth, power, and status. Additionally, the use of fine furnishings hued closely to Brigham Young's instructions that only the best

DEDICATED PLACE 91

materials should be used in constructing the House of the Lord as a tribute to God and out of respect for the sacredness of the structure.

The carpets, drapery, and furniture for the Salt Lake Temple were bought from catalogs and local merchants. Most furniture was purchased from the H. Dinwoodey Furniture Company, a prominent supplier in Salt Lake City founded in the 1850s. Over the course of a year, the church ordered $9,471 worth of furniture from Dinwoodey's. Another $10,000 in furnishings was purchased from ZCMI. The wood for the temple's flooring and trim, at over $2,000, was sourced from Taylor, Romney, and Armstrong, a local mill and lumber operation managed by George Romney, a church bishop. Lighting for the temple exceeded $10,000.[14] Furnishings for the fourth-floor council rooms were purchased with $2,000 in donations from members of the Quorum of the Twelve.[15]

Other distinctive elements in the temple's interior design required custom manufacturing. The Silver Brothers Iron Works Company produced twelve cast-iron, life-size bronzed oxen for the baptismal font in the temple's basement. The oxen, finished in 1892, had silvered horns. The actual font, capable of holding four hundred gallons of water, was four feet deep, cast in iron, and finished in white enamel.[16] A baptismal font supported by twelve oxen first appeared in a Latter-day Saint temple in Nauvoo. Joseph Smith followed the pattern of the Old Testament temple of Solomon, which featured a "molten sea" on top of twelve oxen used by priests to wash before they entered the temple's Holy Place.[17] The oxen, facing the four cardinal directions, represented the twelve tribes of Israel. Temples in St. George, Manti, and Logan all held similar fonts to facilitate the performance of vicarious baptisms for the dead. The font also served as a visual reminder of the ancient and distinctive nature of the church's ritual.

The art in the Salt Lake Temple reinforced institutional values and a cohesive narrative about the church's past. Among other art pieces, church leaders commissioned a stained-glass window to fill an upper-story ordinance room later referred to as the Holy of Holies. During the late nineteenth century, stained-glass pieces became common in new religious buildings in the United States. Inspired by the aesthetic of the Gilded Age, churches commissioned stained-glass works to elevate and set their worship spaces apart. Many stained-glass pieces installed in American churches were purchased with donations from wealthy local patrons. The stained-glass window for the temple required at least $2,500 to commission, but $1,500 of that price was donated by John R. Winder, a member of the church's

92 THE SALT LAKE TEMPLE

Presiding Bishopric who oversaw all work on the temple.[18] In September 1892, Don Carlos Young sent a letter to the Tiffany Glass and Decorating Company in New York, notifying them that "a subject" had been "selected for your artist to sketch out, and submit for approval." The subject selected by church leaders was "the first vision of the Prophet Joseph Smith"—a theophany Smith experienced of Heavenly Father and Jesus Christ in 1820 in upstate New York.[19] The vision, though formative to Smith's maturation into a religious leader and prophet, did not receive sustained attention from the Saints until well after the church was established. Enshrinement in the temple foreshadowed a renewed focus on Smith's vision and other events of the early church.[20]

Don Carlos Young proceeded to detail for Tiffany the entirety of Joseph Smith's vision, pulled from the canonized account found originally in Smith's 1838–39 manuscript history. Yet Young had to take some interpretive license in order to depict the vision visually and to enhance its instructive value. Smith was to be clearly shown as a boy of fourteen surrounded by spring foliage and "kneeling in the attitude of prayer" with "great earnestness" and "deep humility." His facial expression was to indicate "youth and hopefulness." Young described in detail Smith's physical appearance so that his features could be reproduced with some accuracy. Young ambitiously hoped the artists could depict a "healthy boy of good habits and of a thoughtful turn of mind destined for future greatness." The heavenly personages were to be clad in "robes of exquisite whiteness," their heads uncovered and their faces adorned by full beards of "pure white color." Both personages were to be nearly indistinguishable from one another except by age, one being clearly older. Both would be rendered "without wings" to distinguish them from traditional Christian angels. Young hoped the "characteristics of the two personages" would be "so pronounced as to awaken reverence" and to convey the "presence of omnipotence." The bottom of the stained-glass window was to feature the New Testament verse that had prompted Smith's petition: "If any of you lack wisdom let him ask of God. Who giveth to all men liberally and upraideth not and it shall be given him."[21] After Tiffany produced the design, church leaders made revisions to it as late as January 1893.[22]

Most stained-glass windows sought not only to graphically display a holy scene to churchgoers but also to inspire holiness within them. Thus in depicting Smith's theophany, the Tiffany window of the First Vision functioned as a tribute to Smith as well as an instructional work. The piece helped accomplish one of Brigham Young's purposes for constructing the

Salt Lake Temple: solidifying and memorializing the priesthood and temple legacy started by Smith. Importantly, the window expressed an aspirational, democratizing message, communicating a notion that a vision like Smith's was achievable for all Latter-day Saints who entered the holy space. The temple created an expectation that God would manifest himself to and share his power with those who entered his house and asked for it.

The "St. Peter's of the New World": A Temple Open House

Only three days before the temple's scheduled dedication, workers raced to finish and furnish the interior.[23] The announcement of the dedication a year earlier attracted wide publicity and interest. The temple had been a curiosity in promotional literature for the Union Pacific and other railroad guidebooks for years. As a consistent feature of western boosterism, the temple was well recognized before its completion. In the lead-up to the April 1893 general conference and temple dedication, curious outsiders mixed with thousands of Latter-day Saints in descending on Salt Lake City. Church leaders initially had planned to allow only ticketed Latter-day Saints to enter and view the temple at designated dedication sessions, but they changed their minds when they received "numerous applications . . . from Gentiles . . . some of whom had been . . . opponents" to tour the temple.[24] Journalists, business leaders, local dignitaries, and critics of the church received an unexpected invitation to tour the temple on April 5, the evening before the dedication. Somewhere between five hundred and a thousand people filed through the temple in an unprecedented and spontaneous open house.[25]

The decision by church leaders to invite "gentiles" into the temple garnered positive press at a time when the church's public image was suffering. The church was able to showcase the temple's ornate and refined design to the world as the positive fruits of their high-class civilization. Reports of the "secret" temple interior circulated nationwide. The *Chicago Tribune* surmised there was "no finer church edifice in the whole of America." The "St. Peter's of the New World," as the paper dubbed it, boasted features of "striking beauty," worthy of comparison to the greatest architecture in the world.[26] A Kansas newspaper reported that "[t]he temple was thrown open for the only time" for "gentiles" to inspect its "wonders." "All agreed," the paper concluded, "that it was magnificent in every appointment and was without its parallel in the world."[27] Even the *Salt Lake Tribune*, a longtime critic of the church,

94 THE SALT LAKE TEMPLE

declared the temple a "revelation of beauty, gorgeousness and grandeur from the first to the last apartment."[28] A correspondent for the *New York Sun* who received a firsthand look at the temple interior found it "magnificent."[29] The temple, the reporter determined, "will remain for centuries unless destroyed by accident or intentional violence."[30]

Other publications took care to explain the ritual and beliefs that informed the construction of the temple. A full-page feature published in *Harper's Weekly* walked readers through the rooms while explaining their purpose. The article, written by Eugene Young, a grandson of Brigham Young who no longer claimed membership in the church, aimed to accurately explain the temple's intended use.[31]

The temple's completion was admired as an outgrowth of the industrious if still peculiar civilization that Latter-day Saints had constructed in the West. The Salt Lake Temple was a "fitting temple for the rites of a religion which is as fierce and wild in some of its places as the worship of the Druids or the Norseman," the *New York Times* concluded. "Barbaric in its simplicity," the temple conveyed the fortitude of a people who, surrounded by desert, "dug fertility out of the hills." The temple's construction was attributed to "the executive genius of Brigham Young," who the *Times* believed must have received the design through "some unnatural power" since "no such building is to be seen elsewhere in any quarter of the globe."[32]

According to one newspaper account, the temple paradoxically symbolized the church's "permanent endurance," while "Mormonism," with polygamy no longer viable, was "probably in its declining stage at this time." Latter-day Saints could build edifices of unmatched elegance, but such buildings stood in stark contrast to the unsustainable, American-born "religious imposture" that brought them into existence.[33]

Even though the American people remembered the church's contentious showdown with the federal government over polygamy, press reports on the Salt Lake Temple's dedication largely revealed a fascination with the ingenuity of Latter-day Saint pioneer settlement in the face of significant hardship. Latter-day Saints had long been aberrations in the American West, undesirable side-effects of unchecked westward expansion and religious fanaticism. But with polygamy fading, their refugee story seemed more palatable to the American public. The characterization of Brigham Young shifted from indomitable monarch to genius colonizer, and the Salt Lake Temple became a triumph of the human spirit in the taming of the West. At least for a time, the press accepted the church's narrative about the Salt Lake Temple,

DEDICATED PLACE   95

a storyline the church would celebrate in unprecedented fashion at the temple's dedication.

Forty Years to the Promised Land:
The Salt Lake Temple Dedication

A storm raged in Salt Lake City on April 6, 1893, as Latter-day Saints searched for signs from heaven. Wind gusts reached sixty miles per hour, scattering thousands of downtown visitors into nearby buildings for shelter. President Wilford Woodruff later commented on the inclement weather that fumed as church members filled the Salt Lake Temple for the first dedicatory session. "The devil was mad and exercised his power upon the elements," Woodruff told the congregation, but he predicted greater "success and prosperity" for the church following the dedication.[34] Reports in the newspaper on April 6 described a providential scene above the temple during the "violence of the storm." A flock of one hundred seagulls—the bird Latter-day Saints celebrated for saving crops from pestilence in the early settlement years— descended upon the temple spires despite the high winds.[35] After decades of struggle, Latter-day Saints saw signs of heaven-sent deliverance everywhere.

Church leaders promised that spiritual manifestations, like those seen at the dedication of the House of the Lord in Kirtland, would attend the Salt Lake Temple dedication, which was held over nineteen days, from April 6 to 24, and consisted of thirty-one sessions. The anticipated spiritual power came at a high cost, however. According to Apostle Lorenzo Snow, Latter-day Saints had made a "great sacrifice . . . in the issuance of the manifesto relinquishing the practice of plural marriage." In return for leaving polygamy on the sacrificial altar, Snow believed the "Lord would grant some interesting manifestations in the Salt Lake Temple."[36]

Eagerness for the temple's dedication coexisted with anxieties that reached deep into the Latter-day Saint community in the 1890s. The internal confusion about the Manifesto's consequences, mixed with simmering political conflict in Utah Territory, caused dissension, strife, and debate. To prepare for another statehood bid, church leaders in 1891 decided to dissolve the church-supported People's Party to bring the politics of the territory in harmony with the parties of the nation. Latter-day Saints, however, failed to divide evenly among the two national parties, causing conflict that reached into the Quorum of the Twelve Apostles.[37] President Woodruff bristled at the disunity among the Saints, and some wondered if the church had fallen out of divine favor.

To mitigate the contention, the First Presidency issued a churchwide circular two weeks before the Salt Lake Temple's dedication. "We feel now that a time for reconciliation has come," the First Presidency declared, "that before entering into the Temple to present ourselves before the Lord in solemn assembly, we shall divest ourselves of every harsh and unkind feeling against each other." A day of fasting was planned for March 25, 1893, and Latter-day Saints were encouraged to "confess their sins one to another, and draw out ... all feelings of anger, of distrust, or of unfriendliness." Only then would the "edification that is promised ... draw down the choice blessings of the God of Heaven!" The dedicatory events, following the pattern set by other temple dedications, would deliberately include only those church members who were found worthy and were issued "recommends" by their local church leaders to "enter the threshold of the temple" (Figure 5.1).[38]

Yet the Salt Lake Temple's dedication was not only a regional celebration. The call to repentance was issued to the entire church, and thus arrangements were made to accommodate members from all thirty-three organized stakes at a dedicatory session. Latter-day Saints traveled to the dedication from Mexico and Canada, from Europe and the Pacific Isles. In total, over sixty

Figure 5.1 Salt Lake Temple dedication ticket, 1893. Courtesy Church History Library.

Figure 5.2 Latter-day Saints traveling to Salt Lake Temple dedication, 1893. Courtesy Church History Library.

thousand adults and ten thousand children attended the dedicatory sessions in April 1893, more than 30 percent of the total membership (Figure 5.2).[39]

Latter-day Saint temple dedications not only celebrated the end of construction but also ceremonially marked the building for higher forms of worship and divine manifestations. In a communal ritual, Latter-day Saints gathered in the Salt Lake Temple to ask God to accept the building as a House of the Lord. After a formal prayer of dedication, read by a member of the First Presidency or Quorum of the Twelve Apostles, the building was ready for temple worship. Latter-day Saints then participated in the ritual Hosanna Shout, generally led by Apostle Lorenzo Snow. The sacred shout served as a collective prayer of gratitude and thanksgiving that Latter-day Saints believed reached the throne of God.[40] Sacred boundaries around the temple were then in place, and Latter-day Saints bore the responsibility of ensuring no unholy influence profaned God's house. The dedication events in particular reminded Latter-day Saints of Brigham Young's original purpose for building a temple in Salt Lake City: to give Jesus Christ "a place

98 THE SALT LAKE TEMPLE

where he can lay his head."[41] Any spiritual manifestations at the dedication were signs to the participants that the temple had gained heaven's acceptance as an actual House of the Lord.

The dedication, however, sought to accomplish more than to transform a building for sacred purposes. Within the church's newest sacred space, the dedication was also an opportunity to transform an entire people. Apostle Franklin D. Richards believed the Salt Lake Temple had placed the church on the cusp of receiving "heavenly visitors" that would usher in a "new era in the history of the church."[42]

Church leaders had made a concerted push to have the church membership purified prior to the dedicatory services so that God might accept and bless the temple in the same way they felt he had once blessed the land around it. The offering church members were to make prior to entering the temple was of a "broken heart and a contrite spirit."[43] At multiple dedicatory sessions, church leaders predicted forgiveness for those who followed their instructions to prepare spiritually. "If the sixty thousand Latter-day Saints who have or will probably enter into this building ... will humble themselves before the Lord and repent of their sins," Wilford Woodruff promised at an April 18 session, "the Lord will forgive their sins ... and will accept of this people, and they will find their records clear when they come before the judgment seat of God."[44] "This was the day of God's mercy to His people," First Presidency counselor George Q. Cannon added at an April 23 session, "the like of which may not come again for a long time."[45]

The collective forgiveness of the church's sins was accompanied by a ritual act. As part of the dedicatory sessions, church leaders asked for a formal vote from church members on whether or not they accepted the temple and would put it to use. The thousands who attended the dedicatory sessions voted in the affirmative.[46]

The dedication also highlighted changes to the Latter-day Saint's self-image as modern-day Israel. Latter-day Saints frequently found themselves in a recapitulation of biblical narratives. Their self-proclaimed "Restoration" of an ancient gospel blended elements from both the Old and New Testaments. Moreover, because Latter-day Saints proclaimed themselves to be modern Israel, they felt they were heirs to Israelite history and knew the framework of the ancient story well. The narrative became a ritual rite of passage and a perceived pattern for God's movements in human history: exile, then deliverance, then a spiritual outpouring.[47] Latter-day Saints interpreted and reinterpreted the Hebrew-Christian past to find resonance with their reality and to discern their own chosen-ness. For that reason, those exiled from Nauvoo in 1846 felt a kinship with Moses and the children of Israel in search of a promised land, as did Latter-day Saints who saw their Zion threatened by the federal government in the 1880s.

In 1892, anticipating the dedication of the temple the next year, President Woodruff noted the parallels between Israelite history and the forty-year timeline for temple construction: "We have been as long building that Temple as Moses was leading the children of Israel through the wilderness to the land of promise, and I would like to see it finished."[48] The Salt Lake Temple's dedicatory sessions began on April 6, 1893, sixty-three years after the organization of the church. For a church without sacred communal holidays, the dedicatory sessions, like Jewish festivals, approximated a ritual holy day, signaling the beginning of a new era.

The position of Latter-day Saints in Utah Territory had shifted significantly since they had first imagined a temple at the center of their religious civilization. Similar to ancient Israelites, Latter-day Saints had been forced to evolve their frontier gathering place from a mostly autonomous territory to a client state with limited political power, which generated questions about the future viability of a literal kingdom of God.[49] As many wondered about the destiny of Zion, Latter-day Saints gathered to dedicate a sacred space that they had initially viewed as the center of their independent kingdom. Those ambitions, however, had mostly been carried away with the political winds before the 1890s. Still, some saw the Salt Lake Temple as the first step in reclaiming control of a temporal Latter-day Saint kingdom. At a meeting of local and general authorities in between the temple dedication sessions, one leader predicted, "The dominion for God in the midst of this land [would be] restored to this people before long"; Latter-day Saints would again be able to live their religion without fear of external political and legal interference.[50]

For others, however, providential deliverance had already come when, after the Manifesto, the church's properties were returned and church leaders were formally granted amnesty.[51] At a dedicatory session on April 7, President Woodruff prophesied, "[A] better day was dawning, and as the Apostles were now united Satan would not have power to create division among them." "The Lord is going to give His Saints the good things of the earth in greater abundance," he promised.[52] At another session, Woodruff reflected on the past travails of the church: "A little while ago the U.S. Government had possession of this Temple and ground surrounding it and clouds of darkness hung heavy over us." The people of the church wondered

100 THE SALT LAKE TEMPLE

if "the Lord had hid his face" for a time until the present season of "peace and joy." Woodruff declared, "Should we not praise the Lord and thank his most Holy name! He it is that has wrought out this great deliverance and not man."[53] First Presidency counselor Joseph F. Smith expressed similar sentiments at a session the next day, referencing the Manifesto. "Honor and praise to God," Smith said, "who gave his aged servant Wilford Woodruff inspiration and wisdom to take the proper step toward gaining the deliverance of the Saints."[54] Most Latter-day Saints no longer believed they would ever regain full political autonomy. Instead, they turned their focus to the construction of a spiritual kingdom within the American nation.

As Latter-day Saints adjusted their community to be less offensive to the Protestant majority in the United States, their understanding of their relationship to ancient Israel shifted. For a half-century, many church members had obeyed scripture that encouraged them to practice plural marriage, which they viewed as the restoration of an ancient law, practiced by the patriarch Abraham, to grow the seed and lineage of the house of Israel.[55] Latter-day Saints had also busied themselves with the physical work of building a self-sufficient kingdom, and other markers of religious devotion, like Sabbath worship, had been prioritized behind economic production and community-building projects.[56] Latter-day Saints moved away from these narrative connections to ancient Israel but replaced them with a new narrative centered on the temple. As the nature and purpose of a Latter-day Saint kingdom in the Great Basin changed, the Salt Lake Temple became more, not less, important. Private worship and temple ritual soon displaced politics, economic production, and an Abrahamic law as the most pressing priorities of Latter-day Saint life.

With aspects of their self-proclaimed Israelite identity fading, church leaders used other narratives at the temple's dedication to reconnect the church to its chosen place in the American West. Church leaders believed ancient Israel's prophets had seen and anticipated the dedication of the Salt Lake Temple. The dedicatory prayer read at the sessions referenced Isaiah's prophecy: "In past ages thou didst inspire with thy Holy Spirit thy servants, the Prophets, to speak of a time in the latter days when the mountain of the Lord's house should be established in the top of the mountains and should be exalted above the hills. We thank thee that we have had the glorious opportunity of contributing to the fulfillment of these visions of thine ancient seers, and that thou hast condescended to permit us to take part in the great

DEDICATED PLACE **101**

work."[57] Latter-day Saints were not only recapitulating Israelite history but also participating in its fulfillment.

Despite the loss of their political kingdom and an influx of outsiders, Isaiah's prophecy, as interpreted by Latter-day Saints, predicted the permanent establishment of the church in the mountains as the "nations" flowed to the temple. Woodruff highlighted the new trajectory of the post-Manifesto church at a dedicatory session. God had "decreed the establishment of Zion. He had decreed the finishing of this temple. He had decreed that the salvation of the living and the dead should be given in these valleys of the mountains. And Almighty God decreed that the Devil should not thwart it."[58] The Salt Lake Temple dedication provided a crucial moment of collective reflection for church members, one that allowed them to read their chosen-ness and peoplehood no longer through their political status or geography but through their temple space.

The changes the church was undergoing in the 1890s prompted a search for God's presence in a modernizing Israel. In particular, Latter-day Saints hoped the temple would help welcome the real presence of Jesus Christ. The dedicatory prayer petitioned God to make the temple "holy . . . that it may be a house of prayer, a house of praise and of worship; that thy glory may rest upon it, that thy holy presence may be continually in it; that it may be the abode of thy Well-Beloved Son, our Savior; that the angels who stand before thy face may be the hallowed messengers who shall visit it, bearing to us thy wishes and thy will, that it may be sanctified and consecrated in all its parts holy unto thee, the God of Israel, the Almighty Ruler of mankind."[59] Church members took seriously the role of their temple as an abode for the divine and sought confirmation that the temple would provide access to spiritual manifestations.

On April 7, the day after the first dedicatory sessions, Wilford Woodruff told Latter-day Saints in the temple that a revelation the night before confirmed to him that God had accepted the temple. "Heavenly hosts were in attendance at the dedication yesterday," he declared. "If the eyes of the congregation could be opened," he continued, they "would see Joseph and Hyrum [Smith], Brigham Young, John Taylor and all the good men who had lived in this dispensation assembled." The gathered spirits also included "Esais, Jeremiah, and all the holy Prophets and Apostles who had prophesied of the latter-day work." According to Woodruff, Joseph Smith had "gathered all these spirits . . . on this occasion, and they were rejoicing with us in this

102   THE SALT LAKE TEMPLE

building which had been accepted of the Lord, and the shout of Hosanna, which had arisen from this House of God, had reached the throne of the Almighty."[60] Woodruff described how President Brigham Young appeared to him in 1887 before the death of President John Taylor to confer the "keys of the Temple."[61] Others reported seeing the personages of Young and Taylor during dedicatory services. Still others saw halos of light above church leaders or heard angelic singing. Reports of spiritual manifestations were compiled and circulated among Latter-day Saints as proof that the promise of a spiritual outpouring in the temple had been fulfilled and that God had elected to accept his people and their offering of a temple.[62]

With thirty-one dedicatory sessions, a large percentage of the church was able to enter into sacred space and unify behind the messages of priesthood leaders. For the over sixty thousand who attended the dedication, some of whom crossed international borders, the experience amounted to a pilgrimage with the promise of spiritual fulfillment. As the dedication formalized sacred boundaries protecting the temple's atmosphere, the services also delivered clear expectations for those who attended. The Zion-building projects that had directed the church in previous years yielded to a new effort to build a unified church from within the walls of the temple. Woodruff urged the church to use the dedication to unite again behind the leadership of the First Presidency.[63] George Q. Cannon felt the dedication had effectively recommitted the membership to an orthodox path. The "great division among the people" caused by "national politics" had been "healed up" through "the great mercy of the Lord" and the church was "united as never before," he believed.[64] Ultimately, the Salt Lake Temple dedication proved a timely, if only temporary, answer to concerns about the identity of the church and its place in the West as it attempted to reconstitute after the Manifesto. The dedication offered belonging and purpose to a movement searching for a solid footing in a shifting and modernizing political and religious landscape.

"Heirs of the ... Kingdom of God": The Latter-day Saint Family and Temple Work

Just a year after the dedication of the Salt Lake Temple, President Wilford Woodruff made a major statement at the April 1894 general conference that would alter the focus of temple worship. He announced the end of adoptive sealings, a church practice that originated from teachings introduced selectively by Joseph Smith in Nauvoo. Brigham Young had expanded on the theology of adoption, positioning the path to salvation for Latter-day Saints as a communal experience that paralleled the centralized and united communities he had attempted to build in the West. The structure and order of heaven developed as Latter-day Saints connected themselves through nonfamilial sealings to other faithful Latter-day Saints, particularly general authorities, in an eternal priesthood family.[65] Such sealings were seen as necessary to personal salvation. Along with plural marriage, adoptive sealings created and organized eternal kinship relationships for Latter-day Saints, even though questions about the practice persisted.[66] Despite the confusion, the practice continued in Latter-day Saint temples after the Manifesto. Over seven hundred adoptive sealings for the living and dead were performed in the Salt Lake Temple, a fraction of the close to fifteen thousand adoptive sealings that had been performed in temples in the nineteenth century.[67]

As church leaders slowed the quest for a political kingdom of God, Woodruff considered making adjustments to their spiritual kingdom. "I have felt we are too strict in regard to some of our temple ordinances," he told church leaders just days before the April conference. "The Lord has told me that it is right for children to be sealed to their parents, and they to their parents just as far back as we can possibly obtain the records, and then have the last obtainable member sealed to the Prophet Joseph, who stands at the head of this dispensation."[68] In other words, individuals were no longer to be sealed to anyone other than their spouse, parents, and children. Ending adoptive sealings streamlined temple ordinances and stopped the complicated amassing of relationships through nonfamilial sealings. Latter-day Saints instead were governed by a simplified commission to focus strictly on redeeming their ancestors through temple work.

When the procedural change was presented on April 8, 1894, it was suggested the new policy would promote better unity among church members. According to First Presidency counselor George Q. Cannon, adoptive sealings led to a division "into tribes and clans, each man having his own following, and each following looking to the man to whom they had been adopted for counsel and for guidance." "Some men thought to build up kingdoms to themselves," Cannon asserted, and "they appeared to think that by inducing men and women to be adopted into their families they were adding to their own glory."[69] In the future, Latter-day Saints would achieve and experience eternal salvation in the heavenly kingdom of God through a

104   THE SALT LAKE TEMPLE

chain of family relationships, formalized by priesthood authority through temple ritual. This notion, however, required a more generous outlook on the Spirit World, a postmortal probationary state where eternal spirits had the option to formally accept or deny the Latter-day Saint gospel. Some worried about the fate of their eternal salvation if they were sealed exclusively to a parent or spouse who had not accepted the gospel in mortality, potentially breaking the links between faithful Latter-day Saints. Woodruff told the general conference that he believed "there will be very few" of the departed spirits, "if any, who will not accept the Gospel" and be "heirs" in the "kingdom of God." He challenged Latter-day Saints to "go and be adopted to your fathers, and save your fathers, and stand at the head of your father's house, as Saviors upon Mount Zion."[70]

To aid Latter-day Saints in finding their ancestors and performing vicarious temple work for them, the Genealogical Society of Utah was organized in November 1894, with Apostle Franklin D. Richards as its president. The creation of the genealogical society coincided with a rise in similar genealogical and historical societies throughout the United States in the latter half of the nineteenth century, as the American urban middle class took a greater interest in family and local history.[71] Woodruff's renewed commission to perform vicarious work for deceased ancestors facilitated a spike in temple attendance that continued into the twentieth century. Latter-day Saints began to read their place within the church through their individual and eternal family kingdoms, which were forged through intergenerational temple sealings. The expediency of a geographical and political Zion and the power dynamics of expansive adoptive kinship networks faded to the past.

Workers in the Kingdom: Organizing Labor within the Temple

The Salt Lake Temple's completion enabled the church to grow its capacity for temple work near the largest settlement of Latter-day Saints as demand for such ordinances increased. For years, the aging Endowment House on the northwest corner of the Temple Block had filled a critical need as temporary sacred temple space capable of accommodating living and limited vicarious ordinances. But it could not have sustained regular temple work for a growing population like the capacious Salt Lake Temple.

DEDICATED PLACE   105

With a recommend from their ecclesiastical leaders, Latter-day Saints could enter the temple and receive for themselves or their ancestors baptism, initiatories preparatory to the endowment ordinance, the endowment, and marriage and child sealings. Additionally, other rituals brought church members into the temple over the first few decades of its existence. The temple hosted healing rituals which included anointings and blessings for healing as well as rebaptisms for healing, a practice formalized in a font prepared for the Nauvoo Temple in 1841.[72] Such rituals contributed to the perception among temple-goers that the temple was a place of spiritual and physical healing for the faithful. Eventually healing rituals were discontinued in the temple as demand for other essential ordinances strained temple resources.[73]

Church leaders recruited many of the temple's first workers.[74] Some of them had gained temple administration experience in the Endowment House.[75] The first workers were also from prominent Latter-day Saint families in Salt Lake City. Some were the plural wives of general authorities.[76] Temple workers generally were older Latter-day Saints who had fewer employment and household duties to attend to and could commit multiple days in the temple each week. Initially, a daily staff of over sixty attended to the work of the rituals and ordinances and routine maintenance. The volunteer and permanent staff included ushers, janitors, housekeepers, ordinance recorders, marriage sealers, and endowment workers who assisted participants through the ceremony's stages. The endowment was a liturgical performance necessitating acting as participants witnessed a scripted narrative about the Creation, Garden of Eden, and Fall, among other instructions. The administration of ordinances was shared equally; female workers administered to female participants, and male workers to male participants. Generally, ordinance workers in the temple were unpaid. Donations were solicited upon entry to the temple, however, to help offset temple operating costs. The donations also allowed for small payments to some temple attendees, generally the elderly and poor, who performed vicarious ordinance work for individuals too busy or unable to attend.[77]

Presidents and temple matrons were initially selected from the ranks of the General Authorities and officers of the church. The role of matron enabled women to take significant autonomy over the administration of female ordinances as they supervised that half of the labor in the temple. Zina D. H. Young, the third general president of the Relief Society, served as the first temple matron alongside temple president and Apostle Lorenzo Snow.[78]

106   THE SALT LAKE TEMPLE

When Snow became church president in 1898, First Presidency counselor Joseph F. Smith filled the position with temple matron Bathsheba W. Smith, a future Relief Society president and the spouse of Apostle George A. Smith. Apostle Anthon H. Lund followed Smith as president and served alongside Smith's wife, Edna L. Smith.[79] When Apostle George F. Richards became temple president in 1921, it became more common for church leaders to assign couples to serve as president and temple matron together. (Richards served with his wife, Alice A. Robinson Richards, until 1938.)[80]

As the temple aged and demand for ordinances increased, it became necessary to expand the temple's schedule. The temple opened initially in May 1893 for four days a week, Tuesday to Friday. Eventually the temple schedule added a fifth day and extended the hours of operation in 1921 to accommodate an evening endowment session.[81] The increased operations came in response to reports that hundreds were being turned away weekly, especially around general conference, when thousands gathered to the Temple Block to hear church leaders speak because the temple could not meet demand.[82] Expanded operations came with increased challenges for temple administration, which now managed a daily labor force of nearly ninety individuals. The temple also closed for certain events on the Temple Block, like general conference, and for holidays and when repairs and updates needed to be made. It closed for a short period of time during the flu epidemic of 1918–19 following state public health orders.[83]

Despite these occasional disruptions, significant growth occurred in the daily performance of ordinance work over four decades since the temple opened. The number of both living and proxy endowments in the temple in the 1890s was between one hundred to two hundred a day. By the 1910s, output had reached nearly five hundred a day, and by the mid-1920s daily output was between thirteen hundred and eighteen hundred ordinances a day.[84] The accelerating rate at which living and proxy ordinances were performed was aided by church membership growth and by accelerated population growth in Salt Lake City, both of which by 1920 had doubled in size since the temple had opened.[85]

Church leaders expanded the ordinance capacity of the Salt Lake Temple by approving renovations to add more modern conveniences. The structure closed for three months over the summer of 1923 while workers expanded the footprint of the temple's basement floor. New restrooms and expanded dressing rooms were added, along with a laundry facility, kitchen, and dining area. New ordinance recording rooms were added to the Annex. The costly underground renovations were intended to remove the largest barriers limiting the daily capacity of the temple, enabling an estimated fifteen hundred people to engage in temple work.[86]

Church leaders had exerted significant authority and control over many facets of the Salt Lake Temple since its inception, including its construction and design details and its day-to-day operations. But the real engine of temple work—the actual performance of the sacred rites within—was the Latter-day Saint people. Perhaps, given the throngs of individuals who attended both the capstone ceremony and the temple dedication, there was little doubt that the temple would be filled in subsequent years with eager participants. Motivated by a renewed interest in family history and the redemption of their kindred dead, church members routinely busied the temple's ordinance schedule in the early decades of its operation. Lay church members labored, spent, and sacrificed for the temple's construction, and now they attempted to save themselves and others through its sacred rites.

Since the dedication of the first temple in Kirtland, Ohio, attendees sought "God's Holy presence" on the inside of the edifices.[87] A dedicated temple space made manifestations of God's presence expected, but such indications of the divine were anticipated by temple-goers through solemnizing covenants or commitment and work, not by simply waiting for God to materialize. With their political and economic Zion kingdom on the wane, Latter-day Saints sought God's favor in the labor of temples, which promised to forge an eternal and protected spiritual kingdom in God's presence. Such a distinctive purpose, however, had consequences. Unrelenting public demand to prove the religion's fitness for American society in the early twentieth century turned its disapproving gaze on the remaining secretive aspects of Latter-day Saint religious life. With obvious safeguards to preserve the dedicated space, some within the public sought to take their inquiries and exposés beyond the Salt Lake Temple's guarded doors.

6

Public Place

"I have faith enough to go away from this block healed," a female tourist reportedly declared to three missionary guides on Temple Square (the now developed ten-acre Temple Block) in 1934. The three volunteers generally escorted visitors around the square on a scripted tour that showcased the historic and cultural features of The Church of Jesus Christ of Latter-day Saints. The tourist was not a Latter-day Saint but had heard of the church's sacred square and hoped it held a divine power that could heal her hand, which had been disabled for three years. The missionaries briefly explained the traditional liturgy Latter-day Saint priesthood holders performed to heal the sick. She welcomed the laying-on-of-hands blessing, and soon after, she was able to "open and close her hand and move her fingers." Astonished by the miracle, she instinctively offered the missionaries money, which they declined. They instead offered to sell her a Book of Mormon, which she promised to read.[1]

This tourist was only one of thousands who traveled to Temple Square to visit the iconic sacred site of the Latter-day Saints in the first half of the twentieth century. Public interest in the Latter-day Saint people mixed with improved transcontinental travel transformed Salt Lake City into a tourist destination in the West. In response to the interest, church leaders developed a public relations bureau with the Salt Lake Temple as the centerpiece of a strategy to improve the church's public image and attract new converts. Temple Square's clean and welcoming appearance would act as shorthand for the modern Latter-day Saint people, an identity which in turn was shaped by the church's premier sacred space.

Though some visitors came for sacred purposes, many others came out of simple curiosity to better understand the near century-old faith. Independent of their motivation, visitors understood the square as a place of ecclesiastical power. The institutional boundaries around admittance to the temple contributed to public perceptions that the church still harbored critical secrets; visitors without a recommend could enter the temple's gates

The Salt Lake Temple. Scott D. Marianno and Reid L. Neilson, Oxford University Press.
© Oxford University Press 2025. DOI: 10.1093/9780190881580.003.0007

but were stopped short of the temple doors. Such perceptions generated continued exposés and trials of the church and its doctrines in the court of public opinion. In an era of attempted assimilation into American culture, the Salt Lake Temple was one of the last visible symbols of Latter-day Saint distinctiveness and separation from society at large. As polygamy faded as the most recognizable feature of the Latter-day Saint people, the church retreated into what one historian called its "citadels of . . . secrets," where it nurtured a communal identity outside the gaze of the public.[2] As it absorbed repeated critiques that its religious "secrets" transgressed the essence of an acceptable American religion, the church and its leadership would spend the better part of the twentieth century attempting to shrink this perceived distance from American Christianity, with the Salt Lake Temple often at the center of this negotiation.

"A Foreign Mission at Home": Missionary Work at Temple Square

Since 1902, volunteers of the generically named Bureau of Information— founded to upstage unofficial tours of the Temple Block conducted by antagonistic Protestant missionaries—had been guiding people through the square. The Temple Square Mission assumed control of the Bureau in 1922 and curated a standardized tourist experience, starting at their headquarters in the expansive granite Bureau of Information and the adjoining museum on the south side of Temple Square.[3] The entire square was free and open to outsiders, and guides and visitors lauded its peaceful atmosphere and garden-like appearance, calling it by the 1930s a "veritable mecca for tourists who visit the city" (Figure 6.1)[4]

Since its commission as a five-hundred-dollar wooden pavilion in 1902, the Bureau of Information had evolved into the command center of the block. The building was renovated in 1918 to accommodate a museum that housed pioneer relics as well as prehistoric antiquities from the Southwest.[5] The goal of the museum was the same as the Bureau's: to advocate for the industrious and progressive nature of the Latter-day Saint faith. The Latter-day Saints could be at once hardscrabble tamers of the American frontier and a people thoroughly Americanized and modern. This effort was just the first step in the church's larger plan to use the temple and the square to improve its relationship with the public.

Figure 6.1 Temple Block, 1910. Courtesy Church History Library.

This new era in the church's public relations was marked by a straightforward Christian message, progressive cleanliness, and corporate appearance—attributes that were observed by one Methodist reporter and tourist in 1915. He remarked that the Bureau's president, Benjamin F. Goddard, "looked like a prosperous business man." "All men must have such a knowledge of Mormonism before they are received into the church as to be qualified for missionary work anywhere at any time," the reporter surmised. "Mr. Goddard said, 'I can telephone down to the Deseret National Bank and have its cashier here in five minutes to act as a guide.'... The Mormon business man places his church above his business and puts a high premium upon a knowledge of his creed." After the reporter's positive experience on Temple Square, he concluded that the Latter-day Saints had built a community marked by "cleanliness, education and intelligent progressiveness."[6] Temple Square helped Latter-day Saints stake out new public identity markers, ones more palatable to the American republic consumed by the social and moral fault lines of the Progressive Era. Latter-day Saints held the key to resolving society's social ills; their sacred space bore witness to a society that valued the nuclear family, quality education, and patriotic and engaged citizenship. Their administrative center showcased a religion scrubbed of the alleged moral failings decried by Victorian America only decades before.

This image was promoted by a team of approachable missionaries who guided visitors through a coordinated tour of Temple Square and its public buildings, which was to convey a peaceful, restful atmosphere. Male and female guides were recruited from a pool of seasoned missionaries and were celebrated as among the church's most knowledgeable members. These Temple Square guides were asked to be exceptionally hospitable and friendly to visitors. One Bureau president's message to guides was "[B]e kind, sweet. Do not offend. Do not argue. Remember your business is to remove prejudice, not make more prejudice. The Gospel is love, peace and good will to all. Let the Bureau of Information be a model for courtesy and good fellowship."[7] According to Levi Edgar Young, the Temple Square mission president in the 1920s, guides needed to possess "a personality which radiates a religion which will comfort and stabilize mankind. He must be a man who loves to give daily attention to the stranger of whatever color, creed, or standard of intelligence."[8] And according to Apostle Melvin J. Ballard, they were not to attempt to convert visitors but to "speak as . . . moved upon by the Holy Ghost" and to avoid "cut and dried" "mechanical" presentations. Through this hospitality toward outsiders, Latter-day Saints tried to shed their long-standing caricature as isolated agrarians with puzzling family structures.

Though tours around Temple Square were structured, they were not always scripted. The guides told stories of the Latter-day Saints' historical achievements, which were intended to assuage lingering suspicions about Latter-day Saint loyalty to America. They also presented visitors with a printed card of Joseph Smith's creedal Articles of Faith, followed by a walk around the temple grounds and visits to both the Assembly Hall and the Tabernacle. Historical details were mixed with doctrinal topics brought out by the sacred surroundings; discussions often centered on temple work for the dead and on the eternal nature of the Latter-day Saint marriage ceremony. To give their tours some uniformity and consistency, missionaries

112 THE SALT LAKE TEMPLE

regularly met and rehearsed to each other historical information, architectural specifications, and answers to commonly asked questions.[9]

The guides presented aspects of Latter-day Saint culture that highlighted church members' industriousness and spirituality to show that, as President Goddard said, Latter-day Saints were "the best people on earth."[10] The tours also predictably omitted some distinctive aspects of church history and doctrine. Ballard advised guides to present only "the simple story concerning the Church." Plural marriage, for example, was not "an issue that the church is discussing," and the topic was to be addressed only when visitors asked questions about it.[11] Though the temple remained the central attraction of Temple Square, the guides spoke only in general terms about temple worship, avoiding discussions of ritual and covenants that had recently attracted negative attention from US lawmakers and Protestant reformers during the recent hearings in Washington, DC, to determine whether or not to seat Apostle Reed Smoot, the elected US senator from Utah. This approach was also employed because of the Saints' reverence for the sacred rituals performed inside.

For church leaders, the Temple Block was not a commodity to be sold but a free, inspirational experience. According to Joseph J. Cannon, former editor of the *Deseret News*, one tourist remarked, "[W]e sense a calmness here, a feeling of balance, that we have never experienced elsewhere, and we have traveled much." This response was "not surprising" to Cannon. "It is the Holy Spirit which impresses on their hearts the sacred character of the buildings they have visited and of the Pioneer journey and Gospel restoration of which they have been told," Cannon reported. The temple, Tabernacle, and surrounding grounds were designed to be a moving and holy "shrine."[12]

While missionary guides worked to present a positive image to visitors in person, the Bureau also operated a thriving mail ministry. Many wrote to request literature or basic demographic and historical information about the Latter-day Saints, and Bureau correspondence highlights the important role Temple Square played in the church's growing worldwide missionary work and improved public image. The Bureau extended the reach of the church's sacred center beyond its Utah home as it quickly became the inquiring public's initial point of contact with church headquarters. In the words of the *Deseret News*, letters from the Bureau themselves functioned "as missionaries" that could attract proselytes, all while showcasing the church's growing ecclesiastical outreach.[13] Even church leaders occasionally

PUBLIC PLACE   113

forwarded common doctrinal and policy questions to the Bureau to answer on their behalf. The volume of letters flowing into the Bureau during this period suggests that, generally, both Latter-day Saints and outsiders relied on the Temple Square Mission as an authority on church policy and doctrine.

For example, in January 1936 an impoverished mother of four from Kansas wrote to the Bureau of Information asking for money to move to Salt Lake City.[14] After describing the hazardous environment of Kansas—the heart of the Dust Bowl during the Great Depression—she wrote, "I am hoping and praying with all my hear[t] to see good old Salt Lake again. I want my children to see the Temple block."[15] The Bureau kindly declined to help her financially, but the atmosphere on Temple Square had made a positive impression. "I would become a Mormon," she wrote. "I want [to] go through the Temple. I want to learn the truth before it is too late and I want [to] see . . . the temple inside."[16] Her letters modeled how the square might be used to help convert the interested public and move them beyond the walls and into the interior of the temple.

The Temple Square Mission was fittingly celebrated among Latter-day Saints as a "Foreign Mission at home." It was the centerpiece of the church's enterprise to shape perceptions of the church and its people. A referral system was used to put Temple Square tourists in contact with local missionaries in their home region. By the 1930s, since the opening of the Bureau of Information three decades earlier, an estimated 6 million visitors had toured the Temple Block.[17] Over 235,000 people had visited the block in the first eight months of 1936 alone.[18] Missionary guides and Latter-day Saints interpreted the masses coming to what one person termed the "Tourists' Mecca" as a literal fulfillment of Isaiah's prophecy that "in the last days . . . the mountain of the Lord's house shall be established in the tops of the mountains . . . and all nations shall flow unto it" (Isaiah 2:2).[19] The square's success was summarized at the 1948 general conference by Apostle Richard L. Evans: "This square has since become one of the most visited and most talked-of ten acres in the world, I am sure." That year, in fact, about a million visitors converged on Temple Square.[20] To accommodate steady interest from tourists and a growing church membership, Evans forecast the need for changes at Temple Square. Little had changed structurally within the walls of the square since the Bureau of Information had been renovated in the early twentieth century.[21] But the success of the public relations strategy at Temple Square cemented the institutional use of and investment in the square to publicly signal its purpose and values.

114   THE SALT LAKE TEMPLE

In June 1960, the First Presidency announced plans to construct an additional tourist bureau (later called the North Visitors' Center) in the northwest corner of Temple Square. The building's design included a granite exterior to match the temple and tall windows showcasing views of the nearby temple and Tabernacle.[22] The design included a rotunda, which at its focal point featured a *Christus* statue, copied from Bertel Thorvaldsen's original statue of Jesus Christ in Denmark and finished in Italian marble. Plans to obtain a replica of the statue had begun in the 1950s and were meant to give Temple Square a stronger focus on Christ. According to church architect George Cannon Young (the son of Don Carlos Young), church leaders were concerned that depictions of Christ were noticeably absent from the public spaces of the square. Such a shortcoming was noted by Apostle Richard L. Evans, president of the Temple Square Mission: "You know, the world thinks we're not Christians . . . because they see no evidence of Christ on this square. They hear the words, but see no evidence."[23]

Along with the placement of the *Christus* in the North Visitors' Center, the content of the messaging at Temple Square expanded from the church's history and its people to include the Christian nature of the church's doctrine; this shift marked the next frontier for church public relations. In a related move, beginning in 1965 the church annually illuminated Temple Square with Christmas lights and showcased a large crèche.[24] In the ensuing decades, millions of people would walk through Temple Square's gates to celebrate a worldwide Christian holiday with the Latter-day Saints. The large nativity of Christ, a featured attraction of the square, emphasized a shared narrative with the Christian world, collapsing some of the distance between Latter-day Saints and mainstream Christianity.

The church's half-century-long effort to increase the visibility of Temple Square and the Salt Lake Temple paid other cultural dividends as well. With the passage of the congressional Historic Sites Act in 1935, the US Department of the Interior took greater responsibility for the oversight of nationally significant historic properties across America, and in January 1964 a federal advisory board designated Temple Square and the nearby Lion House (the former family home of Brigham Young) as National Historic Landmarks. This same honor was awarded to such sites as Pearl Harbor in Hawaii, the Brooklyn Bridge in New York, the Sandy Hook Lighthouse in New Jersey, and the cable cars in San Francisco.[25]

This welcome announcement came after the temple had been closed for eleven months for renovations and interior remodeling. Concerns about the temple's ability to withstand a seismic event, as well as its outdated plumbing and heating systems, had prompted the largest remodel since the temple's opening. Trenches were dug around the foundation to install concrete abutments. In addition to new electrical, plumbing, heating, and cooling fixtures, the colorful interior aesthetic was updated, altering some of the distinctive pioneer finishes—to the lament of many later temple-goers.[26] Maintenance and cleaning, however, preserved the temple's original exterior, which still offered ample evidence of Latter-day Saint pioneer architecture, now distinct among the church's growing collection of temples. Church leaders wanted to preserve the iconic pioneer landmark but also enhance its functionality for temple patrons, and the interior modernization prompted similar updates at the church's other aging temples. On May 21, 1963, President David O. McKay, who had attended the Salt Lake Temple's original dedication in 1893, rededicated the temple in an invitation-only service within the temple.[27]

Improvements to interior functionality included the addition of a new annex on the temple's north side, completed in 1966, the first major structural addition altering the temple's original exterior. The annex enhanced the temple's capacity to facilitate marriage sealings (seven new rooms) while also adding new locker rooms and a waiting room. The growth of the church and the resulting increased demands placed on the Salt Lake Temple necessitated the significant expansion, nudging the pioneer edifice into a new era when more cost-efficient and functional temples met the demands of a globalizing church.

Public Image, Temple Secrets, and
James E. Talmage's *House of the Lord*

In the years after the dedication, the Salt Lake Temple's public image began to shift as Latter-day Saints participated more fully in American civic life. The public, however, still suspicious about the temple's concealment of secretive plural marriages, began to more carefully scrutinize the temple's religious purpose. The American press held the church close to the political fire, especially after the United States welcomed Utah into the republic in 1896 as the forty-fifth state. Statehood forced the nation to confront the prospect of Latter-day Saints as full citizens. In particular, the election of Seventy Brigham H. Roberts, a Latter-day Saint polygamist, to Congress in 1898

116 THE SALT LAKE TEMPLE

stirred public debate over whether Latter-day Saints abided by Victorian social norms and could be trusted members of the body politic. Roberts was eventually denied his seat in the House of Representatives, and the entire nation received a reminder that polygamous family life did not quickly fade from Latter-day Saint communities after the 1890 Manifesto.[28]

The American public also had reason to believe polygamy continued to grow in Utah. Latter-day Saints entered new plural marriages under certain conditions after 1890. Most new plural marriages from 1890 to 1904 were performed outside of the United States in Latter-day Saint settlements in Mexico and Canada.[29] The Salt Lake Temple was enveloped in scandal, with outsiders speculating that new plural marriages were being performed there as well. In 1903, plural marriage again became a matter of public debate when Apostle Reed Smoot was elected to the US Senate. Smoot was a monogamist, but the church he helped lead was put on trial, and legislators debated questions of Latter-day Saint secrecy and national loyalty in public hearings. The protracted hearings on whether Smoot should take his Senate seat consumed public attention for almost four years and forced the church president and polygamist Joseph F. Smith to testify in Washington, DC.[30]

The public outcry against the church eventually prompted a new statement on plural marriage from President Smith in 1904. Smith declared that new plural marriages were explicitly "prohibited" and any church leader who solemnized such a marriage or entered into one would be "deemed in transgression" and "liable to be dealt with, according to the rules and regulations" of the church.[31] Smith's statement, which helped resolve internal confusion surrounding President Wilford Woodruff's 1890 Manifesto, did not assuage the church's opponents in Congress. The Senate Committee on Privileges and Elections, which had been charged with investigating Smoot, repeatedly interrogated Latter-day Saint witnesses about the temple endowment, including specific language in oaths sworn to by the ritual's participants that, for Congress members, brought the Saints' loyalty to the US government into question. Additionally, Smith and others were questioned about temple records and their contents.[32]

The Reed Smoot hearings reignited public speculation that Latter-day Saint temples were not simply worship spaces but potential guardians of institutional secrets that made them incongruous with American citizenship. Newspaper coverage of the hearings in 1904, for example, included re-creations of the temple endowment, replete with photos of temple clothing and Latter-day Saint undergarments, as well as text from the ritual.[33]

Latter-day Saints who kept these secrets that the temples generated and concealed were thus accused of being complicit in a plot against the nation.

Church leaders eventually determined to make a more public effort to establish distance between the church and the practice of plural marriage. In late 1905 and early 1906, two members of the Quorum of the Twelve Apostles, John W. Taylor and Matthias F. Cowley, were removed from their positions in the Quorum when they dissented from President Joseph F. Smith's new Manifesto. Prior to their dismissal, Smith requested they air their opinions on plural marriage within the council rooms of the Salt Lake Temple before members of the First Presidency and the Quorum of the Twelve.[34]

As the Taylor-Cowley issue simmered for a few years, the Salt Lake Temple became an influential site for the solidification and enforcement of church policy on plural marriage. Church leaders called post-Manifesto polygamist Joseph W. Musser into the temple, for example, in July 1909; he had married a third wife a few years earlier and news of the marriage began to reach the public, causing more negative press.[35] Musser escaped disciplinary action on that occasion but was eventually excommunicated in 1921, when he sought to marry another wife.[36] Some church disciplinary hearings over plural marriage occurred within the Salt Lake Temple itself, as was the case with both Taylor and Cowley in 1911. After multiple meetings with Taylor in the temple, church leaders eventually excommunicated him for "insubordination."[37] A few months later, they barred Cowley from exercising his priesthood authority but stopped short of removing his membership after he expressed remorse within the temple council.[38]

While the Taylor-Cowley affair may have relieved some immediate external pressure for church leaders to act on plural marriage, the public still nurtured an insatiable appetite for exposés on the Latter-day Saints, and Progressive-era muckrakers met the demand. For example, a 1911 series in *McClure's Magazine* described a "Mormon revival of polygamy" throughout the country. The author discerned in the "whole theological system" of the church, "from its conception of the Godhead down," a pervasive "sensualism." President Smith, according to the author, was responsible for a "restoration of old conditions" and openly exhibited "the spirit of Brigham Young," the man who had been viewed by many outsiders as a patriarchal authoritarian. To be sure, the nation's press felt the aging and bearded Smith played the role of oppressive patriarch well, but the comparison to Young moved beyond appearances and the practice of polygamy. *McClure's* feared Smith was building "a great secret society" from within Latter-day Saint temples. The

THE SALT LAKE TEMPLE

key to unlocking the secret of Latter-day Saint polygamy lay in the records that were "held inviolate in the temples," the magazine concluded. The cover of the January 1911 edition of *McClure's* featured an artistic rendering of the Salt Lake Temple with the headline "The Present Status of Polygamy in the United States."[39]

Suspicions about the temple and the persistence of Latter-day Saint polygamy descended naturally from more general fears about the church's subversion of traditional American structures. Borrowing from the themes of the age, Progressive-era journalists imagined the church as a massive trust or an unsympathetic monopoly of religious, economic, and political power. Nineteenth-century literature against the church had called out similar theocratic tendencies in Brigham Young that had also disqualified the Latter-day Saints from being accepted as respectable and moral citizens. The next generation of polemics differed in that they stoked fears that the church was working within the American political and economic system to corrupt it. The church seemed to be beating the country at its own capitalist game while remaining loyal to its own religious empire rather than to the Protestant nation.

Cosmopolitan magazine's 1911 article series "Viper on the Hearth," by Alfred Henry Lewis, intended to expose the church's "plots, plans, and intrigues against American homes."[40] In addition to a lengthy examination of the church's political and economic power, the magazine featured a political cartoon imagining President Joseph F. Smith as an octopus with tentacles reaching into America's cherished institutions and enterprises. Smith's place of power and retreat was the Salt Lake Temple, which loomed in the backdrop. As trustee-in-trust for the church, the magazine asserted, Smith maintained investments in "banks, railroads, mines, smelters, and tariff-protected industries" that gave him and the Latter-day Saints a "money domination of the country."[41] Another cartoon depicted Smith as a wealthy monarch, the nation's industry leaders clamoring at his feet. The kingly Smith clutched purse strings that reached all the way to Wall Street from his throne in front of the Salt Lake Temple.[42] Another of Lewis's headlines, "The Viper's Trail of Gold," was accompanied with an illustration of Smith shoveling piles of gold, acquired from tithing and investment income, into the Salt Lake Temple, where it could be secured in vaults.[43] Press caricatures aside, the church had begun to rid itself of debt only in the early twentieth century, but its foray into private enterprise in an era of antitrust reform spooked progressive journalists. Public calls for institutional transparency

PUBLIC PLACE   119

were aimed at the Salt Lake Temple because, with hidden rituals and limited access, it was the most visible marker of Latter-day Saint secrets.

After the Smoot hearings and during the subsequent magazine crusade against the church, a window opened to profit on fabricated tales of Latter-day Saint sexual deviancy, secret oaths, and strange rites. Two men who attempted to cash in on the public curiosity were Swiss convert Gisbert Bossard and former Salt Lake City theater owner Max Florence, who chose the Salt Lake Temple as their target.[44] Bossard, a convert of six years, was just twenty-one and had apparently grown disgruntled with the church over its business affairs, which he felt were "crooked."[45] Florence, a Russian Jewish immigrant, was much older, at forty-six, and boasted a long but winding career in show business.[46] The two formed an unlikely pair to take on the church and quickly found themselves in a scheme that moved from Salt Lake City to New York City.

Over the summer of 1911, Bossard cultivated a friendship with assistant temple gardener Gottlieb Wutherich. Wutherich enjoyed unrestricted work access to the temple after hours and let Bossard into the temple during a period in June when the temple was closed for cleaning and renovation so he could snap photographs of the interior undetected. The fruits of Bossard's efforts were sixty-eight negatives that showed "almost every nook and corner" of the temple, "from the basement to the steeples."[47] Though Bossard was a trained photographer, the pictures appeared to be hastily taken and some, predictably, under poor lighting. Bossard sat on his ill-gotten images for at least two months while he prepared to blackmail the church. No one besides Latter-day Saints with temple recommends had purportedly seen the interior of the Salt Lake Temple since its dedication in 1893. Bossard anticipated a massive public audience and financial windfall if he released the photographs.

Both Bossard and Florence, however, miscalculated President Joseph F. Smith's interest in the photographs. Florence, now in New York City, where the pair chose to headquarter their enterprise to start generating publicity for their photographs, sent a package addressed to Smith containing enlargements of eight of the photographs and invited his response. Smith's answer was emphatic. By telegram, he told Florence, "I will make no bargain with thieves and traffickers in stolen goods. I prefer to let the law deal with them." In addition, church leaders told the *Salt Lake Tribune* that "they did not care whether photographs of the temple interior were published or not," given that they had let "800 Gentiles" into the temple before its dedication.[48]

120 THE SALT LAKE TEMPLE

Journalists glorified Florence's robber-baron persona as he attempted to promote the photographs in the press. After Smith rejected Florence's initial offer, the *Salt Lake Tribune* featured an interview with Florence from his room at the Imperial Hotel in New York. Florence apparently barked at reporters, with a cigar clenched in his mouth, that "he would rather burn" the photographs "than accept anything so small as $100,000 for them."[49] Reporters pressed him for a purchase price. "Do you think I am a rube?" he retorted. "I'm here for the cash": "Now if any newspaper printed my secret pictures they'd have to hire extra express wagons to haul their papers away. You'd have to pay me a lot of money and give me a share of the profits in the edition besides. Get me? I had a telephone call from a magazine this afternoon asking me if I had made any arrangements to sell the pictures. I said they were here to go to the highest bidder, be he Mormon, Jew, Gentile; I don't care which."[50] The partners distributed their photographs in eight safety deposit boxes throughout New York City to guard against theft. Still, weeks after their foray in the press, no immediate buyer emerged.

Less than a week after news broke of Bossard's photographs, church leaders had devised their own response to undercut any market for the photographs. James E. Talmage, a geologist and professor at Brigham Young Academy, sent a letter to the First Presidency on September 18, 1911, proposing a book on the temple that would include photographs of the interior. The First Presidency quickly accepted Talmage's proposal and released a public statement that the church intended to "publish in book form in the near future interior and exterior views of all . . . temples, giving full and accurate descriptions of the same." The photographs would be made available to any "magazines and moving picture people" that requested them.[51] Talmage and photographer Ralph Savage entered the Salt Lake Temple in late September to take the photographs. On September 30, the views were sent to be copyrighted.[52]

In the meantime, Bossard and Florence's plans began to unravel. The pair attempted to raise the stakes by photographing Bossard in authentic Latter-day Saint temple garb and hosting a magic lantern show displaying their photographs.[53] The show opened on November 11 at the Bijou Theater on Broadway in New York City. A correspondent for the *Deseret News* attended and reviewed the show: "The show is advertised in a way that shocks even the least refined. The chief poster in front of the theater depicts a large bedstead filled with women, all engaged in fighting. . . . The photographs used

PUBLIC PLACE 121

to illustrate the show [include some images] which were pronounced fakes." The lecture was taken from existing anti-Mormon material "written by New York ministers" and was apparently "absolutely unintelligible" in its delivery. A total of eight people attended the first lecture.[54] Just two days before, the Mormon Tabernacle Choir had performed in front of a capacity crowd at Madison Square Garden, only blocks away from the Bijou Theater.[55]

The lantern show and attempts to garner notoriety and riches failed for other reasons. Though Bossard had clandestinely entered the temple in a way that was explicitly forbidden by the church, the prized religious secrets he acquired were less scandalous than the two men had supposed. The nation was infatuated not simply with the Latter-day Saint's sacred space but with the people inside the space and their rituals. While one newspaper billed Bossard's entrance into the dedicated temple "as impossible as profaning the sacred Kaaba at Mecca," the photographs did not show any actual Latter-day Saints or ritual performance—only an elegantly decorated turn-of-the-century religious space.[56] In the end, Bossard and Florence possessed an unintriguing slideshow of Latter-day Saint architecture and design, a problem they eventually attempted to rectify with rough re-creations of temple clothing. Additionally, to the disappointment of the press, Bossard had failed to catch a glimpse of alleged Latter-day Saint marriage records. Florence confessed that attempts to access church records were thwarted by locked vaults.[57] In the realm of popular mystique surrounding the Salt Lake Temple, Bossard and Florence had little to offer. The failed lantern show was the final act for Bossard and Florence's partnership. The miscalculation on their part, however, offered the church an opportunity to clarify the nature and function of temples.

James E. Talmage's *The House of the Lord* was released in October 1912.[58] In the year since first imagining the book, Talmage had been called as an apostle and had spent months contemplating and writing, sometimes within the walls of the Salt Lake Temple. In addition to commentary on ancient and modern temples and ritual, the book featured forty-six photographs of the six temples constructed by Latter-day Saints.[59] Talmage narrated temple-building efforts in antiquity, placing modern temples in a long line of historical temples that connected the church with ancient Israel. "A temple . . . is characterized not alone as the place where God reveals Himself to man," Talmage wrote, "but also as the House wherein prescribed ordinances of the Priesthood are solemnized."[60] He explained that Latter-day Saints, as

122 THE SALT LAKE TEMPLE

inheritors of restored priesthood authority, were the only ones authorized to perform temple ordinances, which set their spaces apart from other holy sanctuaries in the world. The book sought to soften the sensational public perceptions of Latter-day Saint temples by showcasing the theological depth of the church's temple doctrine. And while Talmage's serious treatment of Latter-day Saint temples (at over three hundred pages) was unlikely to persuade the church's critics, *The House of the Lord* displayed a transparency and willingness to communicate on church theology as well as on practices the public worried were being kept secret.

The House of the Lord was only the beginning of Talmage's decade-long effort to exhibit the church's distinctive theology alongside its cultural contributions.[61] While many observers predicted the slow demise of the church after the dedication of the Salt Lake Temple, Talmage argued that those predictions were off the mark. Latter-day Saint theology, when fully practiced, accomplished progressive priorities, including "efficiency, organization, health, and hygiene."[62] The entire system "thrives," he argued, "because its distinctive doctrines are those of progression, in accord with the better manifestations of the spirit of the times, best adapted to meet the vital needs of the age."[63] With the church modernizing as an institution, church leaders hoped outsiders would eventually dispense with tired tropes about the Latter-day Saint people and come and witness the fruits of a religion faithfully lived in Utah.

Since the advent of a transcontinental railroad, more tourists were heading west to see the church up close. Curiosity brought thousands yearly to the Temple Block to see the dedicated Salt Lake Temple from the outside. And while institutional boundaries halted uninitiated tourists at the doors of the temple, those boundaries and the secrets they protected were sensationalized in national debate. Because of the press attacks in the early twentieth century, the church recognized that a positive public image would not grow organically, even after the church had forged more distance from its polygamous past. Scandals and exposés centered the Salt Lake Temple as a main character in the long narrative of the church's Americanization.

Despite sustained public debate about the role of temples in Latter-day Saint practice, the significance of the Salt Lake Temple to believers only strengthened over the course of the twentieth century, aided by its function as the church's administrative center. Brigham Young intended the exterior of the Salt Lake Temple to fix the priesthood as the lifeblood of Latter-day Saint theology and practice. His vision found fulfillment in the use of that priesthood within the walls of the temple to produce major changes to the structure and programs of the church. Even as the public harbored suspicions of a seemingly antidemocratic hierarchy concealed within temple walls, Latter-day Saints awaited and celebrated revelation received from the upper rooms of the Salt Lake Temple by those same leaders.

7

Administrative Place

A sketch of an intelligent and stern Heber J. Grant, the seventh president of The Church of Jesus Christ of Latter-day Saints, graced the cover of *Time*, the weekly newsmagazine, on April 7, 1930. The cover marked the hundredth anniversary of the founding of the church, a milestone the church commemorated worldwide days before the magazine issue circulated. The *Time* article vacillated between two general assumptions about the Utah-based faith: that it operated as something both "exotic" and "American" in its centennial year. The author viewed Latter-day Saints as a "bustling, practical, prosperous" people who built a wealthy settlement from the desert floor. At the head of such an enterprise was Grant. "Tall, bewhiskered," and "graced with patriarchal kindness and authority," Grant presided over the church's ecclesiastical and temporal affairs, which included a list of businesses aiding in the institution's material success. The only remaining "exotic" element, in the author's opinion, was the "holy rites . . . secretly performed in the six-spired Mormon Temple" in Salt Lake City, "open only to Mormon church-members in good standing." The Salt Lake Temple, the author quipped, was "long supposed by superstitious Gentiles to conceal queer ceremonies of polygamous import." Yet Grant, a former polygamist himself, transcended old assessments of the faith as a "startling businessman" who epitomized the prosperity the church now enjoyed.[1] Grant's use of singular priesthood authority apparently no longer attracted the same public outcries of autocracy or oppressive monarchy leveled by critics of church presidents Brigham Young, John Taylor, Wilford Woodruff, or Joseph F. Smith.

Perhaps Grant's prophetic authority was perceived as less threatening to US culture and democracy because the church as a whole—with its embrace of monogamy, capitalism, and overt patriotism—had largely integrated itself with American society by 1930. But the week-long centennial festivities still celebrated much that was distinctive about the Latter-day Saint people. Grant, for example, presided over The Message of the Ages pageant, a

The Salt Lake Temple. Scott D. Marianno and Reid L. Neilson, Oxford University Press.
© Oxford University Press 2025. DOI: 10.1093/9780190881580.003.0008

selective reenactment of world history since the biblical Adam and Eve that positioned the church's organization as a divine postlude to God's overall plan. The finale included a tableau of the church's organizations—the priesthood, Relief Society, temple and family history program, Sunday School, and Primary—with the priesthood on the highest rung. "Hosannah, Lord, and endless praise," the narrator read, "for Temples reared these latter days, Where Saints may serve and dedicate and priesthood seal and consecrate."[2] The celebration of priesthood and temples together observed a significant focus of Grant's administration and of the twentieth-century church. Temple work and church membership grew in tandem.

As the centennial celebration ended, all seven of the church's operating temples were illuminated in the dark night by new floodlights. Despite a growing constellation of temples (new temples were completed in Hawaii in 1919, Alberta in 1923, and Arizona in 1927), the First Presidency considered the Salt Lake Temple the preeminent temple of the church. "But for forty years the hopes, desires, and anticipations of the entire Church have been centered upon the completion of this edifice in the principal city of Zion," they reminded attendees at the Salt Lake Temple's dedication. To the entire body of the church, the Gothic granite structure was to be the "Temple of Temples," the site from which prophetic authority and revelation emanated.[3]

As leaders exercised ecclesiastical authority in the temple's third-floor council chambers (often referred to today as the fourth floor), the Salt Lake Temple became the most visible site for administering the church. While cultural celebrations like the centennial pageant continued to reinforce the importance of temples to the Latter-day Saint world, it was the actual use of priesthood authority within the temple by authoritative figures like Grant that cemented the temple's place as the church's administrative center. Thriving perceptions of the temple's sacredness and its connection to the divine among committed Latter-day Saints bolstered the prophetic authority of Grant and other church leaders, who claimed inspiration within temple walls to modify temple liturgy and church doctrine in the twentieth century. Collective acceptance of the authenticity and validity of prophetic priesthood authority in part rested on the authority of the Salt Lake Temple as a sacred site. Brigham Young's original vision of the temple as a symbol of the priesthood hierarchy materialized in the twentieth century through its weekly use as a place for ecclesiastical councils, setting it apart among the church's expanding collection of temples.

126   THE SALT LAKE TEMPLE

A New Era of Temple Building

The gathering of converts to Utah had slowed, and many faithful Latter-day Saints remained in their home countries, far from the reach of a temple and its higher ordinances. While a young missionary to the Sandwich Islands, President Joseph F. Smith had witnessed the challenge that converts faced when they were far away from temples. As early as 1901, Smith expressed an interest in bringing temples to the people instead of the reigning practice of bringing people to the temple: "I foresee the necessity arising for other temples or places consecrated to the Lord for the performance of the ordinances of God's house, so that the people may have the benefits of the house of the Lord without having to travel hundreds of miles for that purpose."[4]

But for several years, the church could do little to facilitate wider access to temples without more tithing donations. By the October 1912 general conference, the church, now totaling over 400,000 members, was on more solid financial footing, and President Smith announced the first of several new temples to be built outside of Utah. Adding to the excitement, the new temple would be the first one built outside of the United States—in Alberta, Canada, where the church maintained a significant colony of members. Church leaders quietly solicited plans for the temple, and their instructions signaled a radical departure; to cater to the ritual function of temples, leaders invited a design that dispensed with the assembly rooms that crowded all four pioneer-era temples. This innovation was reflected in the plans of young Latter-day Saint architects Hyrum C. Pope and Harold W. Burton, who merged the horizontal and geometric style of American architect Frank Lloyd Wright with pre-Columbian themes seen in Central and South America to create a fresh exterior design. Church leaders selected Pope and Burton's design to deliberately move away from the spired Salt Lake Temple, effectively freezing the Gothic façade in time; as it aged, the Salt Lake Temple would retain its peculiarity among Latter-day Saint architecture.[5]

As construction on the temple in Alberta commenced, other new temples were soon announced. In 1915, after a trip to Hawaii, Smith announced a temple (completed in 1919) to be built in Lāʻie, near the church's sugar plantation and colony. Four years later, new church president Heber J. Grant finalized and announced plans to construct a temple in Mesa, Arizona (completed in 1927). All new temples incorporated elements of Pope and Burton's simplified design, which placed ordinance rooms around the center of the temple, progressing upward toward a higher story that housed the Celestial Room, the culmination point of the endowment ceremony. In addition to bearing the characteristics of a new era in church architecture, each temple reflected elements, both on the exterior and in the interior, of the local culture and landscape.[6]

As more temples were being constructed, the church also finished a new Church Office Building (now the Church Administration Building) in 1917, just east of the Salt Lake Temple. Built in a neoclassical style with Corinthian pilasters, this new office building for church headquarters looked stately and at home among classical American architecture. Don Carlos Young Jr. borrowed elements from the design for the Mesa Arizona Temple. Overall, the church's new temples and buildings shared modern symmetry with public halls, libraries, and justice buildings across the United States. By contrast, the Salt Lake Temple, along with other pioneer-era temples, achieved historic status. As the twentieth century wore on, they were celebrated as unique worship spaces, built by a passing pioneer generation in an architectural style that had aged with them and would never be fully replicated.

Standardizing Temple Work from the Salt Lake Temple

The construction of new temples hundreds of miles from church headquarters clarified the Salt Lake Temple's prominence among all temples and its importance to church members. Before the Salt Lake Temple was dedicated, the St. George Temple, the first pioneer temple in Utah and the first to use a written version of the endowment ceremony, retained a sense of autonomy and preeminence. Church leaders Wilford Woodruff, George Q. Cannon, Brigham Young Jr., John D. T. McAllister, and L. John Nuttall had recorded the ceremony's text for the first time in 1877 to make performing the endowment on behalf of the dead more consistent. Since then, St. George had become the keeper of the ritual's original text. Ritual changes and performance instructions flowed northward to temples in Logan and Manti as their construction was completed. The St. George Temple presidency worked in concert with the First Presidency to prevent unsanctioned innovations or adjustments to the temple script and ordinances. But after 1893, the Salt Lake Temple, with its proximity to the First Presidency and Quorum of the Twelve Apostles at church headquarters, seemed an obvious candidate to replace St. George as the site for administrative decisions regarding temple worship.

128　THE SALT LAKE TEMPLE

President David H. Cannon and the rest of the St. George Temple presidency, however, were reticent to relinquish their leadership role.[7]

Though church leaders had worked to standardize temple ritual, portions and less important procedures remained unwritten, allowing regional adaptations to areas where the First Presidency had given no direction. In 1911, after a discussion with temple workers in St. George on minor differences in temple procedures across temples, Cannon expressed his intent to follow "the order of this temple" in St. George. He continued, "We are not controlled by [the] Salt Lake Temple. . . . This temple has the original of these endowments which w[ere] given by President Brigham Young and we have not nor will we change anything thereof unless dictated by the President of the Church."[8] Cannon's resoluteness was all the more curious because Salt Lake Temple President Anthon H. Lund was also in the First Presidency with President Joseph F. Smith and consulted with him on matters related to the temple's administration.[9] The temple's administration was in essence an extension of church administration and could therefore prescribe procedural changes to other temples.

Following Lund's death, church leaders continued to select the temple's leadership with special consideration. President Heber J. Grant filled the position of temple president with another apostle, George F. Richards. Richards did more to consolidate the authority of the Salt Lake Temple than any president before him.[10] Under the close supervision of an appointed committee of apostles, he drafted new rules and procedures for the disparate temple presidents and spent months revising the wording of the temple ordinances.[11] After almost two years of study and labor, over one hundred changes to temple procedures and ordinances were brought before the First Presidency, Quorum of the Twelve Apostles, and Presiding Patriarch for approval.[12] The ratified changes were packaged in a book, and the presidents of the six operating temples all received copies which they were to follow.

Richards's authoritative book seems to have been inspired primarily by the persistent tension between the leadership of the St. George and Salt Lake temples. Cannon recalled that Richards had "criti[ci]zed him very severely for not adhering to the unwritten part of the ceremonies as he had been instructed to do" by the Salt Lake Temple presidency. Richards later warned Cannon again, "[Y]ou must either conform to our method or we to yours."[13] Cannon eventually relented and appointed a custodian of the new "Temple President's Book" in St. George, who used the book to answer procedural questions. All questions not addressed by the book would be directed to church authorities in Salt Lake City. Furthermore, Cannon was instructed to destroy or send to church headquarters all previous rulings on temple matters.[14]

The standardization of temple ritual brought the church's growing constellation of temples into the controlling orbit of the Salt Lake Temple. For the next few decades (until the administration of temples was taken over by the newly created Temple Department), the Salt Lake Temple was the locus of churchwide temple management. Richards explained his vision for how church leaders would fulfill their administrative role: "The First Presidency could not be expected to be in touch with all the details of Temple work & with the needed changes only as these things are brought to their attention and who should do this if not the Apostle in charge of the Salt Lake & Leading Temple of the church."[15] Following Richards's release as temple president in 1937, he continued to supervise the church's temple work from the Salt Lake Temple as superintendent of all temples until his death in 1950.[16]

The Seat of the Prophets: Administering the Church from the Temple

More obvious signs of the Salt Lake Temple's influence on the general membership existed, reaching back to Brigham Young's explanation of the temple's symbolism. As Young had explained when the cornerstones for the temple were laid, the apostleship was the foundation of the church (and temples) in the latter days.[17] Young's vision of the temple as a symbol of continuing revelation through prophets and apostles borrowed refrains from the New Testament. To the apostle Peter at Caesarea Philippi, Jesus Christ taught that he would build his church upon the "rock" of revelation, inspired by the Holy Ghost, and through the "keys of the kingdom" given to his apostles (Matthew 16:18–19). And for Latter-day Saints, the place where prophets communed with God was the Salt Lake Temple. By the twentieth century, ongoing revelation—although routinized through councils, committees, and processes—was no less real for church members, even if it was less visible. As the meeting place for General Authority councils, the Salt Lake Temple was the seat of institutional revelation and power.

The authority of the Salt Lake Temple and its role in aiding revelation were reflected in its unique floor plan, which remained relatively unchanged (despite several renovations in the twentieth century) since Apostle James E. Talmage had published photographs of the interior in *The House of the Lord*.[18] The temple was divided into several floors, and though its layout and

130   THE SALT LAKE TEMPLE

design were distinctive, several aspects were similar to those of other temples. Like all other temples, for instance, the Salt Lake Temple included rooms where ordinances were performed. The basement or first floor housed a baptismal font and washing and anointing rooms for initiatory rituals. A grand staircase allowed patrons to enter the Creation Room and then the Garden of Eden Room, where the endowment ordinance began. Reached by the same flight of stairs, the second-floor area included the Telestial (World) Room, Terrestrial Room, and Celestial Room, which patrons passed through during the remainder of the endowment ceremony. Several smaller rooms were in the southeast corner of that same floor: the Holy of Holies was situated between the West Sealing Room (for the dead) and the East Sealing Room (for the living), with waiting and reception rooms behind. All temple ordinances for the living and the dead—baptism and confirmation, Melchizedek priesthood ordination, washing and anointing, the endowment, and sealings—were administered on these three lower levels.[19]

Latter-day Saints could travel to any of the church's operating temples to receive and perform sacred ordinances, but what rendered the layout of the Salt Lake Temple unique were the administrative offices on the floor above the ordinance rooms. Since 1893, the presiding priesthood quorums administered the church from the temple's council rooms on the third floor. On the south side of the floor was the Elders' Room (initially used by local elders quorums). The neighboring Council Room of the Twelve Apostles was furnished with twelve leather chairs, small tables, and portraits of the current apostles on the walls. At the end of the hall was the Council Room of the Seventy, where the members of the First Council of the Seventy gathered weekly. On the north side of the corridor was the High Council Room, which was used by local stake presidencies and high councils. And next door was the largest of the council chambers: the Council Room of the First Presidency and the Twelve Apostles (Figure 7.1).[20]

Members of the First Presidency and Quorum of the Twelve Apostles conducted their daily ecclesiastical responsibilities and committee assignments in private offices and shared boardrooms in the neighboring Church Administration Building.[21] But they gathered each Thursday (and still do) as members of the combined Council of the First Presidency and the Quorum of the Twelve Apostles (hereafter Council). In 1979, President N. Eldon Tanner, who was a counselor to four church presidents, provided a rare public glimpse into the Council's weekly meetings in the upper room of the temple:

Figure 7.1 Council Room of the First Presidency and the Quorum of the Twelve Apostles, Salt Lake Temple, 1911. Courtesy J. Willard Marriott Library.

As the First Presidency enters this room at ten o'clock on Thursday mornings, we shake hands with all members of the Twelve, then change to our temple robes. We sing, kneel in prayer, and then join in a prayer circle at the altar, after which we change to our street clothes.

After discussing the minutes of the previous meeting, we consider such matters as the following: approval of changes in bishoprics as recommended by stake presidents—previously discussed in the meeting of the Twelve ... changes in stake, ward, mission, and temple organizations throughout the Church, including boundaries and officers; officers and administration of auxiliary organizations; matters brought in by the heads of different departments; and our reports of stake conferences and other activities during the week, such as funerals, speaking engagements, and so forth. It is in this body that any change in administration or policy is considered and approved, and it then becomes the official policy of the Church....

On the first Thursday of every month the First Presidency meets with all the General Authorities—the members of the Twelve, the Seventy, and the Presiding Bishopric. In this meeting all are advised of any changes in programs or procedures and instructed in their duties or responsibilities.... A recording secretary makes a report of all that is said and done.[22]

Significant decisions affecting the administration of the church came out of the presiding Council's weekly meetings. And while the minutes from those meetings generally remained restricted from public access, the fruits of significant administrative decisions were still visible to general church membership. The temple was used to formulate and even announce these decisions. In July 1899, church president Lorenzo Snow called a solemn assembly in the Salt Lake Temple, inviting leaders from the thirty-two stakes and 388 wards and branches of the church to attend. The total number of guests at the meeting, which focused on improving the number of church members paying tithes and offerings, exceeded six hundred.[23] Every member of the First Presidency and Quorum of the Twelve Apostles was in attendance (Figure 7.2). The meeting became a significant rallying point for institutional

Figure 7.2 Assembly Room, Salt Lake Temple, 1911. Courtesy J. Willard Marriott Library.

efforts to steady the church's finances at the turn of the century as ward and stake leaders relayed the messages to their respective congregations.

Authoritative pronouncements and decisions from the weekly Council meetings in the Salt Lake Temple, some couched in the language of revelation, positioned the Salt Lake Temple as the site where the church adapted to the twentieth-century world. Significant changes aided the collective perception among church members that the temple was the administrative center of the church. These changes included, for example, those regarding succession in the presidency, the scriptural canon, and the translation and presentation of temple ordinances.

Succession in the Presidency

Much like the Sistine Chapel in Vatican City, where the College of Cardinals gather during papal conclaves to elect a new bishop of Rome (the Pope), the third-floor Council Room in the Salt Lake Temple has been the site of deliberations about succession in the church's presidency. Beginning with President Wilford Woodruff's death in 1898, shortly after a church president's funeral, the surviving apostles gather in the Council Room to select the next church president. For example, when President Hebert J. Grant passed away on May 14, 1945, the First Presidency was dissolved, and his counselors J. Reuben Clark and David O. McKay reverted to their places in the Quorum of the Twelve Apostles according to ordination seniority. Days after Grant's funeral, all of the living apostles gathered in the Council Room. Per established pattern, the most senior apostle is considered the new leader of the church and is the next one chosen and set apart as church president. In this instance, that person was George Albert Smith. After each apostle had the opportunity to express his feelings on the matter of succession, George F. Richards, second in seniority, proposed that Smith be appointed as the new church president. McKay seconded the motion, and the entire quorum unanimously sustained the decision. A chair was then placed in the center of the Council Room to ritually set Smith apart as church president. All of the apostles stood in a circle around their new leader and placed their hands on his head. Richards pronounced the blessing. Smith then announced Clark and McKay as his counselors in the First Presidency. Both men were set apart in their roles, and Richards was named and set apart as the president of the Quorum of the Twelve Apostles.[24] Each time a church president (the senior

134 THE SALT LAKE TEMPLE

apostle) or another apostle dies, a replacement apostle is selected by a similar process and set apart by priesthood authority within the Salt Lake Temple.

The Scriptural Canon

Members of the Council of the First Presidency and Quorum of the Twelve Apostles also oversee the open Latter-day Saint scriptural canon. During the twentieth century, new revelations and updates to the standard works (Bible, Book of Mormon, Doctrine and Covenants, and Pearl of Great Price) were approved within the Salt Lake Temple. Only three revelations have been canonized since Wilford Woodruff's 1890 Manifesto on plural marriage (D&C Official Declaration 1): Joseph Smith's 1836 vision of the celestial kingdom (D&C 137), Joseph F. Smith's 1918 vision of the redemption of the dead (D&C 138), and Spencer W. Kimball's 1978 revelation on the priesthood (D&C Official Declaration 2).

In the summer and fall of 1918, President Joseph F. Smith experienced a series of revelations, including a vision in early October of Jesus Christ's postmortal redemption of the dead. "I have not lived alone these five months. I have dwelt in the spirit of prayer, of supplication, of faith and of determination; and I have had my communication with the Spirit of the Lord continuously," Smith told church members in his general conference sermon.[25] Weeks after transcribing his father's vision, Apostle Joseph Fielding Smith presented the revelatory text to the Council for their approval.[26]

Although it was accepted as a divine revelation by the Council in 1918, church leaders did not canonize Smith's vision (along with another vision received by his uncle Joseph Smith in 1836) until six decades later, at a March 25, 1976, meeting of the Council in the Salt Lake Temple.[27] A few years later, the same presiding Council declared that Joseph Smith's vision would become section 137 of the Doctrine and Covenants and Joseph F. Smith's vision would follow as section 138.[28]

Translation and Presentation of Temple Ordinances

The Council oversaw the transformation of the endowment ceremony from an English-language-only dramatization with live actors (temple volunteers) to a multilingual presentation displayed in a motion picture, originally filmed at the Salt Lake Temple. Though temple ordinances were available only in English during the church's first century, that changed soon after Apostle Joseph Fielding Smith toured the Spanish-American Mission in October 1943. At the time, the mission covered Texas, New Mexico, Colorado, Arizona, and California and included large Hispanic and Latino populations. Stake and mission leaders in Arizona asked Smith if the temple ceremonies could be translated into Spanish. "I see no reason why the English language should monopolize the temple session," Smith responded. In 1944, the Council approved a proposal to translate the temple ceremonies and tasked Elder Antoine R. Ivins of the First Council of Seventy and Eduardo Balderas of the church's Translation Department with completing the Spanish translation. On November 6, 1945, Spanish-speaking church members from Mexico and the American Southwest gathered at the Mesa Arizona Temple to perform temple ordinances in their native tongue en masse for the first time, with First Presidency Counselor David O. McKay in attendance.[29]

In 1952, McKay, now church president, traveled to Bern, Switzerland, and purchased land for the first Latter-day Saint temple in Europe (and the first outside of the United States and Canada). With the groundbreaking of the Swiss temple in 1953, the church faced a new reality: temples abroad would be attended by primarily non–English-speaking peoples. To address the challenge, McKay enlisted the help of future apostle Gordon B. Hinckley. McKay tasked Hinckley with figuring out how to deliver the temple instruction in a variety of languages without requiring a large quantity of temple workers. After weeks of prayer and contemplation in the upper rooms of the Salt Lake Temple, Hinckley determined that the best format to present the endowment ceremony in the Swiss and future temples would be through film. A sound stage was set up in the temple's Assembly Room and actors were cast in the ceremony roles. Once the new film was completed and approved in English, subsequent versions were filmed in French, German, Dutch, Finnish, Swedish, Danish, and Norwegian, with new casts for each language. In later months, the presentation was also filmed in Spanish, Tongan, Tahitian, Samoan, and Maori, to serve other temples.[30]

As church members used new temples in their home regions to receive their temple ordinances, pilgrimage to Utah's temples became less pressing for Latter-day Saints. Temple worship remained under the administrative watch of church authorities in Salt Lake City but was increasingly performed regionally, slowly decentering the temple experience for Latter-day Saints.

136   THE SALT LAKE TEMPLE

But the ties that bound the church membership to the Salt Lake Temple never eroded completely. Throughout the twentieth century, when church leaders introduced pivotal revelation to the general church, they often cited the location of the revelation. The phrase "upper rooms of the Salt Lake Temple" and its variants were cues to church members that God had spoken to their leaders and continued to issue divine direction. In other words, the divine and sacred nature of binding prophetic announcements was authenticated by invoking the Salt Lake Temple. The temple therefore served as a unifying symbol of institutional power, authority, and revelation. As the Salt Lake Temple became more globally recognized, the authority of the church's hierarchy was reinforced in tandem.

Temple Spires at the 1964–65 New York World's Fair

The authority of the Salt Lake Temple was broadcast to the public in other ways as well. Thousands continued to stream to Temple Square into the 1960s. With the assistance of the traveling Mormon Tabernacle Choir, prominent Latter-day Saints like businessman and politician George Romney and visible church leaders like President David O. McKay and Apostle Ezra Taft Benson, Latter-day Saints were generally viewed as upstanding, civically engaged American citizens who posed little threat to the fabric of American society. In the eyes of the public, the church was an industrious pioneer faith easily relegated to its corner of the American West. "Those amazing Mormons," as *Coronet* magazine branded them in 1952, were family-centered and vice-free, with a wholesome, corporate appearance.[31] With such encouraging reports in the national media, church leaders determined to scale their public relations efforts nationwide. They created the Church Information Service (CIS; originally the Church Publicity Department) in 1957 to handle media requests and to curate and advertise Latter-day Saint exhibits and events.

CIS found an opportunity to showcase the church on an international stage with the upcoming 1964–65 New York World's Fair, held at Flushing Meadows Park in Queens. The fair's theme, "Peace through Understanding," intrigued church leaders, who felt the fairgrounds offered an unprecedented opportunity to display the church to the anticipated 70 million visitors. By late September 1962, Burton and the church had selected Antonio Raymond and L. L. Rado of New York City to design the pavilion.[32] Adapting early

ADMINISTRATIVE PLACE   137

plans for a chapel-like structure, Rado shared his vision of the pavilion with Burton. According to Rado, the fair would "largely consist of extremely flashy, temporary types of buildings.... Most of the exhibitions [would] represent hard-sell, commercial ventures in contrast to the spiritual intent" of the Utah-based church. Rado advised the church to "take just the opposite expression" to highlight their "spiritual values."[33] The church and Rado eventually parted ways, but the church's planning committee continued to brainstorm design ideas for reconstructing a Latter-day Saint worship space for the fair's Mormon Pavilion.[34]

Some committee members initially recommended a replica of the tortoise-shaped Tabernacle or a mock-up of its world-famous Tabernacle Organ, since these were recognized architectural and musical wonders of the church. "We all agreed it should be something which was readily recognizable—not just a unique architectural shape," Utah advertising executive and CIS member David W. Evans recalled. "I was born and grew up in the [Salt Lake] Avenues. Hundreds of times I had walked down the First Avenue hill looking towards the Temple spires. They were unforgettable as I have viewed them so often towards the sunset. It took no creativity on my part to suggest that we make them our central theme."[35] A 120-foot-tall replica of the temple's east façade, complete with a facsimile golden Angel Moroni, soon became the main feature of the Mormon Pavilion. In mid-November 1962 the committee took a scale model of the structure to the First Presidency and received their approval. Evans also received a letter of encouragement from a colleague: "We feel that the decision to use the façade of the Temple a very happy one and we completely concur with your conclusion that it is the most widely recognized physical symbol of Mormonism."[36]

In a fortuitous development, fair organizers offered the church an empty adjacent lot near the fair's main entrance to extend their display. The lot proved an attractive gateway into the pavilion, especially after it was landscaped and adorned with a reflecting pool. The garden-like atmosphere of the display was inspired by the success of the Temple Square experience. The church's serene presentation served as a buffer amid the hustle and bustle of the fair and allowed for peaceful contemplation before reaching the temple façade. Inside the pavilion, artwork and other visual displays introduced visitors to church history and doctrine. A replica of Thorvaldsen's *Christus* statue of Jesus Christ and a video presentation titled *Man's Search for Happiness*, which the pavilion took as its central theme, introduced visitors to the distinctive elements of Latter-day Saint doctrine and culture. Unlike the Salt Lake Temple, visitors could actually enter the fair's temple façade and view the core tenets of the Latter-day Saint world.[37]

By institutional expectations, the Mormon Pavilion was a massive success. Approximately 6 million visitors viewed the pavilion, and volunteers distributed close to 100,000 copies of the Book of Mormon and passed on nearly a million referrals to the church's global missionary force. In addition, church membership increased in the New York area, and the Eastern States Mission reported a spike in baptisms after the fair closed. The effect of the positive press is difficult to measure, but the pavilion's distinctive temple façade was reproduced in countless press images. The pavilion's success also inspired a revamp of Temple Square and the church's historic and temple sites; new visitors' centers were constructed near these sites to engage the public on a local and regional scale.[38] Though it was a nod toward openness and transparency from the church, this "come and see" strategy came with an asterisk: the displays did not represent the interior rituals of an actual Latter-day Saint temple.[39]

In a new era of corporate public relations, church leaders had settled on a brand image. The Salt Lake Temple symbolized church priesthood authority, but for at least two years at the New York's World's Fair, it also housed the message the church intended to share with the world. By placing the church's quintessential family values and unique doctrine and history center stage, church leaders intended to merge an image with a missionary message. For an audience in the eastern United States, far from Temple Square, the iconic Salt Lake Temple façade announced the church's arrival as a major player on the global religious scene and was shorthand for the Latter-day Saint way of life. But the consolidation of the church's image around a central symbol would have other consequences as the church reentered the realm of national politics. The most recognizable symbol of the faith soon became a site of resistance against the authority it represented.

8

Political Place

In 1965, the year that millions of global tourists streamed through the Mormon Pavilion at the New York World's Fair, Anthony Uzodimma Obinna experienced a life-changing vision in Nigeria.[1] "I was visited in a dream by a tall person carrying a walking stick in his right hand," Obinna recalled. The personage asked Obinna if he had read the great Christian allegory *The Pilgrim's Progress* by John Bunyan. In Bunyan's popular work, the main protagonist wanders an unforgiving landscape, searching for deliverance and a final resting place. Obinna confessed he "had forgotten" the story and was told to read it again. The personage appeared to Obinna on two more occasions and in one instance transported him "to a most beautiful building" and showed him "everything in it."[2]

Obinna initially did not understand the meaning of the dream but, like Bunyan's hero, was apparently being told to seek out the "Celestial City."[3] In 1967, a civil war was ravaging Nigeria, causing mass starvation and death. While restricted to his home because of the war, Obinna found a copy of the September 1958 *Reader's Digest* magazine. "I opened it at page 34 and saw a picture of the same beautiful building I had been shown around in my dream, and immediately I recognized it," Obinna later said. Underneath the headline "The March of the Mormons" was a picture of the Salt Lake Temple belonging to The Church of Jesus Christ of Latter-day Saints. Obinna, who had never heard of the Mormons before, read the entire article.[4] He told his brothers, who were "astonished to hear the story." Obinna confessed he had "no rest of mind any longer" and that the discovery consumed his "whole attention."[5] A war blockade prevented him from sending mail to church headquarters in Utah, so he waited patiently until the embargo was lifted in 1971. He then began to communicate with church authorities, who sent him literature and a copy of the Book of Mormon. Obinna, however, was disappointed to learn that the church would not be organized in Nigeria in the immediate future.[6]

Thousands in Nigeria, like Obinna, were waiting for an official mission to open in their country so that they could be baptized and organized into

The Salt Lake Temple. Scott D. Marianno and Reid L. Neilson, Oxford University Press.
© Oxford University Press 2025. DOI: 10.1093/9780190881580.003.0009

140 THE SALT LAKE TEMPLE

branches. Church leaders had seriously considered sending missionaries there in 1962 but later suspended the plan because it was difficult for missionaries to get visas and because Nigerian natives could not be ordained to the priesthood; priesthood ordination is necessary for most critical administrative roles in the church.[7] Nigerians, as well as other African believers, could not receive the priesthood because of the church's long-standing ban on men of African descent holding the priesthood. This ban extended to the temple, preventing both men and women of African descent from participating in most temple ordinances.[8] The Salt Lake Temple thus presented a paradox for some, like Obinna, who were moved by the temple's heavenly spires to investigate the Latter-day Saint religion but who could not participate in many of the sacred ordinances administered inside.

The church's policies regarding those with an African lineage drew national attention in the mid-twentieth century. During the administration of President David O. McKay (1951–70), the church entered an unprecedented era of growth and building construction. The church's population nearly doubled in the two decades following World War II. Rapid change and increasing visibility, however, brought growing pains.[9] Once an American success story, Latter-day Saints began attracting more scrutiny from people inside and outside of the church for statements and policies on civil rights issues. As tourists and Latter-day Saints alike came to see Temple Square, others came to express dissent and disagreement in the shadow of the most visible symbol of the church's power and authority. The Salt Lake Temple stood at the intersection of public debate over civil and religious freedoms, religious inclusion and exclusion, and individual expression and corporate power.

Center of Policy and Protest

As the House of the Lord for the church's prophets and Utah's capital city— where close to 275,000 people lived by 1950—the Salt Lake Temple aided in the enforcement and evolution of the institutional policy that prohibited peoples of African descent from being ordained to the priesthood and from fully participating in temple ordinances. When Brigham Young fully articulated the priesthood and temple restriction in 1852, he described Black people as "the children of old Cain," who was allegedly cursed and marked with darker skin after slaying his brother Abel.[10] Young's selective reading of the Bible asserting Black inferiority was not of his own creation but borrowed from a decades-old argument deployed to justify slavery in the antebellum American South. His initial explanation of Black ancestry turned into a hardened policy over the remainder of the century. Though the ban was unevenly applied, it affected all men and women of any perceived African lineage. Given the eternal weight of temple ordinances in Latter-day Saint belief, implementing the ban forced painful inequities and exclusions on the church's most sacred of spaces.

The experience of Black Latter-day Saint convert Jane Manning James epitomized the conflicted relationship Black Latter-day Saints had with the Salt Lake Temple. Baptized in October 1843, James had lived and worked in Joseph Smith's Mansion House in Nauvoo, Illinois; had followed Brigham Young and the rest of the church west; and had remained active in her local ward and Relief Society in Salt Lake City. James repeatedly petitioned church leaders to allow her to receive the temple endowment. At one point in 1884, she candidly asked church president John Taylor, "Is there no blessing for me?"[11] Answers to her requests were delayed as church leaders tried to understand precedent on the issue. In the meantime, she was granted a recommend to enter the temple to serve as proxy for her kindred dead in receiving baptism.[12]

When James entered the Salt Lake Temple in 1894, her experience was limited to the temple's lower floor, where baptisms for the dead were performed. That same year, church leaders acquiesced to a modified form of her past requests. James had asserted that in Nauvoo Emma Smith, Joseph Smith's wife, had invited her to be sealed into their family as an adopted child. Not understanding the meaning of the ritual then, James had declined but now wanted the temple blessings she had been offered.[13] She was not permitted into the upper floors of the temple, but one month after church president Wilford Woodruff ended the practice of adoptive sealings,[14] Relief Society president Zina D. H. Young and First Presidency counselor Joseph F. Smith entered the Salt Lake Temple on May 18, 1894, as white proxies for the sealing of James to Joseph Smith. The unprecedented proxy ordinance avoided the traditional language of the adoption sealing and instead sealed James to the Joseph and Emma Smith family as a servant in the eternal world, reflecting her original role in their household. As the stand-in for James, Young verbalized consent for this new role. But James, absent and unable to give her full consent, was not appeased by the unprecedented arrangement.[15]

142   THE SALT LAKE TEMPLE

Her continued petitions to church leaders pushed the First Presidency and Quorum of the Twelve Apostles to discuss the priesthood and temple ban within the walls of the Salt Lake Temple at their regular council meetings. For example, in considering James's case in August 1895, First Presidency counselor George Q. Cannon reasserted the "fiat of the Lord . . . that Cain's descendants should not receive the blessing of the Priesthood until Abel's posterity should come forward and receive tabernacles and the Priesthood."[16] Each successive discussion of the ban within the temple solidified past practice and the ban's rationale, guarding against concessions when the church's racial policy was brought up at future council meetings. The council meetings in the Salt Lake Temple around the start of the twentieth century breathed new life into the racial restriction as church leaders circulated scriptures on lineage, purported statements by the prophet Joseph Smith, and contemporary theories on the risks associated with interracial marriage that, according to Joseph F. Smith, justified denying anyone with a drop of African blood "the priesthood . . . or the blessings of the Temple of God" until a revelation from God sanctioned by the same council in the Salt Lake Temple said otherwise.[17] Restricting temple ordinances based on genealogy, however, proved challenging, and the restriction was generally enforced not at the gates of the temple but through selective proselytizing and in the process of approving temple recommends, which was done at the discretion of local ward and stake leaders.[18]

Without a revelatory injunction, church leaders refused to modify or lift the racial policy, even as the 1960s civil rights movement (as well as the 1968 presidential bid of Latter-day Saint George Romney) shined a light on the restriction. Activists in Utah, for instance, connected the priesthood and temple ban to the stalled civil rights legislation in the Utah legislature. In a state where most residents were Latter-day Saints, the link between the church and politics was inextricable, which led protestors to voice concerns over Utah politics not at the capitol or other municipal buildings but at Temple Square—what one historian has labeled Salt Lake City's "town square."[19] Though the square was considered sacred, it was also the church's most obvious symbol of power, with the Salt Lake Temple at the center of church administration and revelation.

In October 1963, the Utah chapter of the National Association for the Advancement of Colored People (NAACP) had planned to demonstrate outside the gates of Temple Square during general conference until First Presidency counselor Hugh B. Brown calmed tensions with a public

POLITICAL PLACE   143

statement supporting civil rights for all.[20] But a short time later, in 1965, the NAACP suspected the church was working covertly to delay legislation on fair housing and equal employment in Utah, so it held a series of marches around the Church Administration Building, just east of Temple Square.[21] The cause of the delay, the NAACP feared, was "the official L.D.S. doctrine of exclusion of Negroes from the priesthood."[22] Even as proposed civil rights legislation became law in Utah, activists remained focused on the priesthood and temple ban as the source of subtle forms of discrimination in the state. Renewed protests in the late 1960s took place at other visible Latter-day Saint institutions, especially Brigham Young University, the church's flagship college, with about twenty-five thousand students.[23]

As the civil rights movement moved forward, the nation's urban centers became battlegrounds for Black equality, and violence and riots spiked. Church leaders grew concerned that the racial violence would hit Salt Lake City and threaten the pioneer temple. Their concerns seemed to become reality when in the early morning of November 14, 1962, a bomb detonated on the east side of the temple, shattering eleven exterior windows, splintering a large door, and destroying its pioneer hardware. The FBI and a team of US Army explosive experts were called to the scene to investigate. Initially police detained a group of teenagers as suspects but could not uncover enough evidence to tie them to the crime.[24] Though the mystery was never solved, the bombing heightened concerns that the temple was vulnerable to the church's enemies. Fears turned into speculation in Utah as race riots embroiled Los Angeles in 1965 and Detroit in 1967. A source close to the Salt Lake Police Department told one church leader that "carloads" of Black militants "armed with machine guns and bombs were . . . coming to Salt Lake City," and particularly to Temple Square, "for the purpose of inciting a riot." When President David O. McKay heard the rumor, he ordered that "everything possible must be done to guard that sacred spot."[25] The rumor proved false but would resurface just before the April 1970 general conference, prompting increased security on Temple Square.[26]

As the civil rights movement tapered off after succeeding in many of its aims, the temple and priesthood ban remained unchanged, though it was still regularly discussed by church leaders. In 1975, President Spencer W. Kimball extensively reviewed the ban, including its logic and origins, and entreated other church leaders to do the same. The apostles and other general authorities frequently discussed the ban in their regular council meetings in the Salt Lake Temple. The Book of Mormon considered "black and white,

144   THE SALT LAKE TEMPLE

bond and free, male and female" to be "alike unto God" and commanded the gospel to be preached to "every nation, kindred, tongue, and people" (2 Nephi 26:33; 1 Nephi 1:17). The inclusive doctrinal mandates informed the church's expansive missionary program, which found increasing success in the southern hemisphere in places like Brazil. Construction of a temple in São Paulo was announced in 1975, but the temple and priesthood ban posed a barrier for its prospective use by baptized Brazilians of Black or mixed ancestry. The obvious distance between the church's universal message and its historic policies was not lost on church leaders, but Kimball was hesitant to lift the ban or change the policy without a revelation from God and the full support of all his fellow General Authorities. Thus any prospect for change lagged notably behind the racial progress of the civil rights movement in the United States and direct political and cultural pressure to end the race-based policy.[27] While a range of opinions existed among general authorities on the temple and priesthood ban, including growing support for its reversal, their public response reiterated the status quo while study and further discussion about the policy's origins continued quietly behind the scenes.

In the early months of 1978, Kimball spent hours in the temple considering the policy. His contemplation often took place while he was alone in the Holy of Holies, after the temple had closed for the day. In those private moments, he received a personal spiritual witness to end the ban. On Thursday, June 1, 1978, the First Presidency and Quorum of the Twelve Apostles had their regular meeting with the Seventies on the administration floor of the temple. According to prior instruction, the apostles remained behind after the meeting and Kimball led the group in prayer, seeking another confirmation that the policy should be changed. Those in the room reported a Pentecostal-like outpouring akin to one experienced by early church leaders in the House of the Lord in Kirtland, Ohio. According to Apostle Gordon B. Hinckley, "It felt as if a conduit opened between the heavenly throne and the kneeling, pleading prophet." The First Presidency and Quorum of the Twelve Apostles unanimously approved of the decision to end the priesthood and temple ban.[28]

Church leaders kept the decision quiet for over a week as they waited for the rest of the General Authorities to approve the change in a special meeting held on June 8 in the temple's assembly room. The next day, Friday, June 9, the church's Public Communications Department issued an official statement. Sent to media outlets around the world, the statement read in part, "We have pleaded long and earnestly ... spending many hours in the Upper

Room of the Temple supplicating the Lord for divine guidance. He has heard our prayers, and by revelation has confirmed that the long-promised day has come where every faithful, worthy man in the Church may receive the holy priesthood . . . and enjoy with his loved ones every blessing that flows therefrom, including the blessings of the temple."[29] The Salt Lake Temple proved to be center stage for a policy that had found both new life and a dramatic end within its walls. News of the policy change spread quickly, capturing international headlines that again placed the temple at the epicenter of change in the church.[30]

Institutional change had been comparatively slow on the reversal of the temple and priesthood ban for many inside and outside the church, but the ban's end quelled public discontent for a time and stirred celebrations; Latter-day Saints expressed gratitude for the Salt Lake Temple and the prayerful petitions of church leaders. The afternoon after the press release, Darius Gray, a Black Latter-day Saint and businessman, met with his close friend Heber Wolsey in Wolsey's office on Temple Square. According to Wolsey, who was head of public communications for the church, Gray was "looking fondly out the window at the Salt Lake Temple. He rushed to me, and we threw our arms around each other and wept for gratitude and joy." "I always knew," Gray told Wolsey. "I just didn't know if it would happen on this side of the veil [that is, in mortality]." Wolsey recounted, "Darius looked at me, then out the window at the temple, and then at me again. He closed his eyes, opened them slowly and said softly, 'God is good.'"[31]

Lifting the ban allowed African men to be ordained to the priesthood and hold leadership positions, thereby paving the path for the church to be officially established in Africa. In November 1978, the church was organized in Nigeria, and Anthony Obinna and his family were the first in the country to be baptized. Missionaries organized the Aboh Branch, with Obinna as its first president and his wife, Fidelia, as its first Relief Society president. Overjoyed by these events, Anthony and his counselors wrote a letter to President Kimball and the rest of the First Presidency in Utah. "The entire members of the Church of Jesus Christ of Latter Day Saints in this part of Nigeria have the pleasure to thank you and the Latter Day Saints throughout the world for opening the door for the Gospel to come to our people in its fullness," they wrote. "We are happy for the many hours in the Upper Room of the Temple you spent supplicating the Lord to bring us into the fold."[32] Thirteen years had passed since Obinna's initial dream of being led to the Salt Lake Temple, and it was a revelation in that temple that had formally brought the church

146   THE SALT LAKE TEMPLE

to Nigeria. Less than ten years later, in 1985, the ordinances of the temple became available on the African continent when a Latter-day Saint temple was completed in Johannesburg, South Africa. Its exterior featured six spires, reminiscent of the façade of the Salt Lake Temple.

Center of Politics and Protest

As criticism of the church's racial policy faded, the institution made con-certed attempts to improve its public relations. The church's Public Communications Department launched a campaign in the 1970s to improve the institution's cultural cachet in the United States. The most successful and far-reaching of the department's efforts was its "Homefront" public service advertisements. The popular radio and television commercials, produced by professionals in Southern California, avoided obvious reli-gious overtones and instead associated the church with traditional family values while teaching basic moral lessons.[33] The expensive campaign, ac-cording to one Public Communications Department member, was meant to link "Mormons" with "family" in the public mind, displacing more popular associations like "racist," "polygamy," or even "the Osmonds," a popular Utah family music group.[34] By 1976, only four years after the campaign's start, one internal estimate of the church's free radio and television time reached 31 million dollars.[35] The campaign largely worked in rendering Latter-day Saints as a religious people with traditional family values, but church leaders could not always control the narrative.

The institution was also undergoing a corresponding political shift in the 1960s and 1970s, led by individuals in the Quorum of the Twelve Apostles, like Ezra Taft Benson, who served as U.S. president Dwight D. Eisenhower's secretary of agriculture until 1961. Benson frequently decried communism, socialism, and a perceived creeping secularism in American society. The turbulent decades of the 1960s and 1970s nudged the political ideology of a growing number of Latter-day Saints further right on the political spectrum, which mobilized some in the faith to take a public stance on social issues.[36]

In 1976, the First Presidency issued its first official stance on the Equal Rights Amendment, passed by Congress in 1972, formally applying its hard-won moral authority on conservative family values to the arena of national politics just as states began to ratify the amendment.[37] In broad wording, the amendment prohibited discrimination on the basis of sex and guaranteed the equal civil rights of women. Church leaders, including its Relief Society presidency, opposed the amendment on moral rather than political grounds because it carried "deceptively simple language [which] deals with practically every aspect of American life, without considering the possible train of unnatural consequences."[38] The feared consequences of the amendment's ratification included the displacement of women's traditional role within the home, the expansion of abortion access, and general anxiety that any concessions to a burgeoning new feminism might permanently alter the place of the family in society.[39]

Such outcomes seemingly undermined the "Family: Isn't It about Time?" message that aired on American televisions and radios through the Church's Homefront campaign. Any public assertions about the importance of family, however, was firmly rooted in church doctrine on eternal families and a temple theology which espoused traditional and separate roles for males and females in a united divine partnership. The church had spent decades since the end of polygamy sharing its commitment to the traditional nuclear family structure to reassure the American public that it had fully integrated the nation's domestic values. With much invested in the shifting politics of family, the institution encouraged members to contribute to the amendment's defeat.

The church's stance inflamed supporters of the amendment both outside and inside the church. Latter-day Saint Sonia Johnson, for example, rallied fellow congregants to protest the church's position, touching off nationwide protests under the "Mormons for ERA" banner. Though Latter-day Saints protested throughout the country, the largest demonstrations occurred near Temple Square, where a coalition of groups in favor of the ERA gathered at least twice yearly to march during the church's April and October general conferences, "singing, shouting and carrying signs."[40] Airplanes flew above the square, towing banners that read "Mormons for ERA Are Everywhere" and "ERA the Pearl of Great Price."[41] Activists and protestors believed an all-male priesthood unjustly sought to wield influence on an issue affecting basic civil rights for women. They accordingly targeted their protests at the church's administrative center, the Salt Lake Temple and its surrounding square, the preeminent symbol, for critics, of the institution's patriarchy and power.

ERA activists viewed Temple Square as an extension of the church hierarchy; church authorities, along with the thousands who converged on the square to attend general conference, could presumably hear and see the

148   THE SALT LAKE TEMPLE

opposition to church policy as sessions were being held. At the October 1980 general conference, three women vocalized an opposing vote when President Kimball's name was presented during the traditional sustaining of general authorities. When later asked to explain her public dissent, one protestor said, "[I] support Church President Spencer W. Kimball as a religious leader but not as a political leader."[42] Johnson too criticized the General Authorities for entering into what she and many others felt was a political arena; she was eventually excommunicated for her role in the pro-ERA protests. Despite the large demonstrations, most conference attendees were either unfussed or confused by the protesters. "They can march all they want to," said one conference goer, "but I don't know what they hope to accomplish."[43] ERA ratification efforts eventually fizzled and faded on a national scale in the early 1980s. The collective effect, however, of the fraught decades of the 1960s and 1970s (with the church's occasional entrance into politics on moral issues) was to turn Temple Square into a tumultuous crossroads for political expression.

The Illusive Celestial City and the Perspective of Politics

According to Anthony Obinna's later interpretation of his vision in Nigeria, the Salt Lake Temple represented an endpoint for his spiritual yearnings, a "Celestial City" along his pilgrim's quest. By the time Obinna had discovered the true origins of the temple, his country was war-torn and destabilized. Yet the *Reader's Digest* article that connected Latter-day Saints to the temple for Obinna portrayed a self-sufficient, happy, and resourceful people. That image was truly in the eye of the beholder, and for Obinna the religion, seen through its sacred space, seemed to be an idyllic salve to his immediate challenges. Since his conversion, his story has been told and retold by Latter-day Saints largely in the United States. The story's popularity, beyond its appeal to the miraculous, could in part be explained by the fact that Obinna viewed Latter-day Saints exactly as they wanted to be seen as they set their sights on spreading to new areas of the globe. Salt Lake City indeed was their "Celestial City," with the temple at the center of a peaceful and contemplative square that represented the fruits of a successful American-born faith.

Not all, however, bought into such an idealized image, and the visible power center of the church became a site to communicate opposing values and a political cause to church leaders, whose distance from routine public access had grown alongside the church's membership. What indeed was a source of spiritual power to some represented a whole different set of power dynamics for others. Temple Square thus became a site for the mixture of politics and sacred space as the church sought to negotiate its identity as a globalizing faith. In their long tradition of curating the landscape around the temple to match and project church values and peoplehood, church leaders leveled a visual critique at the groundswell of resistance to their ERA stance as one example of this negotiation. In 1979, the church placed two bronze statues on the plaza in front of the Church Office Building. (Similar monuments would soon follow.)[44] The statues, named *In Her Mother's Footsteps* and *Joyful Moment*, were replicas from a series of statues commissioned by the Relief Society for their 136th anniversary in 1978 that were placed in a memorial garden outside the Latter-day Saint visitor's center in Nauvoo, Illinois.[45] Both statues depicted a woman performing her traditional role as a mother, underscoring the centrality of motherhood and families in church values and doctrine. The monuments preached a defiant sermon to the church's critics at a time when its leaders felt traditional family values and womanhood were under assault.

The modern Latter-day Saint image mattered for a church with aspirations to evangelize the globe. The new statues were just a minor part of a series of major costly renovations to the temple and its square in the second half of the twentieth century. If politics were clouding Latter-day Saint messaging at its primary sacred space as millions continued to come to Salt Lake City to see the temple, church leaders responded by modernizing its tourist-hosting strategy in hopes of transforming the tourist's journey of curiosity into a sacred journey.

9

Commemorative Place

By his seventy-seventh birthday, Apostle Spencer W. Kimball's heart was failing. In March 1972, during a consultation that included the First Presidency of The Church of Jesus Christ of Latter-day Saints, cardiologist Ernest L. Wilkinson, and cardiothoracic surgeon Russell M. Nelson, Kimball faced a somber decision. For months his quality of life had deteriorated as he battled fatigue and breathlessness. Nelson, a pioneer in open-heart surgery, understood the risks of operating on the apostle, with his complicated medical history and advanced age. "I am a dying man," Kimball declared to Nelson and others, wishing to decline the surgery and confront the end of his life. First Presidency counselor Harold B. Lee protested Kimball's decision. Rising to his feet and with a voice that jolted the room, Lee exclaimed to Kimball, "You are not to die! You are to do everything you need to do to care for yourself and continue to live."[1] At Lee's pleading, Kimball agreed to surgery under the care of Nelson after the April 1972 general conference.

Before large surgeries or while enduring significant health challenges, Latter-day Saints customarily seek out priesthood blessings for healing. The healing ritual traditionally involves an anointing with oil, after which hands are placed on the petitioner's head and a blessing pronounced by an individual with the priesthood. Just prior to Kimball's surgery, he asked for such a ritual in the Salt Lake Temple. The church had long suspended the performance of regular healing ordinances in the temple, but Kimball's life-threatening condition justified a special meeting of General Authorities.

On April 9, Kimball and his wife, Camilla, entered the temple late in the afternoon. The entire First Presidency and a majority of the Quorum of the Twelve Apostles participated as First Presidency counselor N. Eldon Tanner performed the anointing and Lee spoke the blessing. Lee invoked the setting of the temple as the place for a "special outpouring of the blessings of the Holy Father" because "on many occasions" church leaders had been "closer to Him than elsewhere" within the temple's walls. In addition to praying on behalf of the abilities of the doctors who would perform the surgery, Lee blessed Kimball that he may "bear up physically" to the surgery and that "every

---

The Salt Lake Temple. Scott D. Marianno and Reid L. Neilson, Oxford University Press.
© Oxford University Press 2025. DOI: 10.1093/9780190881580.003.0010

COMMEMORATIVE PLACE   151

organ will function properly" again. He invited God to "cradle [Kimball] as within Thine arms and leave him not alone" and invoked the "united hearts" and faith of the "holy apostleship" in marshaling the powers of heaven to heal him.[2] Kimball's precarious health situation made the occasion notable, but the blessing also represented one instance when the church hierarchy used the Salt Lake Temple to petition for divine power to save one of their own. Years of experience within the Salt Lake Temple had cultivated a special devotion to the site as an access point for spiritual healing and divine power, an expectation shared by other Latter-day Saints who made pilgrimages to or celebrated and commemorated the site.

The Salt Lake Temple sat at the confluence of history, heritage, tourism, and—as we have seen—protest and politics that fostered devotion, curiosity, and public opinion at the site. The diverse motivations of the devotee and the tourist influenced how the space around the temple was curated, interacted with, and remembered by the millions who visited. As the Salt Lake Temple aged toward its centennial year, demands on the structure continued to grow. After World War II, with soaring automobile ownership and improved interstate highways, more Americans took to the road to explore the industrializing West. In an era of "robust consumerism," tourism became an annual ritual of the suburban middle class.[3] Salt Lake City and Temple Square became one waypoint along an improved system of travel around the American West. In the 1960s, the Salt Lake Temple's volunteer staff struggled to manage increased attendance and tourism, especially in the summer months. Accommodating sustained devotion and interest in the historic temple became a pressing challenge for a church administration with global aspirations to spread its message. In an era when institutional priorities ran in many directions, the Salt Lake Temple could have confronted a period of neglect. It instead benefited from reinvestment and sustained engagement that influenced the interpretation and use of the site in the decades to come.

Modernizing Temple Square

For good or for ill, Temple Square captured national attention as a representation of the Latter-day Saint faith. As church leaders opted to amplify the institution's collective voice in national discussions, some members of the public took a renewed interest in Latter-day Saint life. Changes in American life aided in the popularity of Temple Square as automobiles

152 THE SALT LAKE TEMPLE

conveniently whisked tourists there in the second half of the twentieth century. The temple's role as a protest site only served to sustain public engagement. The wave of mixed press reports, which stemmed first from the priesthood and temple policy and later from the excommunication of high-profile activists like Sonia Johnson, brought conflict directly to the sacred site and underscored its pivotal role in institutional messaging to the world about church doctrine and Latter-day Saints in general. With a robust international building program underway in the 1960s, church leaders had their eyes on renovating Temple Square facilities to accommodate persistent interest, initiating a nearly two-decade period of renovation and construction that resulted in drastic changes inside and outside the temple.

The first of a series of projects at Temple Square included updates to the temple itself. According to church president David O. McKay, the primary aim of the 3.5-million-dollar renovation—nearly equal to the original construction cost of the building—was to enhance the temple's capacity to accommodate "more [temple] work . . . by more members of the Church with greater dispatch and comfort."[4] In preparation for the closure on June 29, 1962, the temple reduced its daily endowment sessions from seven to five.[5] The interior renovation was scheduled to last until the end of the year (but took an extra five months to complete) and included the addition of six new sealing rooms, air conditioning and improved heating systems, new lighting, and additional elevator service.[6] While interior renovations occurred at a feverish pace, workers excavated around the temple to prepare for the construction of a new entrance and annex, exposing the original footings.[7] Workers also demolished the original Byzantine-inspired Annex, designed by Brigham Young's son, Don Carlos Young. The replacement annex, designed to match the temple's granite exterior, would house a new subterranean entrance to the temple. The extensive renovation privileged function over fealty to heritage or history, resulting in a selective redesign of the interior furnishings.[8] On May 27, 1963, President McKay, who attended the original Salt Lake Temple dedication, had rededicated the temple and it opened again for use.[9]

The surrounding square remained a construction zone in the ensuing years and even involved a partial renovation of the historic wall.[10] Church leaders decided to construct a new bureau of information to serve as a visitors' center on the north side of the temple. Although largely completed by 1963, the North Visitors' Center functioned initially as a temporary temple annex until the new annex was completed in 1966. The building was then converted into a modern visitors' center by the Church Information Committee. Its transformation continued into the summer, as square guides readied for 700,000 visitors during that year's tourist season. The recent success of the church exhibit at the New York World's Fair in 1964–65 effectively highlighted the positive impact of carefully curated exhibits to tell the church's story to curious tourists, prompting changes to how the church exhibited space around its temple. Beginning in 1966, the new tourist experience at the Temple Square visitor center and at other church sites around the country featured replicas of the displays, paintings, and media components effective in New York, including the Mormon Pavilion's video presentation, *Man's Search for Happiness.*[11]

In the decade after the North Visitors' Center was completed, the crowds of tourists and pilgrims to Temple Square continued to test the square's infrastructure and grounds during peak spring and summer months. The old Bureau of Information and adjoining LDS Church Museum were demolished in 1976 to make space for a new South Visitors' Center in the southeast corner of Temple Square. In comparison to the North Visitors' Center and its seventy-five thousand square feet of floor space, the South Visitors' Center was much smaller, only thirty thousand square feet. Yet despite being 60 percent smaller, the South Visitors' Center's efficient floorplan could accommodate more annual visitors—2 million, as opposed to the North Visitors' Center's capacity of 1.5 million.[12] Four years later, President Spencer W. Kimball announced that the church planned to build two new buildings immediately west of Temple Square: a 65,000-square-foot Museum of Church History and Art and a 136,000-square-foot Genealogical Library.[13] Its ten-acre block overcrowded, Temple Square continued to grow beyond its pioneer footprint to nearly the size of the original forty acres designated for the Temple Block in 1847.

The extensive redesign of the space around the temple continued the square's long tradition of deploying sacred space to transmit Latter-day Saint values and doctrine. The latest attempt demonstrated just how much the church had matured and adapted within American society since earlier attempts to generate tourism at Temple Square. The institution now deployed a systematized corporate public relations strategy to correlate the image of the church in the constructed environment around the square. More than just a rescripting of exhibits, the rebuild of the square's landscape involved an intentional campaign to reconfigure entrenched perceptions about the Latter-day Saint religion in an era when many had heard at least something

154   THE SALT LAKE TEMPLE

about its people. Inasmuch as sacred space served as a representation of both religious practices and the community that supported the practices, the new Temple Square showcased a comfortable merger between the church's unique doctrines and the modern American corporation. Historic structures like the Salt Lake Temple, Tabernacle—which received its own renovation in this period—and the Assembly Hall coexisted with modern, sleek, and functional meeting spaces, surrounded by a carefully landscaped campus befitting a modern and international headquarters. Symbolic of this era of extraordinary growth and change, a new twenty-eight-story skyscraper housing church offices on the east side of Main Street cast a shadow over the Salt Lake Temple in 1972, permanently altering the temple's picturesque mountain backdrop.

The corporate religious aesthetic of the square might seem an odd design choice around a sacred shrine, but the appearance of the square had as much to do with evangelizing perceptions about the church as it did with maintaining the sacred nature of the temple's environs. The global success of the Latter-day Saint faith was on display at Temple Square, a visible representation church leaders hoped would disabuse the public of distorted notions of the faith and eventually lead to new converts. The new South Visitors' Center, for example, featured a replica of the Salt Lake Temple's baptismal font and a 136-seat theater, where visitors could see a new film about the frequently misunderstood nature and purpose of Latter-day Saint temple work. On June 1, 1978, President Kimball dedicated the South Visitors' Center.[14] At the dedication event, Apostle Gordon B. Hinckley talked of the importance of the new building: "[T]his center is dedicated to the telling of two great themes . . . first, the Book of Mormon as the word of God, brought forth in this gospel dispensation by the gift and power of God to the convincing of the Jew and gentile that Jesus is the Christ; and secondly, the reality and importance of the atonement of Christ." Hinckley described the new center as the next step in the church's "effort to correct misrepresentation through self-representation," a significant financial investment in its institutional image.[15] The church had grown its missionary program worldwide in the second half of the twentieth century, and its unprecedented financial investment in the free Temple Square experience was expected to pay dividends in missionary work. Through tourism and missionary work on Temple Square, the church hoped to see a harvest of new members in its worldwide missions.

In 1988 more guests toured Temple Square than visited the American West's legendary national parks, including Yellowstone to the north and the Grand Canyon to the South, making Temple Square the Intermountain West's top tourist attraction. According to a survey that year, of the square's 4,100,000 visitors, about 88 percent came from outside of Utah; most were from the western states, and 9 percent were from outside the United States. Slightly fewer than half (49 percent) of the guests were Latter-day Saints, and Protestants (25 percent) composed the next largest set. Catholics and nonreligionists each represented 7 percent of visitors. Most visited Temple Square with their spouse (37 percent) or as families with children (30 percent). A small minority visited the square alone (6 percent). Surprisingly, barely a quarter of all visitors (26 percent) came for religious reasons. Most tourists (68 percent) were in Salt Lake City on vacation; the majority of non–Latter-day Saints were "just passing through" (27 percent) or touring the larger Intermountain West (28 percent), with Utah just one stop on their itinerary.[16]

The interest among church leaders in controlling the pristine and peaceful environment around the temple and attracting curious outsiders to Temple Square included the commercial development of spaces beyond the square that would act as a hedge against urban blight. In the 1970s, as enclosed shopping malls swept the nation, the church's real estate holding company, Zion Securities Corporation, proposed a dramatic revitalization of the area just south of Temple Square. The multimillion-dollar renovation placed the church's longtime department store, ZCMI, at the center of a sprawling 600,000-square-foot retail development. The ZCMI Center opened in July 1975 and was a striking commentary on the growth of the church's corporate power.[17] Only a couple of decades before, the church had been approaching insolvency with a budget deficit in the millions, but its adoption of corporate reforms and conservative financial principles at the behest of First Presidency counselor N. Eldon Tanner rebuilt its reserves and made the institution more resilient to future economic downturns.[18] Such reforms also grew the church into a modern American corporation capable of absorbing the high costs of global growth. On the heels of past economic crises, the church's move toward self-reliance coincided with a groundswell of political conservatism in its ranks, which valued individualism, capitalism, and free markets. Such retail investments seemed part and parcel with participation in the American experience.

The sleek church-owned mall brought the conveniences of American consumerism within a few tidy downtown blocks of Salt Lake City, inserting the church's sacred space into the cultural rhythms of American daily life. The

156   THE SALT LAKE TEMPLE

new retail center could accommodate two thousand vehicles in a two-story parking structure that catered to automobile-loving suburbanites.[19] The mall was a secular "temple of consumerism" next to the sacred "temple of temples," reflecting the seamless and supportive existence of market space alongside sacred space in the postwar United States.[20] This union of the religious and the secular could be seen particularly in the layout of the American indoor mall, including the one in Salt Lake City, which was partly inspired by some of the nation's iconic worship spaces and their central courts. According to the *Deseret News*, the mall's design was an "affirmation that businessmen can also cope with the problems of the age and urban disuse in an area many had begun to believe was beyond their scope."[21] The thoroughly Americanized Latter-day Saint church shared the Protestant and capitalist ideology in which the secular did not compete with religious life.[22] Latter-day Saints had long nurtured a comfortable marriage between their secular enterprises and spiritual endeavors. Utah's own state emblem—the beehive—emphasized a heritage of self-sufficiency and industry in the state, a heritage visible in downtown Salt Lake City from within the confines of Temple Square. The growth of church resources, however, made the Temple Square model of a beautified, clean, and industrious sacred space exportable to global locales through temple construction.

Bridging Two Eras of Temple Building

The extensive effort to update and expand the church's central square during this period did not come at the expense of developing more temples. In 1965 the church operated only thirteen temples: ten in North America, two in Europe, and one in Oceania. Under the direction of President David O. McKay, however, a new era of temple building began. McKay's interest in constructing new temples was aspirational as well as practical. The existing temples in Utah, for instance, were operating beyond their capacity. According to one report to the First Presidency in 1966, the ordinance workload at the Salt Lake Temple had increased 250 percent since 1950.[23] As church finances improved, President McKay hoped to alleviate the burden on the pioneer temples by authorizing the construction of two new temples in Utah, one in Ogden and one in Provo. He instructed church architect Emil Fetzer to create a temple design that was both "functional" and "economical." According to Fetzer, McKay felt the church was no longer in a position "to build huge monuments": "We have to have temples that the membership can use to do efficient temple work." This meant smaller buildings that clustered six ordinance rooms around a central Celestial Room.[24]

For at least one temple, however, McKay made an exception. In 1962, church leaders purchased a lot near Washington, DC, on a wooded hill just off the planned Capital Beltway in Kensington, Maryland. The land was not developed for another six years, until November 1968, when the church publicly announced a temple would be built near the nation's capital. The First Presidency then privately solicited designs from a handful of Latter-day Saint architects. Keith W. Wilcox drafted the selected exterior design, which featured six iconic spires reminiscent of the Salt Lake Temple. Church architects selected Alabama white marble for the temple's exterior, which caused the 160,000-square-foot structure to glow at night when illuminated. The interior implemented the same six-ordinance-room layout as the Ogden and Provo temples.

According to Wilcox, an iconic, "timeless" design would allow millions of anticipated Beltway drivers to immediately identify the edifice as a "Mormon temple." The structure was also an architectural tribute to "the best known and most easily recognized symbol of the Church, the Salt Lake Temple." The design boldly announced the "literal return of the Church to that part of the United States from whence it was driven."[25] The Salt Lake Temple thus again served as a monument to pioneer sacrifice from a past era of religious violence. Within a short distance of the world's power center, church leaders planted a distinctive and unmistakable reminder that the Latter-day Saints remained and thrived within the American religious and political landscape.

At the ceremony in December 1968, First Presidency counselor Hugh B. Brown called the temple groundbreaking "one of the most significant moments" in Latter-day Saint history. After recounting the painful migration westward of thousands of Latter-day Saint refugees, Brown boldly announced that the temple was the start of a new chapter of church growth beyond the Intermountain West: "We are coming back East."[26] The Washington Temple, dedicated in November 1974, became the first modern Latter-day Saint temple in North America to be constructed east of the Mississippi River. It brought a sizable group of church members in the eastern parts of Canada and the United States within a day's drive of a temple for the first time.[27]

Only three temples had functioned outside of North America—in Bern, Switzerland; Hamilton, New Zealand; and London, England—all built under the direction of internationally minded President McKay. In 1980, President

158 THE SALT LAKE TEMPLE

Spencer W. Kimball told church leaders, "[N]ow begins the most intensive period of temple building in the history of the Church." He looked to the day "when the sacred ordinances of the Church, performed in the temples, will be available to all members of the Church in convenient locations around the globe."[28] A few years earlier he had announced that the church would build temples in São Paulo, Brazil, and Tokyo, Japan. For the first time, Latter-day Saints in South America and Asia could enjoy the blessing of having a temple in their own lands.[29]

Inasmuch as Latter-day Saint architecture contributed to the public image of the organization, the new temples in Japan and Brazil—both designed by church architect Emil Fetzer—exported a functional version of American midcentury architecture abroad.[30] The church's expansion of its network of temples globally also reflected the growth of its resources domestically, which could be reallocated to more distant locales where membership was beginning to grow. Church leaders still accepted the material contributions of local members toward the construction of their temples and meetinghouses, but such construction was offset by finances in Salt Lake City.[31] Church growth overseas coincided with American postwar investments in global markets, making the church a participant in the movement and reach of US power and capitalism abroad. An American-born success story in the twentieth century, the economic capacity of the church corporation in Utah enabled an increase in temple building and a renewed focus on temple worship as a central tenet of a worldwide church.

"We feel an urgency for this great [temple] work to be accomplished," Kimball told church leaders, "and wish to encourage the Saints to accept their responsibility of performing temple ordinances, writing their personal and family history . . . and then continuing their family research to ensure the redemption of their kindred dead."[32] Rather than sacrificing their finances to attend far-off temples, church members were now asked to donate their personal time in nearby houses of the Lord.[33] Between the close of the New York World's Fair in October 1965 and the celebration of the Salt Lake Temple's centennial in April 1993, members of the First Presidency dedicated more than thirty temples, in Africa (one), Asia (four), Europe (three), North America (fifteen), Oceania (four), and South America (four).[34]

Elder William Grant Bangerter, executive director of the Temple Department, announced that by mid-August 1988, over 100 million endowments for the dead had been performed by Latter-day Saints, two-thirds of those being completed since 1970. He estimated that an additional

COMMEMORATIVE PLACE   159

100 million endowments for the dead could be accomplished within the next fifteen years, given the growing number of Latter-day Saints and the proliferation of temples.[35] Less than a decade later, Kahlile B. Mehr, an employee of the church's Family History Library, shared that the total number of proxy endowments performed for the dead was nearing 140 million, just over one-tenth of 1 percent of the earth's estimated historic cumulative population of 105 billion.[36] Rather than being overwhelmed by their task of performing posthumous ordinances for everyone who had ever lived, Latter-day Saints comforted themselves by looking to the Christian Millennium as a time when they believed all outstanding temple ordinances would be completed.[37]

Sustained Devotion and Interest in the Salt Lake Temple

The era of rapid temple building in the latter half of the twentieth century brought these structures, and their respective open houses, closer to international audiences, allowing for an increase in global exposure for the church. Each completed temple shortened the distance some Latter-day Saints had to travel to receive temple ordinances for the first time and expanded the opportunity for curious outsiders to attend temple open houses. Yet even in an era of increased temple access many Latter-day Saints maintained devotion to and interest in the Salt Lake Temple.

The motivations for Latter-day Saints to attend the Salt Lake Temple over others included reasons both practical and personal, such as its proximity to convenient travel infrastructure or to family and friends who could view or participate in the significant ritual milestones. Before the Washington DC Temple was completed in 1974, church members living in the eastern and southern United States traveled to the Salt Lake Temple to receive temple ordinances in part because the city offered more tourist amenities than the smaller Utah communities of Manti, St. George, and Logan. The greater Salt Lake City area, where the bulk of Utah's Latter-day Saint population resided, also afforded travelers the opportunity to visit and lodge with friends and family living there.

Even some international converts, who had few or no family ties in Salt Lake City, elected to travel to the temple to receive ordinances rather than head to newer international temples in Bern (1955), London (1958), or Hamilton (1958). Travel costs to temples in Europe still presented a significant burden for some, requiring the pooling of resources with others or

160   THE SALT LAKE TEMPLE

the accumulation of savings for travel. Converts who elected to use saved resources to travel to Salt Lake City instead of closer temples often did so because they knew missionaries from Utah, who far outnumbered missionaries from other parts of the globe. As they dispersed around the world, these missionaries forged bonds with converts, creating a transnational network that led back to Utah.

For example, Heather Maile, who converted in Australia with her husband in 1963, saved money for ten years to travel to the temple with her family in 1973. Though they could have visited the temple in New Zealand, they chose to journey to Salt Lake City with their five young children after selling their home to finance the trip. Maile explained their choice: "[The New Zealand Temple] was so out of the way, we knew no one there. And all the missionaries [who had played a role in the family's conversion] would say, 'Come over to Salt Lake.'"[38] The family was sealed in the Salt Lake Temple on December 12, 1973. Queenie Chew, a convert from Singapore, gave a similar reason for her 1979 trip to Salt Lake City with her husband. The couple bypassed the temple in Lā'ie, Hawaii, to attend the Salt Lake Temple, near the missionaries who had taught them. "Come, and we'll take care of you," former missionaries had told Chew. "We didn't know anyone in Hawaii at that time," she recalled, justifying the longer journey.[39]

Latter-day Saints outside of Utah also frequently elected to combine a once-in-a-lifetime trip to Salt Lake City for temple ordinances with the church's twice-yearly general conferences, where thousands of like-minded devotees descended on Temple Square to hear from leaders.[40] Many outside of the United States experienced few opportunities to see church leaders speak in person. In addition, leadership training meetings and periodic cultural events coincided with general conference. Temple Square's role as the church's administrative center prompted members to journey from South America, Mexico, Europe, and the South Pacific in the latter half of the twentieth century, especially as global travel capabilities improved. Like Catholics to the Vatican City, Jews to Israel, or Muslims to Mecca, Latter-day Saints saw their trip to Salt Lake City as a rare and priceless pilgrimage to the center of their religious world.

Some of those traveling far distances to experience the Salt Lake Temple were Latter-day Saints living elsewhere in the United States. Their motivation was often history and heritage. As Latter-day Saints migrated away from a central gathering place in Utah in the twentieth century, some hoped to return to the site where their ancestors had experienced temple ordinances. According to Seventy Marion D. Hanks, "Notwithstanding the increasing availability of temples nearer to them offering the same religious experience, many members of the Church [inside and outside of Utah] still travel long distances to receive their individual Endowment in the Salt Lake Temple or to be married or sealed as families in the same building in which parents or perhaps grandparents or other family members were married long ago."[41] To maintain an intergenerational tradition, engaged couples sought marriage in the temple of their descendants. Civilly married couples similarly traveled, some with their families, to be sealed for the first time in the temple.[42] Devotion to the temple deepened through historical and family tradition that continued to draw Latter-day Saints like pilgrims to downtown Salt Lake City.

Generational ties to the Salt Lake Temple were an outgrowth of church demographics at the time of the temple's completion. While Latter-day Saints largely embraced the temple as a shared heritage site regardless of any direct ancestral ties to the temple, many multigenerational Latter-day Saints in the mid-twentieth century had close ancestors who experienced temple ritual there. As a result of a significant transatlantic gathering of Latter-day Saint immigrants to the Salt Lake Valley in the nineteenth century, over 60 percent of church membership resided in Utah by the start of the twentieth century. Since then, a significant outmigration carried church members to other parts of the United States, so that by the 1960s more members lived outside the Intermountain West than within it.[43] Nonetheless, their personal histories frequently passed through the temple.

Church leadership, whose composition was still deeply rooted in Utah and Idaho in the twentieth century, especially reflected the region's importance to temple worship prior to significant church growth outside of the Intermountain West. Of church presidents married after the dedication of the Salt Lake Temple in 1893, all of them, including President Russell M. Nelson, sustained in 2018, were married to their first wife in the Salt Lake Temple. Of the fifteen members of the First Presidency and Quorum of the Twelve present at the October 2000 general conference, ten had been sealed to their wives in the Salt Lake Temple, three in the Logan Temple, and one each in the St. George and Manti temples. Despite shifting demographics worldwide, similar personal ties continued to bind a significant portion of Latter-day Saints to the Salt Lake Temple and sustained personal devotion to

162   THE SALT LAKE TEMPLE

the structure as it aged. As a result, the commemoration for the temple's centennial year was planned on a global scale.

Centennial of the Salt Lake Temple

In 1991, nearly a century after its dedication, the Salt Lake Temple was classed among the "Hundred Wonders of the World," according to a guide published by Rand McNally. The pioneer temple took its place among other human-made wonders in North and Central America, including Chichén Itzá, the Panama Canal, and Mount Rushmore.[44] Not surprisingly, Latter-day Saints celebrated this new accolade.[45] The following year Seventy Marion D. Hanks described the temple's iconic status within the faith and surrounding Utah culture: "The gray granite structure is still recognized as the religious symbol of The Church of Jesus Christ of Latter-day Saints worldwide. Millions of visitors annually have seen the building. Photographs of the temple have gone to scores of countries where people who have never personally seen the structure identify its striking presence with the Church and the city." According to Hanks, the temple is "architecturally and artistically unique and is the most widely known and recognized building in the Church."[46]

By the April 1993 centennial of the Salt Lake Temple, the church was operating forty-four temples around the world, with several more announced or under construction. The centennial was officially commemorated by the church in a series of events and public programming. A special exhibit on the construction of the temple was opened the week before April general conference by the Church Historical Department at the Museum of Church History and Art. Titled *The Mountain of the Lord's House*, the exhibit invited visitors to learn about the temple's forty-year process of construction and its theological purposes.[47] Later that year, the Mormon Tabernacle Choir performed a special musical number in honor of the centennial, and a special entry celebrating the temple was added to the Pioneer Day parade in July. The temple itself was renovated and refurbished in the months leading up to its centenary celebration.[48]

The Salt Lake Temple was a central theme of the April 1993 general conference. Church president Ezra Taft Benson, who had been ailing for a

COMMEMORATIVE PLACE   163

number of years, was unable to attend any of the sessions. In his absence, First Presidency counselor Gordon B. Hinckley, who had personally dedicated twenty-one (nearly half) of the church's operating temples, presided. Second Counselor Thomas S. Monson opened the Saturday morning meetings and highlighted the new exhibition on the temple at the church's museum.[49] Thanks to Monson's prophetic endorsement, the timely theme, and the skilled work of the museum staff, this display became one of the most visited shows in the museum's history.[50]

In between the Saturday morning and afternoon sessions of the conference, the church premiered a new seventy-five-minute film, *The Mountain of the Lord*, on the church's satellite network, broadcast throughout meetinghouses in the United States, Canada, and the Caribbean. It dramatized the construction of the Salt Lake Temple as seen through the eyes of Wilford Woodruff, who was an apostle in 1847, when the temple site was selected, and who, as church president, presided over its 1893 dedication. Making the film was no small undertaking for the church's Temple and Audiovisual departments, as well as the Historical Department, which vetted the script for historical accuracy. The cast and crew totaled over 150, in addition to nearly one thousand extras. The movie was filmed at several Utah locations, including the LDS Motion Picture Studio in Provo; Little Cottonwood Canyon, near the granite quarry; and Temple Square itself. Transforming the square back to the nineteenth century was a monumental task and involved closing Main Street east of the temple in September 1992 so that dirt could be spread and shots could be taken with the temple as a backdrop.[51] The film quickly became a favorite of Latter-day Saint members and missionaries.

On the Sunday of the April 1993 conference, President Hinckley closed the morning session in the Tabernacle with a sermon about the Salt Lake Temple: "Go back with me an even century to this same Temple Square. No, make it an even 101 years. It is April conference of 1892. These grounds are crowded with people. The multitude is the largest ever assembled in this area of the West." Hinckley recounted the temple's capstone ceremony, led by President Woodruff, and then rehearsed the construction history detailed in *The Mountain of the Lord*.[52]

In his remarks on the Salt Lake Temple dedicatory ceremony, Hinckley invited the Mormon Tabernacle Choir to perform the "Hosanna Anthem"

164 THE SALT LAKE TEMPLE

and the congregation and those watching or listening to the broadcast around the world to sing "The Spirit of God," which had been written for and sung at the Kirtland Temple dedication in April 1836.[53]

> The Spirit of God like a fire is burning!
> The latter-day glory begins to come forth;
> The visions and blessings of old are returning,
> And angels are coming to visit the earth.
> (Chorus)
> We'll sing and we'll shout with the armies of heaven,
> Hosanna, hosanna to God and the Lamb!
> Let glory to them in the highest be given,
> Henceforth and forever, Amen and amen![54]

When the song had reverberated around temple walls in 1893, it was in joyful defiance of the church's opponents and in cautious anticipation of a century of uninterrupted temple worship. Now, as the song filled the tabernacle in 1993, Latter-day Saints worldwide united in appreciation for the survival of their crown jewel of a temple and for the successful spread of temple blessings around the globe. Through broadcast technology, President Hinckley linked generations of Latter-day Saints and rallied the church's growing global membership in celebration of the pioneer structure. Like the church itself, the Salt Lake Temple's significance had expanded beyond the borders of the Great Basin Zion as Latter-day Saints everywhere adopted the temple as part of their religious heritage.

10

Media Place

"We're not a weird people," church president Gordon B. Hinckley declared to veteran journalist Mike Wallace in April 1996. The taped television interview with the leader of The Church of Jesus Christ of Latter-day Saints, only a year into his presidency, aired on CBS's nationwide *60 Minutes* program and was a rare sight for the American public. In the age of television, the intrepid Wallace was the first member of the media to receive such open access to the church's president. Disarmingly friendly and quick-witted, Hinckley, with his own background in journalism, felt prepared to tackle Wallace's questions, despite the reporter's reputation as a tough interrogator. Viewers watched as Wallace walked in front of the Salt Lake Temple and discussed the markers of what made Latter-day Saints different in the eyes of the public, including their sacred underwear, known as temple garments. In the interview, Wallace asked questions that reflected over a century's worth of curiosity from outsiders to the faith; he asked about the church's involvement in the daily lives of its members and the church's unique doctrine of eternal families through temple ordinances. The backdrop to all of these questions was footage of the Salt Lake Temple, a striking visual image of the church's purported secrets, power, and peculiarity.

Wallace later confessed he had been surprised when the prophet accepted the interview request, issued at a Harvard Club gathering the pair had attended in November 1995. At the luncheon, Hinckley was asked about boundaries that seemed to prevent candid discussion about the operations of the church. In a statement that reflected the openness of his presidency, Hinckley answered, "There is only one situation that we don't talk about, and that is the sacred work that takes place in our temples . . . but the door is wide open on everything else."[1] In one evening on national television, Hinckley's charisma, candor, and charm reached tens of millions of Americans. Feedback on the segment was overwhelmingly positive. Media requests for Hinckley poured into the church Public Affairs Office from

---

The Salt Lake Temple. Scott D. Marianno and Reid L. Neilson, Oxford University Press.
© Oxford University Press 2025. DOI: 10.1093/9780190881580.003.0011

166   THE SALT LAKE TEMPLE

notables such as CNN's Larry King, the *New York Times, Time* magazine, and the BBC, resulting in an informal media tour for Hinckley over the next few years. Through media engagement and unprecedented openness, Hinckley championed a modern Latter-day Saint image by demystifying church members for outsiders. Latter-day Saints could be good neighbors and citizens while remaining comfortably peculiar in their religious observance.[2] Hinckley's public relations push proved prescient. In the ensuing decade, a wave of media coverage would usher in a "Mormon Moment," placing the entire church in the public spotlight.

As church leaders sought to broker an understanding with the media and the public, they continued to use the Salt Lake Temple to protect their worldwide flock of believers against a secular world. In the 1990s, relationship trends, including same-sex marriage, divorce, and teen pregnancy, fueled fears that the fabric of the traditional nuclear family was eroding. In his first address as church president, Howard W. Hunter, Hinckley's predecessor, warned "that the disintegration of the family brings upon the world the calamities foretold by the prophets." He encouraged Latter-day Saints to "look to the temple of the Lord as the great symbol of [their] membership."[3] At a time when traditional values were receding, the temple became an institutional rallying point for a retrenchment advocating worthiness, purity, and obedience. To help communicate these ideals, church materials and media were also rebranded, placing the iconic image of the Salt Lake Temple at the center of a global outreach campaign to inspire church members to stay the orthodox course in their religious life.

As the world entered a new century and a novel digital age, no singular Mormon Moment crowned the church as an American Christian faith; rather, a series of moments showcased the resiliency of the Latter-day Saint image in the face of worldwide scrutiny. In the wake of Hinckley's presidency, Americans grew increasingly comfortable with Latter-day Saints in their neighborhoods, corporate boardrooms, and sporting contests. However, they seemed less comfortable with Latter-day Saints in their politics, or at least that was the case for the 2008 presidential bid of businessman and former Massachusetts governor Mitt Romney. During the presidential race, the timeworn tropes of ecclesiastical authoritarianism and institutional secrets resurged, and though the church received sizable press coverage, that coverage engaged only superficially with the church's theology.[4] In the media and during this period of unprecedented interest in the church, the Salt Lake Temple was shorthand for the nation's cursory understanding of Latter-day

MEDIA PLACE   167

Saint core beliefs and its lingering suspicion of the church's power; in other words, the temple symbolized Latter-day Saint distinctiveness for those within and outside of the faith.

The 2002 Winter Olympics in Salt Lake City

"Not since the ancient Olympiads were held under the gaze of Zeus and his randy band of gods and goddesses have the Games been staged in a locale so thoroughly saturated by a single religion," wrote Kenneth L. Woodward, religion reporter for *Newsweek*. Woodward made this statement in September 2001, just months before the Olympic torch would be lit in Utah.[5] Since 1995, when Salt Lake City was announced as the site for the global contest, questions had swirled about how visible the church would be at the games. In the lead-up to what reporters branded the "Molympics," international media worked to understand the Latter-day Saint people while jesting (with an underlying hint of seriousness) that "a stiff drink" might not be available in "Zion."[6] For their part, church leaders tried to reassure the public that they would be friendly, supportive hosts. President Gordon B. Hinckley announced in 2000 that the church would not use the Olympics to proselytize to the world. Instead, the church offered its quiet support to the Salt Lake Olympic Committee (SLOC) and its eventual president, Mitt Romney, as they planned the global games.

Church leaders opted for a more subtle public relations campaign, understanding that, with Olympic venues at the doorstep of Temple Square, the church's presence would be unavoidable. "We're not going to throw a shroud over" the Salt Lake Temple, church spokesperson Michael Otterson related to the *Los Angeles Times* (although the temple was closed during the entirety of the games). "It is going to be a widely seen image" because of its prominence in the Salt Lake City skyline, much like the Opera House was for the 2000 Summer Games in Sydney.[7] A portion of the Joseph Smith Memorial Building, adjacent to the Salt Lake Temple, was converted into a News Resource Center, which hosted over three thousand reporters throughout the games. Bilingual volunteers answered media questions about Utah and the church, and a formal website, prepackaged video clips, and press guides facilitated accurate journalism about the church. Latter-day Saint efforts to welcome visitors to the Winter Games adopted a theme—"Friends to All Nations"—and on its welcome pamphlet appeared both the theme and an

168   THE SALT LAKE TEMPLE

official logo, featuring the façade of the Salt Lake Temple.[8] In addition to providing volunteers on Temple Square, the church encouraged its members to staff the SLOC's thousands of volunteer positions to help present a clean, friendly image to the world.

Of course, a public relations approach that highlights the best of Latter-day Saint culture was not new for the church; guides on Temple Square had been attempting to befriend the public for much of the twentieth century. The *Washington Post* called this "subtle approach" to public relations "a brilliant move by the church." "The only religious shenanigans and Bible-thumping at the Winter Games," the report continued, "came courtesy of angry other denominations, whose members circled Temple Square with anti-Mormon signs and pamphlets and posters. . . . Everyone looked nutty except the Mormons, who looked golden."[9]

Because of this subtle strategy, in the end the 2002 Winter Olympics became the "'Mormon' Olympics that weren't."[10] Latter-day Saints were everywhere and nowhere at the same time, woven seamlessly into the fabric of the events. According to a reporter for the *Washington Post*, "The Mormon Tabernacle Choir shared top billing with the celebrities; Temple Square got almost as much TV time as Bob Costas. The very theme of the Games— 'Light the Fire Within'—is straight out of a more self-determined, Oprah-affirmative modern Mormon theology."[11] Indeed, the Salt Lake Olympics seemed to cast a distinctive Latter-day Saint tone while still remaining palatable to an international audience that relished the quaintness of Utah culture. The Public Affairs Office tracked the news coverage of the church closely and classified approximately 95 percent of the thousands of articles about the church as "positive" or "fair."[12] The "Molympics" ultimately "rang true and warm" for many who attended.[13]

NBC's official television coverage featured Utah's mountainous landscape, a natural fit for the Winter Games, but it was the intermittent shots of the Salt Lake Temple that reminded viewers the scenery was more than an attractive skiing destination—it had been set apart as holy ground by a religious minority. Centralizing the Salt Lake Temple at the Winter Games was no accident. Romney privately admitted to a member of the SLOC that he wanted to make the Salt Lake Temple "serve for the Salt Lake Games the role that the Buddhist Temple served for the Nagano Games, namely the structure the world remembers."[14] To render the temple more visible, the church offered the SLOC use of a large downtown parking lot between North and South Temple and 200 and 300 West, along with 5 million dollars to develop the

Olympic Medals Plaza, just one block from Temple Square and facing the plaza, so that the Salt Lake Temple was an unmistakable presence. Nothing else on the plaza—a free venue capable of accommodating twenty thousand people—explicitly related to the Latter-day Saint religion. Its location brought 1 million people within the shadow of the temple, and that was justification enough for church leaders to invest such a large sum. Renowned musical artists Macy Gray, the Foo Fighters, the Goo Goo Dolls, the Dave Matthews Band, and others performed nightly at the venue after the medals were awarded.[15] Salt Lake City projected a thoroughly modern, urban appearance within the church's approving gaze and, at times, on its actual property.

For a religious movement that repeatedly sacralized its Great Basin settlement using statements made by both ancient and modern prophets, Latter-day Saints had no problem seeing the 2002 Winter Olympics as the fulfillment of prophecy. Before and after the Olympics, including at the April 2002 general conference, President Hinckley repeated a statement attributed to Brigham Young in 1849 about the future destiny of the Saints' home in the mountains: "We shall build a city and a temple to the Most High God in this place. We will extend our settlements to the east and west, to the north and to the south, and we will build towns and cities by the hundreds, and thousands of the Saints will gather in from the nations of the earth." For Hinckley, the Olympics had fulfilled Young's promise that Utah would become "the great highway of the nations" where the "Kings and emperors and the noble and wise of the earth" would visit.[16]

At the same April general conference, Apostle Robert D. Hales mentioned the Olympics and specifically referenced the Salt Lake Temple, connecting it to Isaiah's prophecy that the "nations shall flow" to the "mountain of the Lord's house . . . in the top of the mountains." Hales summarized, "The nations of the earth and many of their leaders have come. They have seen us serving alongside our friends in this community and our neighbors of other faiths. They have seen the light in our eyes and felt the clasp of our hands. 'The mountain of the house of the Lord,' with its brightly lit spires, has been witnessed by 3.5 billion people around the world."[17] Making the temple a visible symbol of the Latter-day Saint faith for a captive worldwide audience was a victory for church leaders. The 2002 Winter Olympics allowed Latter-day Saints to display a hard-earned confidence in their place in American society. The people of the United States could celebrate the achievements of both the nation and the Latter-day Saints side by side. For the seventeen days

170 THE SALT LAKE TEMPLE

of the Olympic Games, Salt Lake City showcased a comfortable alliance between its public and religious space.

Public versus Private Space: The Battle for
Main Street Plaza

The church's cooperative image showcased during the Olympics and the seeming alliance between public and religious matters hid a long-simmering legal battle taking place in downtown Salt Lake City over public versus sacred real estate. This conflict stemmed from the dual role of Temple Square as a public and a private space. The desire of church leaders to maintain a peaceful atmosphere at church headquarters often came into direct conflict with the space's improvised role as the "town square" of Salt Lake City.[18] Protestors still routinely came to the square to air grievances against church policies or the institution's involvement in local and national politics.

The church maintained an interest in Salt Lake City's downtown environment because it directly affected the atmosphere in proximity to their temple space. Beginning in the 1960s, the church worked closely with the city to alleviate the deterioration of the downtown core, a problem plaguing other American cities, that was marked by vandalism, boarded-up storefronts, and decayed buildings. City planners created the "Second Century Plan," with fourteen specific projects to keep the city center "vital and alive."[19] One project proposed closing one block of Main Street (the road between the Salt Lake Temple and the Joseph Smith Memorial Building to the east—then the Hotel Utah) for "a quiet haven for tourists" and to "unify the peaceful, contemplative garden space and funnel visitors into the commercial districts just south of the Church campus."[20] According to the plans, if the church agreed to fill the space with greenery, reflecting pools, and fountains to create a "visual anchor" on the north end of the city, the land would be provided to the church at no cost. By the 1990s most of the objectives of the Second Century Plan had been achieved, though Main Street still remained city property, open to car traffic.[21]

In 1993, the church purchased underground rights to the section of Main Street between North and South Temple to build a parking structure, and in 1998 the city council agreed to sell the church the entire block for approximately 8 million dollars, the amount needed by the city to "undertake other public projects of benefit to the people of the city."[22]

MEDIA PLACE   171

The Main Street block appealed to church leaders who hoped not only to unify their administration and temple blocks but also to exert more control over protestors who congregated in the space, particularly during the twice-yearly general conferences. A unified block with restrictions would also restore a peaceful atmosphere to the immediate vicinity of the temple, benefiting patrons who accessed the temple through a connecting annex on Main Street. During a proposal period to settle the terms of the block's sale, the church met with citizen groups and eventually presented a plan that promised the plaza would "remain open to all citizens and visitors as a place of quiet beauty . . . [and] would be regulated like the Church administration block—people would be free to come and go but not disrupt the peaceful atmosphere with protests or demonstrations."[23] After two public hearings and revisions to the original plan, the Salt Lake City Council agreed to the sale on April 1, 1999.

The sale immediately attracted critics, who decried what they saw as an unholy union between church and state. The American Civil Liberties Union (ACLU) of Utah, with support from its parent organization, agreed to legally represent groups in Utah who viewed the Main Street block adjacent to Temple Square as "the literal and symbolic intersection of church and state in Utah."[24] In November 1999, the ACLU filed a lawsuit on behalf of the First Unitarian Church, Utahns for Fairness, and the Utah National Organization for Women to protect the constitutional right to exercise free speech on the space east of the temple.[25] A legal battle ensued even as the block was closed, renovated, and eventually dedicated along with the church's new Conference Center, adjacent to the plaza, on October 1, 2000. The city eventually ceded all rights to the plaza to the church as the court cases pressed forward.

In 2003, the church, with the help of a private donor, gave Salt Lake City close to 2.5 acres of land on the city's west side and 1 million dollars in exchange for the plaza's public easement, effectively granting the church and its security team the power to determine the rules governing the plaza.[26] By October 2005, all legal battles were quieted when the Tenth Circuit Court of Appeals ruled that the church's clear ownership of the property and its easement rendered "Main Street Plaza no longer a public forum."[27] Pedestrian access remained, but protestors were relegated to the sidewalks on the south and north sides of the temple block, outside the temple walls.

Under the church's ownership, the Main Street plaza no longer functioned as a place for public expression but was now an "ecclesiastical park" with restrictions to preserve the atmosphere around the temple.[28] Some groups

172   THE SALT LAKE TEMPLE

tested the invisible boundaries around the plaza and found the church well prepared to enforce its property rights. In 2009, two gay men were cited for trespassing after kissing on the plaza; in response, supporters of LGBTQ rights staged a "kiss-in" that eventually moved into the plaza. Church security acted quickly by calling the police and instructing the protestors to move to designated public spaces outside the area. A few weeks later, at the entrances to the plaza, new signs appeared asserting the church's private property rights.[29]

Four years later the rules governing the plaza and square were again tested, this time by a group known as Ordain Women, a collective of current and former Latter-day Saints as well as sympathetic non–Latter-day Saints advocating for the priesthood ordination of women. With no signs or chants to indicate a formal protest, the women marched directly through the square's north gates to the entrance of the Tabernacle, where they sought tickets to the all-male priesthood session of the October 2013 general conference. They were met by church security and a church spokesperson who knew of the group's public intentions and turned them away.[30]

The protest was renewed at the April 2014 general conference, predictably with the same result.[31] Three months later, Kate Kelly, the leader of Ordain Women, was excommunicated by the church for her public advocacy of female priesthood ordination. The ecclesiastical charges against her included defiance of requests from church leaders not to protest on Temple Square.[32] Kelly and church leaders shared an understanding of the power of Temple Square, including its ties to the church's public image and proselytizing goals. The Salt Lake Temple, as a representation of the institutional ideals and peoplehood of the church, raised the stakes within the square. By violating the behavioral norms expected on the square, Kelly attracted media attention and extra institutional scrutiny. By excommunicating Kelly, the church both policed orthodox boundaries of church practice and reinforced the boundaries of its sacred space.

Personal Purity and the Salt Lake Temple as Cultural Symbol

Latter-day Saint temple building took a major turn in June 1997, after President Gordon B. Hinckley traveled to northern Mexico to visit the Latter-day Saints still living in the Mormon colonies in the northwestern state of Chihuahua. While there, Hinckley contemplated the struggles of the region's isolated church members, who had to drive far distances to attend temples in Mexico or the United States. "They've been so very faithful over the years," he said. "They've gone on missions in large numbers. These stakes have produced very many mission presidents who served faithfully and well." The church president continued, "I thought of these things and what could be done. The concept of . . . smaller temples came into my mind." He later sketched a simplified floor plan for such a temple, which did not have a laundry, cafeteria, or other amenities that were customarily provided but not necessary to temple worship. Smaller temples, Hinckley imagined, would increase financial savings and decrease construction time.

Once back at church headquarters, he showed his rough sketch to church architects, who then fleshed out the concept. Months later, at the October general conference, he shared his inspiration with the church membership and announced plans to build three smaller temples in Monticello, Utah; Anchorage, Alaska; and the Mormon colonies in northern Mexico. "There are many areas of the Church that are remote, where the membership is small and not likely to grow very much in the near future. Are those who live in these places to be denied forever the blessings of the temple ordinances?" he asked. Within nine months, the temple in Monticello was dedicated, marking the beginning of a new era of temple building.[33]

Emboldened by the concept of small temples, Hinckley announced over thirty new temples at the April 1998 general conference. He also declared that he intended to have one hundred temples operating by the end of 2000.[34] That goal was met when the temple in Boston was dedicated on October 1, 2000.[35] One hundred seventy years after the church was organized, it had built one hundred temples around the world. As the number of worldwide temples rose, church members developed attachments to temples in their region; meticulously planned cultural celebrations were held to welcome each new temple, reflecting the diversity of the growing church membership. Attended by the church authorities who came to formally dedicate the temple, these celebrations consisted of reenactments of church history as well as presentations of local history and culture, incorporating distinctive ethnic and cultural heritages into the Latter-day Saint legacy.

Latter-day Saints were instructed to go to the temple regularly and to strengthen their personal relationships with God there. While nineteenth-century Latter-day Saints had worked to form eternal communal bonds through temple ritual, the feverish temple-building efforts of the 1980s and 1990s emphasized individual worthiness and purity. As part of President Howard W. Hunter's effort to make the temple the "symbol of [church]

174 THE SALT LAKE TEMPLE

membership," for example, he advised Latter-day Saints, regardless of proximity to a temple, to maintain a current temple recommend. His counsel that "every adult member . . . be worthy of—and carry—a current temple recommend" became a frequent mantra at general conference and inspired a renewed focus on individual preparation for temple worship.[36]

At the October 1995 general conference, Hinckley delivered a similar message, labeling temple ordinances "the most profound expressions" of Latter-day Saint theology. "I urge our people everywhere," he continued, "with all of the persuasiveness of which I am capable, to live worthy to hold a temple recommend, to secure one and regard it as a precious asset. . . . There is need occasionally to leave the noise and the tumult of the world and step within the walls of a sacred house of God, there to feel His spirit in an environment of holiness and peace."[37] Similarly, Apostle Russell M. Nelson in 2001 encouraged Latter-day Saints to engage in "personal preparation for temple blessings." In a "world smitten with spiritual decay," Nelson said, "temple blessings make a difference." Through temple worship, the "covenant people" would be "armed with righteousness and with the power of God in great glory" to face the world.[38]

This pervasive focus on temples extended even to the church's youth programs. In 2002, the president of the Young Women's organization, Margaret D. Nadauld, advised the young women to envision themselves in the temple, particularly the Salt Lake Temple: "Can you imagine the reverence you would feel to walk the same halls the Savior walked? Do you picture yourself there, pure and clean, a daughter of God, prepared to receive His finest blessings?"[39] The consolidation of Latter-day Saint religious life around the temple called for greater personal purity, modesty, worthiness, and orthodoxy.

The brand image for the church's emphasis on temple worthiness was the Salt Lake Temple. After becoming a universally recognized church icon in the 1960s, the pioneer temple served as a visual messenger for new church initiatives beginning in the 1990s. During that era and later, the temple's façade featured prominently on church-published materials. For example, temple recommends—issued to church members around the world who met worthiness requirements—were streamlined in the 1990s to include membership information on a wallet-size card embossed with an image of the Salt Lake Temple.

The east façade of the Salt Lake Temple also appeared as the backdrop for a poster titled "My Gospel Standards," distributed by the Primary organization in 1996. After 2002, young men ages twelve to eighteen who completed the new Duty to God program—which emphasized community service, talent development, and adherence to gospel standards—received a golden medallion engraved with the Salt Lake Temple spires. A similar program for the Young Women's organization known as Personal Progress also received a small overhaul; the necklace medallion awarded upon completion of the program, once displaying a young female, now featured the spires of the Salt Lake Temple. Church leaders intended the new emblem to "signify what we are trying to accomplish in Young Women, for girls to be prepared to make and keep sacred temple covenants."[40] At the same time, *For the Strength of Youth*, a pamphlet containing the catechism of moral standards for teenagers, received a new cover displaying the temple spires. Institutional efforts to inspire church members to progress along the "covenant path" (that is, to receive ordinances and lead a life in adherence to the church's worthiness standards) were marketed most often by an image of the Salt Lake Temple.

In an era of digital marketing and global brand imaging, the Salt Lake Temple made sense as an identifiable visual aid to communicate the distinctive ideals and aspirations of church membership. The church's youth magazine, the *New Era*, frequently used the Salt Lake Temple in shareable posters with inspirational sayings, known as "Mormonads." In an attempt to bridge the gap between religious and youth culture, the church produced several of these posters, which featured contemporary images of the Salt Lake Temple and encouraged Latter-day Saint youth to "set [their] sights" on the temple, to go on their "dream date" to the temple, and to become "best friends forever" by being sealed to a spouse in the temple.[41]

The Salt Lake Temple also appeared alongside messages from church leaders that leaned on popular culture to encourage Latter-day Saints to prepare for entering the temple. Tapping into the literary conventions of fairy tales and animated Disney films, First Presidency counselor Dieter F. Uchtdorf in 2010 gave a widely circulated general conference sermon encouraging the church's youth to find their "happily ever after."[42] In the address, Uchtdorf pointed his young audience to the standards outlined in the *For the Strength of Youth* pamphlet and promised that living them would bring a "happily ever after" that culminated in "sacred covenants in the temple."[43] Uchtdorf's address inspired a host of memes on digital platforms like Pinterest and Instagram with the phrase "happily ever after" backdropped by the Salt Lake Temple.

176   THE SALT LAKE TEMPLE

If nineteenth-century Latter-day Saints saw the castellated temple as a defense against persecution, modern Latter-day Saints were encouraged to view it as the culminating point in their eternal love story. Lay individuals created inspirational prints and artistic renderings of the Salt Lake Temple, usually aimed at young women: the image of the castle-like temple was used to encourage them to "find their prince" in eternal marriage. Drawing from the doctrine and language of temple ordinances, other inspirational materials celebrated young women as "royal spirit daughters of Almighty God" and "princesses, destined to become queens."[44]

The temple was used to shore up the church's youth at a time when global religious leaders worried young people were leaving organized religion in higher numbers than in previous generations. In 2010 global Latter-day Saint church membership exceeded 14 million. Overall Latter-day Saint activity rates only modestly declined over the first two decades of the twenty-first century even as religious disaffiliation among US millennials (generally those born between 1981 and 1996) spiked.[45] Though church activity among Latter-day Saint millennials actually held steady for those who married and started families, the institutional push toward greater use of the temple was not just a global initiative to encourage church members to frequently use new temples but also a method of ministering to ensure the church fortified the faith of its younger membership. Amid modern trends to leave religion altogether, Latter-day Saint culture began to retrench, hedging against what some outside the faith labeled a "crisis of faith." And the Salt Lake Temple was the most common image representing that retrenchment.[46]

The "Mormon Moment": The Salt Lake Temple as a Visual Critique

The world emerged from the 2002 Winter Olympics knowing more about the Latter-day Saints. The Salt Lake Temple and the Tabernacle, frequent subjects of Olympic television coverage, became more recognizable as distinctly Latter-day Saint places. The games left participants and spectators with a good impression about church members, but the years that followed tested the public on what they actually knew about the church's doctrine and practice. In early 2006, Massachusetts governor and Latter-day Saint businessman Mitt Romney announced his entrance into the 2008 presidential race, bringing his religion with him into the public spotlight. The

American political landscape had changed since Romney's father, George, had run for president in 1967–68. The Republican Party, to which Mitt Romney belonged, was now beholden to a vocal coalition of socially conservative Christians who had hit their stride in American politics in the 1970s and 1980s. Modern American Latter-day Saints, predominantly conservative, found much to like in social-political movements like Baptist minister Jerry Falwell's Moral Majority of the 1980s. But the admiration was not mutual; Protestant evangelicals held Latter-day Saints at arm's length, believing they were not Christian enough. The same fears were expressed by Protestants during Catholic John F. Kennedy's presidential campaign in 1960. Evangelical Protestants were leery of ecclesiastical meddling in the presidency if a Catholic or Latter-day Saint—both responsive to hierarchical leadership structures—assumed the nation's highest office.

Romney attempted to appease religious conservatives with a speech on faith, promising that "no authorities of my church, or of any other church for that matter, will ever exert influence on presidential decisions. Their authority is theirs, within the province of church affairs, and it ends where the affairs of the nation begin."[47] His promise to keep his ecclesiastical superiors out of government affairs and his praise for other Christians did little to move the needle among the vital conservative Republican base. Americans in the end remained suspicious, perceiving a blurred line between Romney's religious affiliation and his civic duties. Further, according to one scholar of religion, Romney's actual religious views were less problematic than the general "sense that there is something vaguely troubling or unfamiliar in the Mormon manner or worldview."[48] Latter-day Saints were well known by now but still not well understood by the public.

In the absence of pervasive understanding of Latter-day Saint beliefs, the public fell back on timeworn tropes about the church and its people— namely, that the church kept curious secrets and that Latter-day Saints were strange and cultish. Romney's involvement in "secret, sacred temple rites and garments" reminded some of the "church's murky past," including its earlier "embrace of polygamy."[49] The temple marked a "hidden sacramentalism" that to outsiders seemed weird or cultish and clouded Latter-day Saint loyalties. If the temple was used by church leaders to fortify faith and to guard against full assimilation into the world, the collective engagement of Latter-day Saints in temple rituals proved to outsiders that a Latter-day Saint was unfit for the highest office in the United States. Religious secrets transgressed long-negotiated democratic principles and signaled

178   THE SALT LAKE TEMPLE

a "defiance, entrenchment, and resistance" of individualistic American ideals.[50]

Reporters covering Romney's run for the presidency naturally asked about his religious beliefs. American audiences seemed to relish primetime exposés about his "Mormonism." In their television, internet, and newspaper coverage of Romney's political campaigns in 2008 and 2012, news media routinely used photographs and clips of the Salt Lake Temple, confirming that the temple had achieved notoriety as an icon of the Latter-day Saint faith. The temple's distinctive nineteenth-century architecture and the fact that only recommended Latter-day Saints could enter reinforced the narrative that Romney, like all Latter-day Saints, was hiding something. The Salt Lake Temple was a visual representation of the lingering distance between Latter-day Saints and mainstream society.[51] For example, the four-hour PBS *Frontline* documentary *The Mormons* (2007) opened with exterior shots of the Salt Lake Temple and the promise that the "mysteries of the Mormons" would be laid bare. Viewers watched the story of the church, described as "one of the most powerful, feared, and misunderstood religions in American history."[52] The perception that Latter-day Saints remained "unusually secretive" fed misconceptions about the church during this time of increased media coverage known as the "Mormon Moment."[53]

During this period, other events drew the public's attention to the Latter-day Saint faith, often casting it in a negative light. Around the time that Romney's campaign was capturing extensive media attention, law enforcement arrested Warren Jeffs, the leader of the Fundamentalist Church of Jesus Christ of Latter-day Saints (FLDS), a sect whose members still practice polygamy. Jeffs was tried in Texas on charges that included rape and the sexual assault of a minor. The trials went on for years until he was convicted and sentenced in 2011 to life in prison plus twenty years. At each stage of the legal battle, including raids on Jeffs's Texas compound, the sordid details of his life as leader of the religious sect sparked public ire and condemnation—but also confusion. While many media outlets differentiated the FLDS from the LDS Church in their coverage, others were less careful. In April 2008, Latter-day Saint church leaders criticized international media after photos of the Salt Lake Temple's exterior appeared in stories about the FLDS Church.[54] Even American media, which better clarified the distinction between the two churches, found the Salt Lake Temple an intriguing backdrop for their reporting on Jeffs.[55]

Public confusion was compounded by the popularity of HBO's television series *Big Love* (2006–11), a fictional drama about a polygamous family living in Salt Lake City's suburbs. The series subtly characterized and critiqued the institutional church and its "slick bureaucrats" in Salt Lake as "an elaborate hierarchy" that reached "into the economic, social, and political lives of its members."[56] However, it was the familiar geography that lent the most legitimacy to *Big Love*'s storyline. Scenes featured recognizable landmarks around Salt Lake City, including shots of the Salt Lake Temple. The fundamentalist polygamist story unfolded within mainstream Latter-day Saint culture and near the church's headquarters, suggesting the church and its powerful hierarchy bore some enduring responsibility for the fundamentalist lifestyle. The visuals were enough to bring the church in perilous proximity to polygamy, a practice it had sought distance from for over a century, and prompted denunciations from church leaders, who worried the church's hard-earned public image would be tarnished if old critiques were vaulted back into the public consciousness.

Perhaps the Salt Lake Temple was used in media such as *Big Love* because no other visual marker signaled as effectively the power, culture, and reach of the church. The towering Church Office Building to the east showcased the church's administrative modernization, but it fit in too seamlessly with 1970s corporate America and with the other soaring skyscrapers of America's cities to be instantly recognizable to outsiders. Instead, the Salt Lake Temple was used to draw readers into stories about a curious and often misunderstood faith.

Digital and print media increasingly used images of the Salt Lake Temple as the lead photo in stories about the church. For example, the Salt Lake Temple was featured in reports on the church's involvement in California's 2008 "Yes on Proposition 8" campaign, which supported a prohibition on gay marriage; in later stories discussing LGBTQ issues and the church;[57] in stories on race and church corporate power;[58] and in national news reports on the church's lobbying against a 2018 medical marijuana initiative in Utah.[59] The Salt Lake Temple, placed alongside hot-button social and political issues, subtly reinforced perceptions that Latter-day Saint religious authority could reach and influence civil, social, and political matters. Ever in the spotlight, the Salt Lake Temple served as a critique of the institution it supported, signaling the difference between Latter-day Saints and the rest of society.

180 THE SALT LAKE TEMPLE

The Salt Lake Temple at 125 Years

Though the media flattened the image of the Salt Lake Temple, perpetuating old caricatures of Latter-day Saint culture and doctrine, the church countered with attempts to inspire a more robust and informed conversation around the temple. In May 2010, church leaders unveiled a seven-foot-tall, 1:32 scale replica model of the Salt Lake Temple to the public. Housed in the South Visitors Center on Temple Square, the new exhibit offered a cutaway view of the temple's interior. (The south and east exterior walls of the model temple were absent.) Providing a detailed look at the floor plan and rooms removed some of the perceived secrecy surrounding the temple. Helpful kiosks allowed visitors to sort through photos and videos of the Salt Lake Temple's many rooms.[60] Elder Richard G. Hinckley, executive director of the church's Missionary Department, commented on the purpose of the replica: "Like all temples, once the building is dedicated it is used for sacred Church purposes and not open to the general public, but this exhibit will provide the public with a glimpse of the interior and a feeling of the Spirit that is present there."[61] The interactive temple replica softened the restrictions governing the actual structure, allowing those not allowed to enter the building a chance to experience the temple's interior on a miniature scale. In addition, the exhibit reminded the public that it was temple experiences and rituals that rendered the structure sacred for Latter-day Saints.

Critiques of the church as an institution rippled outward in the wake of the Mormon Moment. Many still viewed the temple as a harbinger of Latter-day Saint secrets, rendering them cultish and unchristian. In the spirit of President Gordon B. Hinckley's declaration to Mike Wallace that Latter-day Saints were not "weird," the church used media to demystify the temple experience. In 2015, they released an unprecedented video showing actual temple garments and explaining their significance: "The nun's habit. The priest's cassock. The Jewish prayer shawl. The Muslim's skullcap. The saffron robes of the Buddhist monk. All are part of a rich tapestry of human devotion to God." Like these items of sacred clothing, the video explained, Latter-day Saints wear religious vestments both inside and outside the temple during their everyday lives as a reminder of their covenants.[62] In 2018, the church issued a series of videos addressing common questions like "What is a temple endowment?," "Can I go inside a Latter-day Saint temple?," "What are temple weddings like?," and "What are 'baptisms for the dead?'"[63] The videos

MEDIA PLACE   181

defended Latter-day Saint temple worship as akin to other ritual practices common to the world's religions.

The videos also emphasized the Christ-centeredness of Latter-day Saint temple worship, tracing some of the temple practices back to the Bible. This campaign modeled the church's defense of its version of Christianity: church practice and doctrine were Christ-centered but not subsumable within Protestant Christianity. Latter-day Saints searched for understanding and belonging within Christian circles even as they hoped to remain set apart. As an official church essay on the topic stated in 2013, the institution would seek to contribute to a global "Christian conversation" but remained unwilling to "compromise the distinctiveness of the restored Church of Jesus Christ."[64] Latter-day Saints were peculiar Christians, but they were, in fact, Christians. If Latter-day Saints were seen as oddly Mormon in the wake of the Mormon Moment, church leaders recommitted to publicizing the church's more Christian elements.

In 2018, Russell M. Nelson, recently sustained as church president, requested that press and public alike eliminate their use of the term "Mormon" as a descriptor for the institution and its associated organizations, such as the Mormon Tabernacle Choir (now the Tabernacle Choir at Temple Square). And two years later, at the April 2020 general conference, Nelson unveiled a new "symbol" for the institution to complete the rebranding. The symbol was a visual depiction of the replica *Christus* statue of Jesus Christ by Bertel Thorvaldsen (displayed for years on Temple Square) with the official name of the church below. Nelson intended the symbol to serve as a "visual identifier for official literature, news, and events of the Church" that emphasized the church's connection to the "living Christ" and the "Savior's Church."[65] The rebrand was the culmination of an institution-wide refocusing on an underlying Christ-centered core, buttressed by Latter-day Saint scripture, that had been underway for almost three decades, as church leaders responded to questions about the institution's belonging under the larger umbrella of Christianity.[66] While Protestants especially have leveled critiques at the Book of Mormon's supernatural origins, the book's narrative and doctrine, as one scholar of religion remarked, rendered Latter-day Saints "more Christian than many mainstream Christians" on the point of the divinity of Jesus Christ.[67] Latter-day Saints simply had to bring to the forefront the elements of their doctrine saturated with Christ. The new symbol offered up a formal Christian marker to displace unofficial markers for the church, like the distinctive Gothic spires of the Salt Lake Temple.

182 THE SALT LAKE TEMPLE

In 1994, sociologist Armand Mauss proposed two distinctive symbols—the angel and the beehive—to represent Latter-day Saint interaction with the forces of assimilation and retrenchment over its history. The beehive signified the Latter-day Saint embrace of political, social, and economic structures in secular society, while the angel represented the remaining distinctive elements of Latter-day Saint culture, like temple work, prophets, and an ambitious missionary program, to name a few.[68] As the church moves into the twenty-first century, the core of the organization's identity remains in flux, suspended between two distinctive poles: its peculiar past, as represented by its historic temple spires (or the Angel Moroni atop the temple), and its newer Christian present, as represented by the official adoption of a depiction of Christ as a worldwide symbol.

Latter-day Saints may be comfortable continuing to operate within the tension between their past and present. Though early Saints imagined themselves as new Israel reliving the biblical history of persecution, deliverance, and exodus, modern Saints have seen the church's Christian elements supersede that distinctive quest.[69] Yet the church's robust temple program continues to sound echoes of its past kingdom-building aspirations, preserving distance from general evangelical Christianity. The Saints, according to scholar John Turner, have "chartered their own Christian course" among religious movements. Its mixture of the peculiar with the decisively Christian continues to nurture a unique "temple Christianity" for modern times.[70]

The historic Salt Lake Temple and its surrounding square stand ready to manifest any institutional course changes, as they have throughout their history. And at 125 years in 2018, they were due for a major update. Concerns mounted that the pioneer temple would be significantly damaged in the event of a major earthquake. The decades-old mechanical and plumbing systems showed major wear. Accordingly, after over ten years of study and planning, President Russell M. Nelson shared at the October 2018 general conference that the Salt Lake Temple, along with the church's three other nineteenth-century temples, would be renovated.[71]

At the April 2019 general conference, Nelson described the extensive and costly renovations. "We now have 162 dedicated temples," the church president began. "The earliest ones stand as monuments to the faith and vision of our beloved pioneers. Each temple constructed by them resulted from their great personal sacrifice and effort. Each one stands as a stunning jewel in the crown of pioneer achievement. Ours is a sacred responsibility to care for them. Therefore, these pioneer temples will soon undergo a period of renewal and refreshing and, for some, a major restoration. Efforts will be made to preserve the unique historicity of each temple wherever possible, preserving the inspiring beauty and unique craftsmanship of generations long-since passed."[72]

Two weeks later, during a press conference, Nelson announced that the Salt Lake Temple would close on December 29, 2019, with an anticipated public open house and rededication in 2024 (which was eventually delayed until 2027). "This project will enhance, refresh, and beautify the temple and its surrounding grounds," he explained to the media. "Obsolete systems within the building will be replaced. Safety and seismic concerns will be addressed. Accessibility will be enhanced so that members with limited mobility can be better accommodated." The most ambitious upgrade would be the installation of a base isolation system to structurally separate the temple from the earth around it, ensuring the preservation of the temple's fragile and historic footings and the walls in the event of a major earthquake. Installing the complex system would require extensive digging under the temple and the reinforcement of its granite walls. Interior plans, in line with the intent to "preserve the unique historicity" of the temple, included restoring the interior to more closely resemble the original finishes, where possible.[73] Significant updates were to be made to existing floorplans to accommodate ordinance work in eighty-six languages, a change that would shift the live endowment presentations common to the Salt Lake Temple to a video format and make the temple the largest multilingual temple in the church. Church leaders hoped the financial investment in the Salt Lake Temple would pay spiritual returns for church members from around the world who made pilgrimages to the site.

The historic renovations were not limited to the temple itself but also extended to the surrounding square. Improvements there included the demolition of a few existing buildings, such as the South Visitors' Center and Temple Annex. New temple entry pavilions, an underground grand hall into the temple, and guest waiting areas were planned for the north side of the temple, and two new visitors' centers were proposed for the south side. An overhaul was scheduled for the landscaping around the temple, including the Main Street plaza to the east. To increase access and the visibility of the temple, portions of the historic wall around the square would be removed or modified and opened. For over a century, the church had strived to cultivate an open, peaceful atmosphere in the square where visitors could contemplate near but be separated from the sacred temple. The adjustments signaled a shift toward greater openness. A garden-like atmosphere would welcome visitors just as it had in the past, but the temple, "a beacon of light to all the world," according to Nelson, would be far more visible and accessible from areas around the square.[74] Exhibits at the visitors' centers would "emphasize and highlight the life, ministry, and mission of Jesus Christ in His desire to bless every nation, kindred, tongue and people," Nelson declared.[75]

Church leaders acknowledged that the Salt Lake Temple is "one of the largest operating temples of the Church" and "serves thousands of patrons in the Salt Lake Valley as well as many other Church members who visit Salt Lake City from around the world."[76] The renovations would support the temple's ability to handle increasing demand for its ordinance sessions. But given the Salt Lake Temple's continued importance to the church, the multimillion-dollar renovation is about more than operational efficiency or historical preservation—it is about a sustained sense of peoplehood.

Throughout its life of over 125 years, and in the forty years before it opened, the Salt Lake Temple has not been a passive bystander to the many changes within the faith, but has been a main character in the church's unfolding story. The pioneer craftsmen who built the temple walls intended them to stand resolute and unchanged over centuries of use, but the significance of the temple within Latter-day Saint culture evolved over the years. Nineteenth-century Latter-day Saints created out of the mountains a symbol of resistance and poured into it their communal and millennial aspirations in the face of American intrusions. Subsequent generations of Latter-day Saints reverenced the temple as a monument to a fading era of pioneer peculiarity. The temple still thrived as a place of institutional revelation and change and as a pervasive symbol of the Latter-day Saint claim to divine power and prophethood. And in a modern era in which the church's critics wondered if the Salt Lake Temple still housed too many secrets for modern sensibilities, church leaders worried that Latter-day Saints had assimilated too thoroughly into secular society, and the temple soon served as a rallying point for internal purity, orthodoxy, and family values.

Given the temple's iconic status, the public open house after the renovation's completion is sure to be on a scale and scope yet unseen in the church's history. The open house will also be an opportunity for the public to walk through the halls and rooms of the previously closed temple and to view Temple Square's updated exhibits and messages. The church's longtime Protestant critics might see the universal Christian message that is anticipated at the renovated square as easily betrayed by the nineteenth-century Gothic temple, with its distinctive rituals and secrets, still at the square's center. But such a paradox is perhaps core to Latter-day Saints' peoplehood, which remains, not an ex nihilo creation, but a culture shaped by history and heritage, priesthood and policy, old and new scripture, and ancient and modern times.

The strengthening of the temple's historic exterior alongside the wholesale remaking of the temple's interior and square to support pilgrims from all corners of the globe point to a people and a movement adapted for change. Latter-day Saints believe their prophets speak to immediate and future times. This responsiveness to prophetic revelatory authority reconciles the church to forces both old and new—its historical and distinctive truth claims, for example, and a crystallizing Christian message that has grown membership outside of the United States to exceed membership within it. The renovated temple will support a new age of global church membership, one increasingly diverse and more vocally Christian, with a visual anchor that cements a collective foot in the past.

Gone from Latter-day Saint culture is the theocracy and overt millenarianism of the church's Zion-building project that raised the temple from the valley floor. But Brigham Young's Judeo-Christian quest for a physical refuge to gather in Israel, emboldened by Joseph Smith's imaginative temple building, remains alive in other ways. Latter-day Saints still retreat from worldly influences to the inside of their temples to unify in a spiritual kingdom and to gather their ancestors into a heavenly Israel through vicarious ritual. The historic Salt Lake Temple still conjures the church's claim to ritual, priesthood, and revelation—features of its distinctive mixture of old and new Christianity. In safeguarding the temple's unique exterior, the temple's historic restoration and renovation will ultimately preserve a material manifestation of the church's restoration message, of the effort by obedient, impoverished Latter-day Saints to bring about "the ancient order of things" through building a temple in the Salt Lake Valley.[77] As a result, when the temple's doors open to the public, Latter-day Saints will likely embrace the opportunity to bring the world to the foundational site of their most ancient and revolutionary claim: that prophets learn and speak heaven's wishes from within granite walls carved out of the American West.

Notes

Introduction

1. James E. Talmage, *The House of the Lord: A Study of Holy Sanctuaries Ancient and Modern* (Salt Lake City: The Church of Jesus Christ of Latter-day Saints, 1912), 192–94.
2. LeRoi C. Snow, "An Experience of My Father's," *Improvement Era* 35, no. 11 (September 1933): 677.
3. Snow, "Experience of My Father's," 677.
4. George Q. Cannon, journal, September 13, 1898, Church History Library, The Church of Jesus Christ of Latter-day Saints, Salt Lake City (hereafter CHL); Journal History of the Church, September 13, 1898, Historical Department, CHL.
5. Because of the lack of contemporary documentary evidence for the vision, some have questioned the authenticity of surviving accounts. See John P. Hatch, "From Prayer to Visitation: Reexamining Lorenzo Snow's Vision of Jesus Christ in the Salt Lake Temple," *Journal of Mormon History* 42, no. 3 (July 2016): 155–82.
6. Snow, "Experience of My Father's," 677, 679. Previously the Quorum of the Twelve Apostles led the church for a period of time before a new church president was eventually selected.
7. John A. Widtsoe to Noah S. Pond, October 30, 1946, Noah S. Pond Correspondence, CHL; Hatch, "From Prayer to Visitation," 168.
8. "Ministry of Lorenzo Snow: A Vision of the Lord," Churchofjesuschrist.org, May 2012, video, https://www.churchofjesuschrist.org/media/video/2012-05-0504-ministry-of-lorenzo-snow-a-vision-of-the-lord?lang=eng; Susan Arrington Madsen, "Lorenzo Snow and the Sacred Vision," *Friend* 23, no. 8 (August 1993): 14.
9. "Minutes of the General Conference," *Deseret News* (Salt Lake City), April 16, 1853.
10. Patrick Q. Mason, "God and the People: Theodemocracy in Nineteenth-Century Mormonism," *Journal of Church and State* 53, no. 3 (Summer 2011): 349–75; Benjamin E. Park, "The Council of Fifty and the Perils of Democratic Governance," in *The Council of Fifty: What the Records Reveal about Mormon History*, ed. Matthew J. Grow and R. Eric Smith (Salt Lake City: Deseret Book, 2017), 43–54.
11. Richard E. Bennett, "'We Are a Kingdom to Ourselves': The Council of Fifty Minutes and the Mormon Exodus West," in Grow and Smith, *Council of Fifty*, 153–66.
12. See *Doctrine and Covenants* (hereafter D&C), 57.
13. Samuel B. Brown, "Early Mormon Adoption Theology and the Mechanics of Salvation," *Journal of Mormon History* 37, no. 3 (Summer 2011): 3–52; Jonathan A. Stapley, "Adoptive Sealing Ritual in Mormonism," *Journal of Mormon History* 37, no. 3 (Summer 2011): 53–117.
14. David Chidester and Edward T. Linenthal, eds., *American Sacred Space* (Bloomington: Indiana University Press, 1995), 15.
15. Louis P. Nelson, ed., *American Sanctuary: Understanding Sacred Spaces* (Bloomington: Indiana University Press, 2006), 1–14; Jeanne Halgren Kilde, *Sacred Power, Sacred Space: An Introduction to Christian Architecture and Worship* (New York: Oxford University Press, 2008).
16. Tad Walch, "Salt Lake Temple to Close for Four Years as Temple Square Undergoes Seismic Change," *Deseret News*, April 18, 2019.
17. See, for example, Wallace A. Raynor, *Everlasting Spires: The Story of the Salt Lake Temple* (Salt Lake City: Deseret Book, 1965); C. Mark Hamilton, *The Salt Lake Temple: A Monument to a People* (Salt Lake City: University Services, 1983); and Richard Neitzel Holzapfel, *Every Stone a Sermon: The Magnificent Story of the Construction of the Salt Lake Temple* (Salt Lake City: Bookcraft, 1992).
18. Wilford Woodruff, George Q. Cannon, and Joseph F. Smith, "An Address to the Officers and Members of the Church of Jesus Christ of Latter-day Saints," March 18, 1893, [1], CHL.
19. Temples of the Church of Jesus Christ of Latter-day Saints, "Temple Locations," Statistics, https://churchofjesuschristtemples.org/statistics/locations/.

188   NOTES TO PAGES 7–12

Chapter 1

1. Joseph Smith introduced plural marriage, or the practice of being sealed through a marriage ordinance to more than one wife, to select associates in Nauvoo in the early 1840s. Elizabeth A. Kuehn and others, eds., *Documents*, vol. 10: *May–August 1842*, vol. 10 of the Documents series of *The Joseph Smith Papers*, ed. Matthew C. Godfrey, R. Eric Smith, Matthew J. Grow, and Ronald K. Esplin (Salt Lake City: Church Historian's Press, 2020), xix–xl.
2. James B. Allen, *Trials of Discipleship: The Story of William Clayton, a Mormon* (Urbana: University of Illinois Press, 1987), 198–203; William Clayton, journal, April 15, 1846, in *An Intimate Chronicle: The Journals of William Clayton*, ed. George D. Smith (Salt Lake City: Signature Books, 1991), 270–71.
3. In March 1844, Joseph Smith organized the Council of Fifty in Nauvoo, Illinois, an administrative organization of around fifty men, which discussed, among other subjects, the eventual migration of Latter-day Saints westward. The council intended to find a place where the rights of church members to worship in peace would be preserved. The minutes make no specific mention of the design or location of a temple in the West. Matthew J. Grow and others, eds., *Council of Fifty, Minutes, March 1844–January 1846*, vol. 1 of the Administrative Records series of *The Joseph Smith Papers*, ed. Ronald K. Esplin, Matthew J. Grow, and Matthew C. Godfrey (Salt Lake City: Church Historian's Press, 2016).
4. Only retrospective sources of Brigham Young's vision survive. George Albert Smith, in *Journal of Discourses*, 26 vols. (Liverpool: F. D. Richards, 1855–86), 13:85–86; Ronald K. Esplin, "'A Place Prepared': Joseph, Brigham and the Quest for Promised Refuge in the West," *Journal of Mormon History* 9 (1982): 101; Wilford Woodruff, "Zion's Camp—Mormon Battalion—Pioneers," *Elders' Journal* 4, no. 6 (December 15, 1906): 122–130.
5. John D. Lee, journal, January 13, 1846, CHL; Esplin, "Place Prepared," 101.
6. Terryl L. Givens, *By the Hand of Mormon: The American Scripture That Launched a New World Religion* (New York: Oxford University Press, 2002), 67–68.
7. "Old Testament Revision 1," 16, The Joseph Smith Papers, https://www.josephsmithpapers.org/paper-summary/old-testament-revision-1/18; see also Moses 7:18–19; Thomas A. Wayment, "Intertextuality and the Purpose of Joseph Smith's New Translation of the Bible," in *Foundational Texts of Mormonism: Examining Major Early Sources*, ed. Mark Ashurst-McGee, Robin Jensen, and Sharalyn D. Howcroft (New York: Oxford University Press, 2018), 74–76.
8. C. Mark Hamilton, *Nineteenth Century Mormon Architecture and City Planning* (New York: Oxford University Press, 1995), 14–20.
9. Gerrit J. Dirkmaat and others, eds., *Documents*, vol. 3: *February 1833–March 1834*, vol. 3 of the Documents series of *The Joseph Smith Papers*, ed. Ronald K. Esplin and Matthew J. Grow (Salt Lake City: Church Historian's Press, 2014), 243–57; Craig S. Campbell, *Images of the New Jerusalem: Latter Day Saint Faction Interpretations of Independence, Missouri* (Knoxville: University of Tennessee Press, 2004), 50–55; Alma 13:6; Doctrine and Covenants 107:10.
10. "Minute Book 1," 21 (June 6, 1833), Joseph Smith Papers, https://www.josephsmithpapers.org/paper-summary/minute-book-1/25; Karen Lynn Davidson, Richard L. Jensen, and David J. Whittaker, eds., *Histories*, vol. 2: *Assigned Historical Writings, 1831–1847*, vol. 2 of the Histories series of *The Joseph Smith Papers*, edited by Dean C. Jessee, Ronald K. Esplin, and Richard Lyman Bushman (Salt Lake City: Church Historian's Press, 2012), 151.
11. Hamilton, *Nineteenth Century Mormon Architecture and City Planning*, 35–39.
12. David J. Howlett, *Kirtland Temple: The Biography of a Shared Mormon Sacred Space* (Urbana: University of Illinois Press, 2014), 26–27; Elwin C. Robison, *The First Mormon Temple: Design, Construction, and Context of the Kirtland Temple* (Provo, UT: Brigham Young University, 1997), 9–16.
13. Joseph Smith Jr., journal, November 12, 1835, in *Journals*, vol. 1: *1832–1839*, ed. Dean C. Jessee, Mark Ashurst-McGee, and Richard L. Jensen, vol. 1 of the Journals series of *The Joseph Smith Papers*, ed. Dean C. Jessee, Ronald K. Esplin, and Richard Lyman Bushman (Salt Lake City: Church Historian's Press, 2008), 98; Jonathan A. Stapley, *The Power of Godliness: Mormon Liturgy and Cosmology* (New York: Oxford University Press, 2018), 14–15.
14. Howlett, *Kirtland Temple*, 21–24; Stapley, *Power of Godliness*, 15.
15. Joseph Smith Jr., journal, September 11, 1842, in *Journals*, vol. 2: *December 1841–April 1843*, ed. Andrew H. Hedges, Alex D. Smith, and Richard Lloyd Anderson, vol. 2 of the Journals series of *The Joseph Smith Papers*, ed. Dean C. Jessee, Ronald K. Esplin, and Richard Lyman Bushman (Salt Lake City: Church Historian's Press, 2011), 143–50.

NOTES TO PAGES 12–19   189

16. Mark L. Staker, *Hearken, O Ye People: The Historical Setting of Joseph Smith's Ohio Revelations* (Salt Lake City: Greg Kofford Books, 2010), 391–558.
17. Susan Easton Black, "How Large Was the Population of Nauvoo?," *BYU Studies* 35, no. 2 (1995): 91–94.
18. Simon Baker, statement, in Journal History of the Church, August 15, 1840, Historical Department, CHL; Alexander L. Baugh, "'For This Ordinance Belongeth to My House': The Practice of Baptisms for the Dead outside the Nauvoo Temple," *Mormon Historical Studies* 3, no. 1 (Spring 2002): 47–58; Ryan G. Tobler, "'Saviors on Mount Zion': Mormon Sacramentalism, Mortality, and the Baptism for the Dead," *Journal of Mormon History* 39, no. 4 (Fall 2013): 182–238.
19. Baugh, "For This Ordinance Belongeth to My House," 53; "Minutes of a Conference of The Church of Jesus Christ of Latter-day Saints, Held in Nauvoo, Ill., Commencing Oct. 1st, 1841," *Times and Seasons* (Nauvoo, IL) 2 (October 15, 1841): 577–78.
20. Kathleen Flake, "'Not to Be Riten': The Mormon Temple Rite as Oral Canon," *Journal of Ritual Studies* 9, no. 2 (Summer 1995): 1–21; Philip L. Barlow, "Toward a Mormon Sense of Time," *Journal of Mormon Studies* 33, no. 1 (Spring 2007): 33–35.
21. "History, 1838–1856, volume C-1 [November 2, 1838–July 31, 1842]," 1328, Joseph Smith Papers, https://www.josephsmithpapers.org/paper-summary/history-1838-1856-volume-c-1-2-november-1838-31-july-1842/502.
22. "History, 1838–1856, volume C-1," 1328.
23. Steven C. Harper, "Freemasonry and the Latter-day Saint Temple Endowment Ceremony," in *A Reason for Faith: Navigating LDS Doctrine and Church History*, ed. Laura Harris Hales (Salt Lake City: Deseret Book, 2016), 143–57.
24. Philip L. Barlow, "To Mend a Fractured Reality: Joseph Smith's Project," *Journal of Mormon History* 38, no. 3 (Summer 2012): 37–38.
25. Samuel B. Brown, "Early Mormon Adoption Theology and the Mechanics of Salvation," *Journal of Mormon History* 37, no. 3 (Summer 2011): 3–52.
26. Lisle G. Brown, comp., *Nauvoo Sealings, Adoptions, and Anointings: A Comprehensive Register of Persons Receiving LDS Temple Ordinances, 1841–46* (Salt Lake City: Smith-Petit Foundation, 2006), viii.
27. Jonathan A. Stapley, "Adoptive Sealing Ritual in Mormonism," *Journal of Mormon History* 37, no. 3 (Summer 2011): 62–67.
28. On the competing claims to succession in the church hierarchy beginning in 1844, see Ronald K. Esplin, "Joseph, Brigham, and the Twelve: A Succession of Continuity," *BYU Studies* 21, no. 3 (Summer 1981): 301–41.
29. This argument is articulated in Andrew F. Ehat, "Joseph Smith's Introduction of Temple Ordinances and the 1844 Mormon Succession Question" (master's thesis, Brigham Young University, 1982).
30. Minutes, August 8, 1844, quoted in Esplin, "Joseph, Brigham, and the Twelve," 324–25.
31. "Trial of Elder Rigdon," *Times and Seasons* 5 (September 15, 1844): 647–48.
32. Richard E. Bennett, "'The Upper Room': The Nature and Development of Latter-day Saint Temple Work," *Journal of Mormon History* 41, no. 2 (April 2015): 4–6.
33. Roger Friedland and Richard Hecht, "The Bodies of Nations: A Comparative Study of Religious Violence in Jerusalem and Ayodhya," *History of Religions* 38, no. 2 (November 1998): 101–49.
34. Phillip L. Barlow, *Mormons and the Bible: The Place of the Latter-day Saints in American Religion* (New York: Oxford University Press, 2013), 75, emphasis in original.
35. Richard Bennett, "'Has the Lord Turned Bankrupt?' The Attempted Sale of the Nauvoo Temple, 1846–1850," *Journal of the Illinois State Historical Society* 95, no. 3 (Autumn 2002): 235–63.
36. Journal History of the Church, October 6, 1845.
37. Wilford Woodruff, journal, December 20, 1846, CHL.
38. Richard E. Bennett, *Mormons at the Missouri: Winter Quarters, 1846–1852* (Norman: University of Oklahoma Press, 1987), 14–15.
39. Journal History of the Church, October 6, 1845.
40. Esplin, "Place Prepared," 99–101; Brent M. Rogers, *Unpopular Sovereignty: Mormons and the Federal Management of Early Utah Territory* (Lincoln: University of Nebraska Press, 2017), 37–39.
41. Richard E. Bennett, *We'll Find the Place: The Mormon Exodus, 1846–1848* (Salt Lake City: Deseret Book, 1997), 40.

190 NOTES TO PAGES 19–27

42. Thomas L. Kane, *The Mormons: A Discourse Delivered before the Historical Society of Pennsylvania: March 26, 1850* (Philadelphia: King & Baird, 1850), 31; Bennett, *We'll Find the Place*, 43; Matthew J. Grow, *"Liberty to the Downtrodden": Thomas L. Kane, Romantic Reformer* (New Haven, CT: Yale University Press, 2009).
43. Clayton, journal, May 29, 1847, in Smith, *Intimate Chronicle*, 324–33.
44. Woodruff, journal, May 13, 1847.
45. Esplin, "Place Prepared," 105–8.
46. Woodruff, journal, July 24, 1847.
47. Brigham Young's use of a cane to declare the spot for the Salt Lake Temple was recalled and shared by Wilford Woodruff, but the only known retellings occurred after the death of Young. Woodruff does not mention the incident in his journal for July 26, 1847. "At the Tabernacle," *Deseret Evening News* (Salt Lake City), August 30, 1897; "Pioneers' Day," *Deseret Evening News*, July 26, 1880; "Pioneer Day," *Deseret Evening News*, July 25, 1888; "Discourse," *Deseret Weekly*, April 25, 1891.
48. Woodruff, journal, July 26, 1847.
49. Thomas Bullock, journal, July 28, 1847, CHL.
50. Norton Jacob, journal, July 28, 1847, CHL.
51. Levi Jackman, "A Short Sketch of the Life of Levi Jackman," 30 (July 28, 1847), CHL.
52. Brigham Young, in *Journal of Discourses*, 1:133.
53. Ronald O. Barney, *Mormon Vanguard Brigade of 1847: Norton Jacob's Record* (Logan: Utah State University Press, 2005), 227.
54. Though Young claimed to have seen in vision the colors and design for the flag to be raised on Ensign Peak, no evidence exists that the group that reached the top of the hill on July 26, 1847, actually raised a flag there. Instead, it seems likely they waved a yellow bandana provided by Heber C. Kimball. Dennis A. Wright and Rebekah E. Westrup, "Ensign Peak: A Historical Review," in *Salt Lake City: The Place Which God Prepared*, ed. Scott C. Esplin and Kenneth L. Alford (Provo, UT: Religious Studies Center, Brigham Young University, 2011), 27–46.
55. Woodruff, journal, August 1, 1847.
56. See Isaiah 2:2.
57. Hamilton, *Nineteenth Century Mormon Architecture and City Planning*, 26; Journal History of the Church, August 2, 1847.
58. Journal History of the Church, August 7, 1847.
59. Journal History of the Church, August 26, 1847.
60. "An Epistle of the Council of the Twelve of the Church of Jesus Christ of Latter-day Saints to the Saints in California," August 7, 1847, in Journal History of the Church, August 7, 1847.
61. Minutes, Big Sandy, WY, September 3, 1847, 1, box 1, folder 57, Historian's Office General Church Minutes, 1839–77, CHL.
62. Bennett, *Mormons at the Missouri*, 210–14.
63. Woodruff, journal, December 27, 1847.
64. Minutes, December 27, 1847, 19, box 1, folder 61, Historian's Office General Church Minutes; John G. Turner, *Brigham Young: Pioneer Prophet* (Cambridge, MA: Harvard University Press, 2012), 174.
65. "Destruction of Mormon Temple," *Millennial Star* (Liverpool) 11, no. 3 (February 1, 1849): 46–47.

Chapter 2

1. Miles Romney, journal, February 11, 14, 1853, CHL.
2. J. Earl Arrington, "William Weeks, Architect of the Nauvoo Temple," *BYU Studies* 19, no. 3 (1979): 354–59.
3. Willard Richards, "The Temple," *Deseret News* (Salt Lake City), February 19, 1853, italics in original.
4. Wilford Woodruff, journal, February 14, 1853, CHL.
5. Woodruff, journal, February 14, 1853.
6. Woodruff, journal, February 14, 1853.
7. Richards, "The Temple"; Woodruff, journal, February 14, 1853.
8. Construction on the Old Tabernacle, an adobe brick meetinghouse on the Temple Block designed by Truman O. Angell, began in May 1851. The building was completed by April 1852. The meetinghouse was torn down in the 1870s, and all meetings shifted to the Great Tabernacle still in use today. Elwin C. Robison, *Gathering as One: The History of the Mormon Tabernacle in Salt Lake City* (Provo, UT: Brigham Young University Press, 2013), 55–81.
9. "To the Saints," *Deseret News*, April 16, 1853.

NOTES TO PAGES 28–35   191

10. "Minutes of the General Conference," *Deseret News*, April 16, 1853.
11. Woodruff, journal, April 6, 1853; Brigham Young, President's Office Journal, April 6, 1853, box 72, folder 2, Brigham Young Office Files, 1832–78, CHL.
12. "Minutes of the General Conference." The stones were approximately six feet long, four feet wide, and two feet thick. They were made of sandstone quarried from Red Butte Canyon in the mountains above Salt Lake City. Romney, journal, April 6, 1853.
13. "Minutes of the General Conference"; Brent M. Rogers and others, eds., *Documents*, vol. 5: *October 1835–January 1838*, vol. 5 of the Documents series of *The Joseph Smith Papers*, ed. Ronald K. Esplin, Matthew J. Grow, and Matthew C. Godfrey (Salt Lake City: Church Historian's Press, 2017), 194–95.
14. "Minutes of the General Conference."
15. John G. Turner, *Mormon Jesus: A Biography* (Cambridge, MA: Harvard University Press, 2016), 72–80, 121–42.
16. "Celebration of the Anniversary of the Church," *Times and Seasons* (Nauvoo, IL) 2, no. 12 (April 15, 1841): 375–77. High priest is an office within the higher priesthood, the Melchizedek Priesthood.
17. "Celebration of the Anniversary of the Church"; John S. Dinger, "'A Mean Conspirator' or 'The Noblest of Men': William Marks's Expulsion from Nauvoo," *John Whitmer Historical Association Journal* 34, no. 2 (Fall–Winter 2014): 12–38.
18. "Sermon by President Young on the 6th of April, 1853 2 O'clock P.M.," 11, Historian's Office Report of Speeches, 1845–85, CHL.
19. "Sermon by President Young on the 6th of April," 10–11; Richard E. Bennett, *Temples Rising: A Heritage of Sacrifice* (Salt Lake City: Deseret Book, 2019), 161–63. Priesthood "keys" refers to special ecclesiastical authority to administer in the church.
20. "Minutes of the General Conference."
21. "Who Designed the Temple," *Deseret News*, April 23, 1892.
22. "Who Designed the Temple"; Richard O. Cowan, "The Design, Construction, and Role of the Salt Lake Temple," in *Salt Lake City: The Place Which God Prepared*, ed. Scott C. Esplin and Kenneth L. Alford (Provo, UT: Religious Studies Center, 2011), 48.
23. Heber C. Kimball, in *Journal of Discourses*, 26 vols. (Liverpool: F. D. Richards, 1855–86), 1:162.
24. "Minutes of the General Conference," *Deseret News*, November 6, 1852; Jacob W. Olmstead, Josh Probert, and Elwin Robison, "Myths and Realities of the Salt Lake Temple Foundation," *Journal of Mormon History* 48, no. 4 (October 2022): 40.
25. "Sermon by President Young on the 6th of April," 4.
26. Paul L. Anderson, "Truman O. Angell: Architect and Saint," in *Supporting Saints: Life Stories of Nineteenth-Century Mormons*, ed. Donald Q. Cannon and David J. Whittaker (Provo, UT: Religious Studies Center, Brigham Young University, 1985), 146–47, 151; C. Mark Hamilton, *Nineteenth Century Mormon Architecture and City Planning* (New York: Oxford University Press, 1995), 45.
27. Jeanne Halgren Kilde, *When Church Became Theatre: The Transformation of Evangelical Architecture and Worship in Nineteenth-Century America* (New York: Oxford University Press, 2005), 56–111.
28. Laurel B. Andrew, *The Early Temples of the Mormons: The Architecture of the Millennial Kingdom in the American West* (Albany: State University of New York Press, 1978), 141–45.
29. Ezra T. Benson, in *Journal of Discourses*, 2:348.
30. Ann Eliza Secrist to Jacob F. Secrist, May 30, 1853, Jacob F. Secrist Collection, 1841–74, CHL.
31. "Minutes of the General Conference," *Millennial Star* (Liverpool) 15 (July 23, 1853): 484.
32. Truman P. Angell, "The Temple," *Deseret News*, August 17, 1854.
33. Parley P. Pratt, in *Journal of Discourses*, 1:14.
34. George A. Smith, "Description of the Temple," *Millennial Star* 16 (October 7, 1854): 636, italics in original.
35. "History, 1838–1856, volume C-1 [November 2, 1838–July 31, 1842]," 1328, Joseph Smith Papers, accessed April 12, 2019, https://www.josephsmithpapers.org/paper-summary/history-1838-1856-volume-c-1-2-november-1838-31-july-1842/502.
36. Lisle G. Brown, "'Temple Pro Tempore': The Salt Lake City Endowment House," *Journal of Mormon History* 34, no. 4 (Fall 2008): 2–4.
37. Brown, "Temple Pro Tempore," 4.
38. Brown, "Temple Pro Tempore," 5, n16, 65.
39. Brown, "Temple Pro Tempore," 6; Bennett, *Temples Rising*, 166.
40. Journal History of the Church, March 5, 1855, Historical Department, CHL; Brown, "Temple Pro Tempore," 7.

192 NOTES TO PAGES 35-42

41. Brown, "Temple Pro Tempore," 54.
42. "Temple Pro Tempore," box 1, folder 6, Truman O. Angell Architectural Drawings, 1851–67, CHL.
43. Leonard J. Arrington, *Great Basin Kingdom: An Economic History of the Latter-day Saints, 1830–1900* (Urbana: University of Illinois Press, 2005), 109.
44. Arrington, *Great Basin Kingdom*, 108–10, 134.
45. "Minutes of Conference," *Deseret News*, September 18, 1852; Reid L. Neilson and R. Mark Melville, eds., *The Saints Abroad: Missionaries Who Answered Brigham Young's 1852 Call to the Nations of the World* (Provo, UT: Religious Studies Center, Brigham Young University, 2019).
46. George Q. Cannon, journal, June 9, 1853, CHL.
47. "News from Deseret," *Millennial Star* 15 (July 9, 1853): 441–43, italics in original. The British Mission's *Millennial Star* reprinted an account of the groundbreaking from the *Deseret News* in June 1853. "The Temple," *Millennial Star* 15 (June 18, 1853): 391–93.
48. Arrington, *Great Basin Kingdom*, 97–98.
49. "Second General Epistle of the First Presidency, October 1849," in *Settling the Valley, Proclaiming the Gospel: The General Epistles of the Mormon First Presidency*, ed. Reid L. Neilson and Nathan N. Waite (New York: Oxford University Press, 2017), 87–88; Fred E. Woods, "Perpetual Emigrating Fund," in *Encyclopedia of Latter-day Saint History*, ed. Arnold K. Garr, Donald Q. Cannon, and Richard O. Cowan (Salt Lake City: Deseret Book, 2000), 910.
50. Arrington, *Great Basin Kingdom*, 133–41.
51. "First Fruits," *Deseret News*, June 18, 1853.
52. "To the Saints," *Deseret News*, July 30, 1853.
53. "Sixth General Epistle of the Presidency of the Church of Jesus Christ of Latter-day Saints," *Deseret News*, November 15, 1851.
54. "Sixth General Epistle of the Presidency"; Arrington, *Great Basin Kingdom*, 131.
55. Arrington, *Great Basin Kingdom*, 111.
56. "Fifth General Epistle of the Presidency of the Church of Jesus Christ of Latter-day Saints," *Deseret News*, April 8, 1851; Edward Hunter, "Notice to the Bishops," *Deseret News*, March 20, 1852; "Temple Block," *Deseret News*, August 7, 1852.
57. "Temple Wall," *Deseret News*, May 14, 1853; "General Items," *Deseret News*, May 28, 1853.
58. George A. Smith to Franklin D. Richards, April 27, 1855, in *Millennial Star* 17 (August 11, 1855): 508; Journal History of the Church, December 7, 1851; James E. Talmage, *The House of the Lord: A Study of Holy Sanctuaries Ancient and Modern* (Salt Lake City: The Church of Jesus Christ of Latter-day Saints, 1912), 138.
59. "Railway," *Deseret News*, May 3, 1851.
60. "Sixth General Epistle of the Presidency"; Wallace A. Raynor, *Everlasting Spires: The Story of the Salt Lake Temple* (Salt Lake City: Deseret Book, 1965), 72.
61. Smith to Richards, April 27, 1855, 507.
62. "Temple Wall."
63. Smith to Richards, April 27, 1855, 507.
64. Historian's Office History of the Church, 1839–ca. 1882, June 30 and August 21, 1855, 72, 89, box 9, volume 25, CHL; Wallace Alan Raynor, "History of the Construction of the Salt Lake Temple" (master's thesis, Brigham Young University, 1961), 27; Olmstead, Probert, and Robison, "Myths and Realities of the Salt Lake Temple Foundation," 44–46.
65. "The Temple," *Deseret News*, August 1, 1855; Brigham Young to John Taylor, July 25, 1855, Brigham Young Letterbook, 4:252, Brigham Young Office Files.
66. Smith to Richards, April 27, 1855, 507; Brigham Young, "Notice," *Deseret News*, April 25, 1855; Daniel H. Wells, "Discourse," *Deseret News*, March 19, 1856.
67. David L. Cook and others to John Sharp, July 31, 1855, box 81, folder 1, Brigham Young Office Files; Brigham Young to George A. Smith, June 30, 1856, box 5, folder 12, George A. Smith Papers, 1834–77, CHL; "Big Cottonwood Canal," *Deseret News*, March 25, 1857; Raynor, "History of the Construction of the Salt Lake Temple," 98–99.
68. Truman O. Angell, journal, April 1856, 1, in Daughters of Utah Pioneers Collection, 1828–1963, CHL.
69. Angell, journal, April 1856, 2.
70. Anderson, "Truman O. Angell," 158.
71. Brent M. Rogers, *Unpopular Sovereignty: Mormons and the Federal Management of Early Utah Territory* (Lincoln: University of Nebraska Press, 2017), 40–49.
72. Arrington, *Great Basin Kingdom*, 99.

NOTES TO PAGES 42–48   193

73. Paul H. Peterson, "The Mormon Reformation of 1856–1857: The Rhetoric and the Reality," *Journal of Mormon History* 15 (1989): 61.
74. Peterson, "Mormon Reformation of 1856–1857," 62–65.
75. Wells, "Discourse."
76. Brigham Young, "Discourse," *Deseret News*, March 26, 1856.
77. Wells, "Discourse."
78. Ronald W. Walker, Richard E. Turley Jr., and Glen M. Leonard, *Massacre at Mountain Meadows* (New York: Oxford University Press, 2008), 24–25; Brigham Young, in *Journal of Discourses*, 3:222.
79. Marie Cornwall, Camela Courtright, and Laga Van Beek, "How Common the Principle? Women as Plural Wives in 1860," *Dialogue: A Journal of Mormon Thought* 26 (Summer 1993): 149.
80. Walker, Turley, and Leonard, *Massacre at Mountain Meadows*, 24–27.
81. Justin S. Morrill, "Utah Territory and Its Laws—Polygamy and Its License," February 23, 1857, appendix to the *Congressional Globe*, U.S. Cong., House (34-2), in *At Sword's Point, Part 1: A Documentary History of the Utah War to 1858*, ed. William P. MacKinnon (Norman, OK: Arthur H. Clark, 2008), 87.
82. Rogers, *Unpopular Sovereignty*, 135.
83. Rogers, *Unpopular Sovereignty*, 8.
84. MacKinnon, *At Sword's Point, Part 1*, 145–47.
85. "The Temple," *Deseret News*, June 24, 1857.
86. Brigham Young, in *Journal of Discourses*, 5:170.
87. Brigham Young, in *Journal of Discourses*, 4:319.
88. Richard D. Poll, "The Move South," *BYU Studies* 29, no. 4 (1989): 66; William P. MacKinnon, ed., *At Sword's Point, Part 2: A Documentary History of the Utah War, 1858–1859* (Norman, OK: Arthur H. Clark, 2016), 310.
89. MacKinnon, *At Sword's Point, Part 2*, 215; Matthew J. Grow, *"Liberty to the Downtrodden": Thomas L. Kane, Romantic Reformer* (New Haven, CT: Yale University Press, 2009), 162–73.
90. Historian's Office History of the Church, March 18, 1858, 266, box 12, volume 28, CHL; Arrington, *Great Basin Kingdom*, 182.
91. Brigham Young, *A Series of Instructions and Remarks by President Brigham Young at a Special Council, Tabernacle, March 21, 1858* (Salt Lake City: n.p., 1858).
92. Poll, "Move South," 77.
93. Journal History of the Church, March 25, 30, 1858; Historian's Office History of the Church, March 30, 1858, 291, box 12, volume 28, CHL; Brigham Young to John M. Bernhisel, May 6, 1858, Brigham Young Letterbook, 4:148.
94. Young, *Series of Instructions*, 8.
95. Poll, "Move South," 82; MacKinnon, *At Sword's Point, Part 2*, 580–98; Arrington, *Great Basin Kingdom*, 193–94; William P. MacKinnon, "Utah War: Impact and Legacy," *Journal of Mormon History* 29, no. 2 (Fall 2003): 195.
96. John G. Turner, *Brigham Young: Pioneer Prophet* (Cambridge, MA: Harvard University Press, 2012), 296.
97. Turner, *Brigham Young*, 296–98; Poll, "Move South," 85; Kenneth L. Alford, "'We Have Now the Territory on Wheels': Direct and Collateral Costs of the 1858 Move South," *Journal of Mormon History* 45, no. 2 (April 2019): 107.

Chapter 3

1. Leonard J. Arrington, *Great Basin Kingdom: An Economic History of the Latter-day Saints, 1830–1900* (Salt Lake City: University of Utah Press, 2005), 196–99; William Clayton to George Q. Cannon, July 16, 1861, in *Millennial Star* (Liverpool) 23 (August 31, 1861): 566.
2. Jacob W. Olmstead, Josh Probert, and Elwin Robison, "Myths and Realities of the Salt Lake Temple Foundation," *Journal of Mormon History* 48, no. 4 (October 2022): 53.
3. Wilford Woodruff, journal, December 7, 1859, CHL; Historical Department, Office Journal, 1844–2012, December 7, 1859, CHL.
4. "Progress of the Work Connected with the Building of the Temple," *Deseret News*, June 25, 1862; Brigham Young to Daniel H. Wells, June 4, 1862, Brigham Young Office Files, 1832–78.
5. Brigham Young, discourse, August 9 and 10, 1864, Church History Department Pitman Shorthand Transcriptions, 2013–17, CHL.
6. Olmstead, Probert, and Robison, "Myths and Realities of the Salt Lake Temple Foundation," 55.

194   NOTES TO PAGES 48–56

7. Brigham Young, discourse, July 13, 1865, Church History Department Pitman Shorthand Transcriptions.
8. Brigham Young, in *Journal of Discourses*, 26 vols. (Liverpool: F. D. Richards, 1855–86), 10:254.
9. Rock Book A, June 30, 1860, box 11, folder 1, Public Works Account Books, 1848–87, CHL; "Summary of News and Passing Events: American," *Millennial Star* 22, no. 34 (August 25, 1860): 542; Brigham Young to John W. Hess, September 18, 1861, Brigham Young Office Files Transcriptions, 1974–78, CHL.
10. "Improvement of the State Road," *Millennial Star* 24, no. 17 (April 26, 1862): 268–69.
11. Brigham Young, "Remarks," *Deseret News*, May 14, 1862.
12. "Emigration and the Temple," *Millennial Star* 25, no. 38 (September 17, 1864): 600–602; Brigham Young to Daniel H. Wells and Brigham Young Jr., August 31, 1864, in *Millennial Star* 26, no. 45 (November 7, 1864): 716–18.
13. Woodruff, journal, August 23, 1862.
14. Truman O. Angell to Brigham Young, March 31, 1867, Brigham Young Office Files.
15. Truman O. Angell, journal, April 11–13, 17–18, 22, 29, 1867, CHL.
16. "Thirty-Seventh Annual Conference," *Deseret News*, April 10, 1867.
17. Young, in *Journal of Discourses*, 11:371.
18. "Apportionment to the Wards of the No. of Loads of Rock," October 12, 1867, Letterbook, 10:423, Brigham Young Office Files Transcriptions; Edward Hunter and J. C. Little to "Bishop," October 17, 1867, Letterbook, 10:424.
19. Edward W. Tullidge, *The History of Salt Lake City and Its Founders* (Salt Lake City: E. W. Tullidge, 1886), 697; Brigham Young, "Governor's Message," *Deseret News*, January 23, 1867; Arrington, *Great Basin Kingdom*, 258–62.
20. Brigham Young to Henry Eccles and all the masons and stonecutters on the Temple Block, Salt Lake City, August 10, 1868, Brigham Young Office Files.
21. "Wanted Immediately! 2,000 Men," *Deseret News*, July 29, 1868; "Wanted Immediately! 500 Men," *Deseret News*, August 21, 1868; Arrington, *Great Basin Kingdom*, 263.
22. Arrington, *Great Basin Kingdom*, 258–65.
23. Arrington, *Great Basin Kingdom*, 265–70.
24. Woodruff, journal, January 10, 1870.
25. At the occasion of the temple's groundbreaking, Young declared, "The Rail Road must be completed before we can do much towards laying the foundation of this Temple." Willard Richards, "The Temple," *Deseret News* (Salt Lake City), February 19, 1853.
26. James E. Talmage, *The House of the Lord: A Study of Holy Sanctuaries Ancient and Modern* (Salt Lake City: The Church of Jesus Christ of Latter-day Saints, 1912), 143.
27. James H. Anderson, "The Salt Lake Temple," *The Contributor* 14, no. 6 (April 1893): 264; Angell, journal, May 29, 1867; Wallace Alan Raynor, "History of the Construction of the Salt Lake Temple" (master's thesis, Brigham Young University, 1961), 79–83.
28. "The Wasatch and Jordan Valley Railroad," *Deseret News*, April 5, 1873.
29. Richard Neitzel Holzapfel, *Every Stone a Sermon: The Magnificent Story of the Construction and Dedication of the Salt Lake Temple* (Salt Lake City: Bookcraft, 1992), 22.
30. Granite Ward manuscript history and historical reports, 1877–1984, CHL; Raynor, "History of the Construction of the Salt Lake Temple," 70–73.
31. Arrington, *Great Basin Kingdom*, 98.
32. William Dobbie Kuhre, "Recollections of Temple Quarry, Little Cottonwood Canyon, and Old Granite," 6, CHL.
33. Kuhre, "Recollections of Temple Quarry," 5; Raynor, "History of the Construction of the Salt Lake Temple," 75.
34. Kuhre, "Recollections of Temple Quarry," 7.
35. Anderson, "Salt Lake Temple," 264.
36. Robert Campbell, "Correspondence," *Deseret Evening News* (Salt Lake City), July 2, 1877.
37. Raynor, "History of the Construction of the Salt Lake Temple," 77; Kuhre, "Recollections of Temple Quarry," 6–7.
38. Kuhre, "Recollections of Temple Quarry," 4.
39. James Campbell Livingston, "Sketch of the Life of James Campbell Livingston," 3, undated, CHL.
40. Young to Hess, September 18, 1861.
41. Campbell, "Correspondence."
42. Raynor, "History of the Construction of the Salt Lake Temple," 130–37.
43. "The Temple," *Deseret Evening News*, November 28, 1874.
44. Anderson, "Salt Lake Temple," 265.

NOTES TO PAGES 56–66   195

45. "The Temple," *Deseret Evening News*, August 16, 1873.
46. "Rocklaying Resumed," *Deseret Evening News*, May 23, 1878; Raynor, "History of the Construction of the Salt Lake Temple," 142.
47. "The Salt Lake Temple," *Deseret Evening News*, June 10, 1881.
48. "The Temple," *Deseret News*, November 20, 1878.
49. "Fatal Accident," *Deseret News*, October 4, 1881; "Feramorz L. Young," *The Contributor* 3 (November 1881): 38; Raynor, "History of the Construction of the Salt Lake Temple," 144.
50. "Fell Thirty Feet," *Deseret Evening News*, January 20, 1890.
51. Joseph Young, A. P. Rockwood, H. S. Eldredge, and John Van Cott to "Dear Brother," November 10, 1876, Hiram W. Mikesell Collection, 1836–93, CHL.
52. James Livingston and quarrymen to John Taylor and the Council of the Apostles, May 17, 1880, First Presidency (John Taylor) Correspondence, 1877–87, CHL.
53. Young to Hess; Priscilla Merriman Evans, "Account of Relief Society in 1856–1870, as Recorded in Autobiography, circa 1907," in *The First Fifty Years of Relief Society: Key Documents in Latter-day Saint Women's History*, ed. Jill Mulvay Derr, Carol Cornwall Madsen, Kate Holbrook, and Matthew J. Grow (Salt Lake City: Church Historian's Press, 2016), 224.
54. Young, in *Journal of Discourses*, 16:186; Richard O. Cowan, *Temples to Dot the Earth* (Salt Lake City: Bookcraft, 1989), 73.
55. Woodruff, journal, January 24, 1868; Richard E. Bennett, *Temples Rising: A Heritage of Sacrifice* (Salt Lake City: Deseret Book, 2019), 204.
56. Richard E. Bennett, "'Line upon Line, Precept upon Precept': Reflections on the 1877 Commencement of the Performance of Endowments and Sealings for the Dead," *BYU Studies* 44, no. 3 (2005): 38–77.
57. Annals of the Southern Utah Mission, ca. 1903–06, 9–10, CHL.
58. George Q. Cannon, journal, November 9, 1876, CHL.
59. Woodruff, journal, January 1, 1877.
60. Bennett, *Temples Rising*, 213–14.
61. Woodruff, journal, January 19, 1851; Richard E. Bennett, "'Which Is the Wisest Course?': The Transformation in Mormon Temple Consciousness, 1870–1898," *BYU Studies* 52, no. 2 (2013): 9.
62. Bennett, *Temples Rising*, 229–30.
63. Bennett, *Temples Rising*, 208–9; Woodruff, journal, January 14, 1877; Cannon, journal, April 13–14, 1877.
64. Bennett, *Temples Rising*, 213.
65. Bennett, *Temples Rising*, 196–202.
66. William G. Hartley, "The Priesthood Reorganization of 1877: Brigham Young's Last Achievement," *BYU Studies* 20, no. 1 (1980): 3–36.
67. "Remarks by Prest. Brigham Young," *Deseret Evening News*, May 5, 1877.
68. "Prayer Offered by Elder Orson Pratt," *Deseret Evening News*, May 18, 1877.
69. "Funeral of President Brigham Young," *Deseret News*, September 5, 1877.
70. "Funeral of President Brigham Young."

Chapter 4

1. Pleasant Grove Branch Relief Society Minutes and Records, 1868–1901, 397–98, CHL.
2. Jill Mulvay Derr, Carol Cornwall Madsen, Kate Holbrook, and Matthew J. Grow, eds., *The First Fifty Years of Relief Society: Key Documents in Latter-day Saint Women's History* (Salt Lake City: Church Historian's Press, 2016), 236–47.
3. "Ladies' Cooperative Retrenchment Meeting, Minutes, February 10, 1870," in Derr et al., *First Fifty Years of Relief Society*, 341.
4. Derr et al., *First Fifty Years of Relief Society*, 243.
5. Pleasant Grove Branch Relief Society Minutes and Records, 517.
6. Mary Isabella Horne and others, "To the Presidents and Members of the Relief Society of Salt Lake Stake of Zion, Greeting!," *Woman's Exponent* 6, no. 16 (January 15, 1878): 123.
7. J. Spencer Fluhman, *"A Peculiar People": Anti-Mormonism and the Making of Religion in Nineteenth-Century America* (Chapel Hill: University of North Carolina Press, 2012), 103–10.
8. Kathryn M. Daynes, *More Wives Than One: Transformation of the Mormon Marriage System, 1840–1910* (Urbana: University of Illinois Press, 2001), 14.
9. Sarah Barringer Gordon, *The Mormon Question: Polygamy and Constitutional Conflict in Nineteenth-Century America* (Chapel Hill: University of North Carolina Press, 2002), 4–6.

196 NOTES TO PAGES 67–73

10. The Church of Jesus Christ of Latter-day Saints, "Plural Marriage and Families in Early Utah," Gospel Topics Essays, https://www.churchofjesuschrist.org/study/manual/gospel-topics-essays/plural-marriage-and-families-in-early-utah.
11. Gordon, *Mormon Question*, 81–83.
12. Gordon, *Mormon Question*, 113–45.
13. Thomas G. Alexander, *Things in Heaven and Earth: The Life and Times of Wilford Woodruff, a Mormon Prophet* (Salt Lake City: Signature Books, 1991), 235–37.
14. Wilford Woodruff, journal, December 28, 1880, CHL. He received the revelation on January 26, 1880.
15. Woodruff, journal, December 28, 1880, January 19, 1881; Alexander, *Things in Heaven and Earth*, 237–39.
16. "An Epistle of the First Presidency of the Church of Jesus Christ of Latter-day Saints, Read at the Semi-Annual Conference, Held at Coalville, Summit County, Utah, October, 1886," 11, Digital Collections, Harold B. Lee Library, Brigham Young University, Provo, UT, https://contentdm.lib.byu.edu/digital/collection/NCMP1820-1846/id/22669.
17. "Epistle of the First Presidency of the Church," 11; Richard E. Bennett, *Temples Rising: A Heritage of Sacrifice* (Salt Lake City: Deseret Book, 2019), 260.
18. Salt Lake Stake General Minutes, vol. 3, December 28, 1881, CHL.
19. Salt Lake Stake General Minutes, vol. 3, April 4, 1885.
20. Gordon, *Mormon Question*, 149–55; B. Carmon Hardy, *Solemn Covenant: The Mormon Polygamous Passage* (Urbana: University of Illinois Press, 1992), 46–54.
21. Gordon, *Mormon Question*, 154–61.
22. Truman O. Angell to John Taylor, March 8, 1886, First Presidency (John Taylor) Correspondence, 1877–87, CHL.
23. The Church of Jesus Christ of Latter-day Saints, "Plural Marriage and Families in Early Utah"; Kathryn M. Daynes, "Striving to Live the Principle in Utah's First Temple City: A Snapshot of Polygamy in St. George, Utah, in June 1880," *BYU Studies* 51, no. 4 (2012): 70.
24. Franklin L. West, *Life of Franklin D. Richards* (Salt Lake City: Deseret News, 1924), 190–203.
25. Gustive O. Larson, *The "Americanization" of Utah for Statehood* (San Marino, CA: Huntington Library, 1971), 165–82; Franklin D. Richards, journal, October 21 and November 5, 1887, Richards Family Collection, 1837–1961, CHL; Charles P. Adams and Gustive O. Larson, "A Study of the LDS Church Historian's Office, 1830–1900," *Utah Historical Quarterly* 40, no. 4 (Fall 1972): 386.
26. Gordon, *Mormon Question*, 185–208.
27. Edwin Brown Firmage and Richard Collin Mangrum, *Zion in the Courts: A Legal History of the Church of Jesus Christ of Latter-day Saints, 1830–1900* (Urbana: University of Illinois Press, 1988), 252–54; Larson, *"Americanization" of Utah*, 213–16.
28. George Q. Cannon, journal, September 1, 1890, CHL.
29. Thomas G. Alexander, "The Odyssey of a Latter-day Prophet: Wilford Woodruff and the Manifesto of 1890," *Journal of Mormon History* 17 (1991): 197–201.
30. Cannon, journal, June 30, 1890.
31. Cannon, journal, July 16, 1890; Alexander, *Things in Heaven and Earth*, 265–66; Ronald W. Walker, *Wayward Saints: The Godbeites and Brigham Young* (Urbana: University of Illinois Press), 349–50.
32. Alexander, "Odyssey of a Latter-day Prophet," 185.
33. Cannon, journal, September 1, 1890.
34. Woodruff, journal, September 25, 1890.
35. Alexander, "Odyssey of a Latter-day Prophet," 190.
36. Lisle G. Brown, "'Temple Pro Tempore': The Salt Lake City Endowment House," *Journal of Mormon History* 34, no. 4 (Fall 2008): 51–53.
37. Arthur Winter, "Remarks Made by President Woodruff, at Cache Stake Conference, Held at Logan, Sunday Afternoon, November 1st, 1891," *Deseret Weekly* (Salt Lake City), November 14, 1891.
38. Jan Shipps, "The Principle Revoked: A Closer Look at the Demise of Plural Marriage," *Journal of Mormon History* 11 (1984): 65–77.
39. "Sermon by President Young on the 6th of April, 1853 2 O'clock P.M.," 11, Historian's Office Report of Speeches, 1845–85, CHL.
40. "Who Designed the Temple?" *Deseret Evening News* (Salt Lake City), April 16, 1892.
41. Truman O. Angell, "The Salt Lake City Temple," *Millennial Star* (Liverpool) 36, no. 18 (May 5, 1874): 273–75.

NOTES TO PAGES 74–80 197

42. Truman O. Angell, "The Temple," *Deseret News* (Salt Lake City), August 17, 1854.
43. James H. Anderson, "The Salt Lake Temple," *The Contributor* 14, no. 6 (April 1893): 275.
44. Salt Lake Temple Architectural Drawings, 1853–93, CHL.
45. Some have theorized that Orson Pratt helped create the temple's moon stones. These same sources assert that he helped run a government-sponsored observatory on the southeast corner of the Temple Block. Little contemporary evidence, however, substantiates Pratt's involvement with the observatory and the temple stones. See Richard Neitzel Holzapfel, *Every Stone a Sermon: The Magnificent Story of the Construction and Dedication of the Salt Lake Temple* (Salt Lake City: Bookcraft, 1992), 29; C. Mark Hamilton, "A Symbolic Statement of Mormon Doctrine," in *The Mormon People: Their Character and Traditions*, ed. Thomas G. Alexander (Provo, UT: Brigham Young University Press, 1980), 107–8.
46. "Buttress Blocks Representing Moon Phases of 1878," Salt Lake Temple Architectural Drawings, 1853–93; Doctrine and Covenants 20:1.
47. Anderson, "Salt Lake Temple," 276.
48. Salt Lake Temple Architectural Drawings, 1853–93.
49. Angell, "Temple."
50. "A Lady Temple Builder," *Deseret Evening News*, August 20, 1880.
51. "Sermon by President Young on the 6th of April, 1853 2 O'clock P.M.," 4.
52. Terryl Givens and Brian M. Hauglid, *The Pearl of Greatest Price: Mormonism's Most Controversial Scripture* (New York: Oxford University Press, 2019), 138–40; "The Book of Abraham," *Times and Seasons* (Nauvoo, IL) 3, no. 10 (March 15, 1842): 721–22 [Abraham 3].
53. Brigham Young, in *Journal of Discourses*, 26 vols. (Liverpool: F. D. Richards, 1855–86), 2:122.
54. Journal History of the Church, August 13, 1857, Historical Department, CHL.
55. Steven C. Harper, "Freemasonry and the Latter-day Saint Temple Endowment Ceremony," in *A Reason for Faith: Navigating LDS Doctrine and Church History*, ed. Laura Harris Hales (Provo, UT: Religious Studies Center, Brigham Young University, 2016), 143–57.
56. James E. Talmage, *The House of the Lord: A Study of Holy Sanctuaries Ancient and Modern* (Salt Lake City: The Church of Jesus Christ of Latter-day Saints, 1912), 179.
57. "Fiftieth Semi-Annual Conference," *Deseret Evening News*, October 11, 1880.
58. Truman O. Angell, journal, March 9–August 6, 1855, CHL; "The Temple," *Deseret News*.
59. Woodruff, journal, April 15, 1856; Truman O. Angell to Orson Pratt, September 19, 1856, in *Millennial Star* 18, no. 41 (October 11, 1856): 652–55.
60. Truman O. Angell to John Taylor, October 18, 1881, First Presidency (John Taylor) Correspondence.
61. Franklin D. Richards to John Taylor, April 20, 1886, First Presidency (John Taylor) Correspondence.
62. Richards to Taylor, April 20, 1886.
63. Franklin D. Richards to John Taylor, April 23, 1886, First Presidency (John Taylor) Correspondence.
64. Richards to Taylor, April 23, 1886; Truman O. Angell to John Taylor, April 29, 1886, First Presidency (John Taylor) Correspondence; Cannon, journal, April 30, 1886. The shorter west towers were actually depicted in the original design. See "The Temple," *Deseret News*; Cannon, journal, May 3, 1886.
65. Franklin D. Richards to John Taylor, May 3, 1886; Franklin D. Richards to John Taylor, May 6, 1886, First Presidency (John Taylor) Correspondence; Franklin D. Richards, journal, May 3, 1886, CHL.
66. Cannon, journal, May 8, 1886.
67. Richards, journal, May 10, 1886.
68. Truman O. Angell Jr. to John Taylor, April 28, 1885, First Presidency (John Taylor) Correspondence.
69. Truman O. Angell Jr. to John Taylor, May 8, 1878, First Presidency (John Taylor) Correspondence.
70. Truman O. Angell to John Taylor, March 11, 1885, First Presidency (John Taylor) Correspondence.
71. John Taylor to Truman O. Angell, May 13, 1886, quoted in Paul L. Anderson, "Truman O. Angell: Architect and Saint," in *Supporting Saints: Life Stories of Nineteenth-Century Mormons*, ed. Donald Q. Cannon and David J. Whittaker (Provo, UT: Religious Studies Center, Brigham Young University, 1985), 167.
72. B. H. Roberts, *The Life of John Taylor, Third President of The Church of Jesus Christ of Latter-day Saints* (Salt Lake City: George Q. Cannon and Sons, 1892), 409.

198 NOTES TO PAGES 80–88

73. Angell, "The Temple."
74. Anderson, "Truman O. Angell," 167.
75. "Death of T. O. Angell, Sr.," *Deseret Evening News*, October 17, 1887.
76. "To Complete the Temple," *Deseret Evening News*, April 16, 1892.
77. "Who Designed the Temple," *Deseret Evening News*, April 16, 1892.
78. P. Bradford Westwood, "The Early Life and Career of Joseph Don Carlos Young (1855–1938): A Study of Utah's First Institutionally Trained Architect to 1884" (master's thesis, University of Pennsylvania, 1994), 15–20.
79. Cannon, journal, February 16, 1888.
80. "The Last Tile," *Deseret Evening News*, August 15, 1889.
81. "The Temple," *Deseret Evening News*, October 26, 1889.
82. "Otis Elevator Company drawings and bid sheet, 1889 June 11–13," Salt Lake Temple Architectural Drawings, 1853–93; Cannon, journal, December, 9, 1890, September 8, 24, 1892.
83. Cannon, journal, June 20, 1890.
84. Linda Jones Gibbs, *Harvesting the Light: The Paris Art Mission and Beginnings of Utah Impressionism* (Salt Lake City: The Church of Jesus Christ of Latter-day Saints, 1987), 35–37.
85. "Dedicated to the Lord," *Salt Lake Herald*, April 7, 1893; Gibbs, *Harvesting the Light*, 37.
86. Martha Elizabeth Bradley and Lowell M. Durham Jr., "John Hafen and the Art Missionaries," *Journal of Mormon History* 12 (1985): 91–105; Cannon, journal, April 12, 20, 1892.
87. William Clayton, "An Interesting Journal," *Juvenile Instructor* 21, no. 10 (May 15, 1886): 157–58.
88. Cannon, journal, September 24, 1891.
89. Cannon, journal, April 5, 1892.
90. Inside the capstone was placed a Book of Mormon, Doctrine and Covenants, Bible, Pearl of Great Price, as well as Parley P. Pratt's *Voice of Warning*, a hymn book, renderings of Joseph Smith, Hyrum Smith, Brigham Young, John Taylor, Wilford Woodruff, George Q. Cannon, and Joseph F. Smith, and select other documents. "At the Tabernacle," *Deseret Evening News*, April 6, 1892.
91. "At the Tabernacle."
92. Jacob W. Olmstead, "From Pentecost to Administration: A Reappraisal of the History of the Hosanna Shout," *Mormon Historical Studies* 2, no. 2 (Fall 2001): 13–16.
93. Woodruff, journal, April 6, 1892.
94. "At the Tabernacle."
95. Cannon, journal, October 7, 1891.
96. Cannon, journal, July 21, October 22, 1891; Albert L. Zobell Jr., "Cyrus E. Dallin and the Angel Moroni Statue," *Improvement Era* 72, no. 4 (April 1968): 5; Levi Edgar Young, "The Angel Moroni and Cyrus Dallin," *Improvement Era* 56, no. 4 (April 1953): 234–35.
97. Cannon, journal, September 22, 1891.
98. Zobell, "Cyrus E. Dallin and the Angel Moroni Statue," 6; Woodruff, journal, March 28, 1892.
99. Cyrus E. Dallin to Gaylen S. Young, July 30, 1938, CHL.
100. *Temple Souvenir Album, April 1892* (Salt Lake City: Magazine Printing Company, 1892), 8. Apostle Marriner W. Merrill viewed the angel on display on the Temple Block prior to the general conference. He identified the angel as "Moroni." Both the *Deseret Weekly* report for the April 1892 general conference as well as Woodruff subsequently identified the bronze statue as Moroni. Marriner W. Merrill, journal, April 2, 1892, CHL; "At the Tabernacle"; Woodruff, journal, April 6, 1892.
101. Armand L. Mauss, *The Angel and the Beehive: The Mormon Struggle with Assimilation* (Urbana: University of Illinois Press, 1994), 196.
102. Joseph Smith, "Church History," *Times and Seasons* 3, no. 9 (March 1, 1842): 707.

Chapter 5

1. "Thanksgiving and Prayer," *Deseret Evening News* (Salt Lake City), April 23, 1892.
2. "Thanksgiving and Prayer."
3. H. C. Barrell and Laron Pratt to Wilford Woodruff and counselors, May 1, 1892, First Presidency (Wilford Woodruff) Correspondence, 1887–98, CHL.
4. "Temple and Grounds," *Salt Lake Herald* (Salt Lake City), March 16, 1895; "Utah News," *Millennial Star* (Liverpool) 57, no. 14 (April 4, 1895): 223; Wallace Alan Raynor, "History of the Construction of the Salt Lake Temple" (master's thesis, Brigham Young University, 1961), 63–65.

NOTES TO PAGES 88–98   199

5. "Discourses," *Deseret Evening News*, December 17, 1892.
6. "Presiding Bishops' Office. Expenditures. 6 months to July 1, 1893," Joseph F. Smith Papers, 1854–1918, CHL.
7. James H. Anderson, "The Salt Lake Temple," *The Contributor* 14, no. 6 (April 1893): 283.
8. George Q. Cannon, journal, January 4, 1893, CHL.
9. "In the Social Realm," *Salt Lake Herald*, July 8, 1894.
10. Anderson, "Salt Lake Temple," 291–92.
11. Kristine Wright, "'We Baked a Lot of Bread': Reconceptualizing Mormon Women and Ritual Objects," in *Women and Mormonism: Historical and Contemporary Perspectives*, ed. Kate Holbrook and Matthew Bowman (Salt Lake City: University of Utah Press, 2016), 82–100.
12. "Donated to the Salt Lake Temple," March 31, 1893, Joseph F. Smith Papers.
13. Statement of debt, June 15, 1893, Joseph F. Smith Papers.
14. Statement of debt.
15. Anthon H. Lund, journal, April 16, 1893, CHL.
16. James E. Talmage, *The House of the Lord: A Study of Holy Sanctuaries Ancient and Modern* (Salt Lake City: The Church of Jesus Christ of Latter-day Saints, 1912), 184.
17. D. M. McCallister, *A Description of the Great Temple, Salt Lake City, and a Statement concerning the Purposes for Which It Has Been Built* (Salt Lake City: Bureau of Information and Church Literature, 1904), 9–10; 1 Kings 7:23–26.
18. Steven C. Harper, *First Vision: Memory and Mormon Origins* (New York: Oxford University Press, 2019), 121.
19. Joseph Don Carlos Young to Tiffany and Co., September 20, 1892, in Joseph Don Carlos Young Letterpress Copybook, 1888–93, 160, CHL.
20. Harper, *First Vision*, 123; Kathleen Flake, *The Politics of American Religious Identity: The Seating of Senator Reed Smoot, Mormon Apostle* (Chapel Hill: University of North Carolina Press, 2004), 118.
21. Young to Tiffany and Co., 162–71.
22. Young to Tiffany and Co., 169–71; Cannon, journal, January 4, 1893.
23. Cannon, journal, April 3, 1893.
24. Cannon, journal, April 6, 1893.
25. M. Guy Bishop and Richard Neitzel Holzapfel, "The 'St. Peter's of the New World': The Salt Lake Temple, Tourism, and a New Image for Utah," *Utah Historical Quarterly* 61, no. 2 (Spring 1993): 136–49.
26. "Mormons' Gala Day," *Chicago Tribune*, April 7, 1893.
27. "The Temple Dedicated," *Leavenworth (KY) Times*, April 7, 1893.
28. "The Temple Dedication," *Salt Lake Tribune*, April 6, 1893.
29. "The Great Mormon Temple," *The Sun* (New York), April 6, 1893.
30. "The Mormon Temple," *The Sun*, April 8, 1893.
31. Eugene Young, "Inside the New Mormon Temple," *Harper's Weekly* 37 (May 27, 1893): 510; "The Great Temple," *St. Louis (MO) Post-Dispatch*, April 6, 1893.
32. "After Forty Years' Labor," *New York Times*, April 7, 1893.
33. "The Mormon Temple," *The Sun*.
34. Andrew Jenson, journal, April 8, 1893, CHL.
35. "A Singular Circumstance," *Deseret Evening News*, April 6, 1893.
36. Rudger Clawson, journal, October 23, 1892, quoted in Brian H. Stuy, "Come, Let Us Go Up to the Mountain of the Lord," *Dialogue: A Journal of Mormon Thought* 31, no. 3 (Fall 1998): 105.
37. Thomas G. Alexander, *Mormonism in Transition: A History of the Latter-day Saints, 1890–1930* (Urbana: University of Illinois, 1996), 6–8.
38. Wilford Woodruff, George Q. Cannon, and Joseph F. Smith, "An Address to the Officers and Members of the Church of Jesus Christ of Latter-day Saints," March 18, 1893, CHL.
39. Cannon, journal, April 24, 1893; Jenson, journal, April 24, 1893. Total church membership had surpassed 214,000 by 1893. *Deseret News 2013 Church Almanac* (Salt Lake City: Deseret News, 2013), 212.
40. Jacob W. Olmstead, "From Pentecost to Administration: A Reappraisal of the History of the Hosanna Shout," *Mormon Historical Studies* 2, no. 2 (Fall 2001): 25–26.
41. "Minutes of the General Conference," *Deseret News* (Salt Lake City), April 16, 1853.
42. Jenson, journal, April 15, 1893.
43. Jenson, journal, April 23, 1893.
44. Cannon, journal, April 18, 1893.

200 NOTES TO PAGES 98–105

45. Jenson, journal, April 23, 1893.
46. Jenson, journal, April 18, 1893.
47. Jan Shipps, *Mormonism: The Story of a New Religious Tradition* (Urbana: University of Illinois Press, 1985), 58.
48. Wilford Woodruff, June 12, 1892, in *Collected Discourses Delivered by President Wilford Woodruff, His Two Counselors, the Twelve Apostles, and Others*, 5 vols., ed. Brian H. Stuy (Burbank, CA: Brian H. Stuy, 1987–92), 3:82; Stuy, "Come, Let Us Go Up to the Mountain of the Lord," 105.
49. Shipps, *Mormonism*, 63.
50. Franklin D. Richards, journal, April 19, 1893, CHL.
51. B. Carmon Hardy, *Solemn Covenant: The Mormon Polygamous Passage* (Urbana: University of Illinois Press, 1992), 143–44.
52. Quoted in Stuy, "Come, Let Us Go Up to the Mountain of the Lord," 111.
53. Quoted in Stuy, "Come, Let Us Go Up to the Mountain of the Lord," 114.
54. Jenson, journal, April 18, 1893.
55. See Doctrine and Covenants 132:32: "Go ye, therefore, and do the works of Abraham; enter ye into my law and ye shall be saved."
56. Shipps, *Mormonism*, 59–63.
57. Doctrine and Covenants 132:32.
58. The Church of Jesus Christ of Latter-day Saints, "Excerpts from Three Addresses by President Wilford Woodruff regarding the Manifesto," Official Declaration 1, https://www.churchofjesu schrist.org/study/scriptures/dc-testament/od/1.
59. "Annual Conference," *Deseret Evening News*, April 6, 1893.
60. Jenson, journal, April 7, 1893.
61. Francis A. Hammond, journal, April 10, 1893, CHL; Wilford Woodruff, journal, "A Synopsis of Wilford Woodruff Labors in 1893," 54, CHL; Stuy, "Come, Let Us Go Up to the Mountain of the Lord," 117.
62. John Nicholson, "Temple Manifestations," *The Contributor* 14, no. 2 (December 1894): 116–18.
63. Clawson, journal, April 19, 1893, quoted in Stuy, "Come, Let Us Go Up to the Mountain of the Lord," 118.
64. Hammond, journal, April 10, 1893; Stuy, "Come, Let Us Go Up to the Mountain of the Lord," 117.
65. Samuel B. Brown, "Early Mormon Adoption Theology and the Mechanics of Salvation," *Journal of Mormon History* 37, no. 3 (Summer 2011): 3–52.
66. Jonathan A. Stapley, "Adoptive Sealing Ritual in Mormonism," *Journal of Mormon History* 37, no. 3 (Summer 2011): 73–82.
67. Richard E. Bennett, *Temples Rising: A Heritage of Sacrifice* (Salt Lake City: Deseret Book, 2019), 277, 300.
68. Abraham H. Cannon, journal, April 5, 1894, quoted in Stapley, "Adoptive Sealing Ritual in Mormonism," 108.
69. "Discourse by President George Q. Cannon," *Millennial Star* 56, no. 23 (June 4, 1894): 355.
70. Wilford Woodruff, April 8, 1894, in *Collected Discourses*, 4:74; Stapley, "Adoptive Sealing Ritual in Mormonism," 110.
71. James B. Allen, Jessie L. Embry, and Kahlile B. Mehr, *Hearts Turned to the Fathers: A History of the Genealogical Society of Utah, 1894–1994* (Provo, UT: Brigham Young University, 1995).
72. Jonathan A. Stapley and Kristine L. Wright, " 'They Shall Be Made Whole': A History of Baptism for Health," *Journal of Mormon History* 34, no. 4 (Fall 2008): 75–77.
73. Stapley and Wright, "A History of Baptism for Health," 108–110.
74. Amy Brown Lyman, "General Conference of Relief Society," *Relief Society Magazine* 8, no. 6 (June 1921): 342; Alice Louise Reynolds, "Susan West Smith," *Relief Society Magazine* 8, no. 12 (December 1926): 610.
75. See, for example, H. G. Richards, "A Brief Sketch of the Life of Levi W. Richards," *Juvenile Instructor* 49, no. 5 (May 1914): 302.
76. Emma Woodruff (wife of Wilford Woodruff), Sarah J. Cannon (George Q. Cannon), Margaret Y. Taylor (John Taylor), Lucy B. Young (Brigham Young), and Bathsheba W. Smith (George A. Smith) all served in the temple's early years of operation.
77. Devery S. Anderson, *The Development of LDS Temple Worship, 1846–2000* (Salt Lake City: Signature Books, 2011), 140, 212.

NOTES TO PAGES 105–113   201

78. "Circular of Instructions to Officers and Members of the Relief Society," *Relief Society Magazine* 2, no. 3 (March 1915): 114; Andrew Jenson, *Latter-day Saint Biographical Encyclopedia* (Salt Lake City: Deseret News, 1901), 1:30.

79. "Circular of Instructions to Officers and Members of the Relief Society," 114; "A Friend of the Helpless Dead," *Relief Society Magazine* 4, no. 9 (September 1917): 483–86.

80. Anderson, *The Development of LDS Temple Worship*, xviii; "Announce Changes in Heads Various Church Auxiliaries," *Deseret Evening News*, November 27, 1918; Lund, journal, November 27, 1918; Mary C. Kimball, "Alice Robinson Richards," *Relief Society Magazine* 19, no. 5 (May 1932): 261.

81. *Ninety-First Annual Conference of the Church of Jesus Christ of Latter-day Saints* (Salt Lake City: Deseret Book, 1921), 4.

82. "Guide Lessons," *Relief Society Magazine* 3, no. 3 (March 1916): 172.

83. Lund, journal, October 11, 1918, January 13, 1919.

84. *Ninety-Second Annual Conference of the Church of Jesus Christ of Latter-day Saints* (Salt Lake City: The Church of Jesus Christ of Latter-day Saints, 1922), 98; *Ninety-Sixth Annual Conference of the Church of Jesus Christ of Latter-day Saints* (Salt Lake City: The Church of Jesus Christ of Latter-day Saints, 1926), 3.

85. *Deseret News 2013 Church Almanac*, 212; "Population: Utah," in *Fourteenth Census of the United States: 1920, Bulletin* (Washington, DC: Government Printing Office, 1921), 2.

86. "Temple Notices," *Deseret News*, July 3, 1923; "Temple Additions Are Contemplated," *Ogden (UT) Standard-Examiner*, June 2, 1923. The renovations were nearly complete by the October 1923 general conference. See *Ninety-Fourth Semi-Annual Conference of the Church of Jesus Christ of Latter-day Saints* (Salt Lake City: The Church of Jesus Christ of Latter-day Saints, 1923), 6–7.

87. Doctrine and Covenants 109:12.

Chapter 6

1. Temple Square Mission Historical Record, 1902–42, 120, CHL.

2. J. Spencer Fluhman, "Secrets and the Making of Mormon Moments," in *Faith in the New Millennium: The Future of Religion and American Politics*, ed. Matthew Avery Sutton and Darren Dochuk (New York: Oxford University Press, 2016), 224.

3. Edward H. Anderson, "The Bureau of Information," *Improvement Era* 25 (December 1921): 137–39.

4. "A Mecca for Tourists," *Deseret News* (Salt Lake City), December 17, 1932.

5. Anderson, "Bureau of Information," 137–39; Glen M. Leonard, "Antiquities, Curiosities, and Latter-day Saint Museums," in *The Disciple as Witness: Essays in Honor of Richard Lloyd Anderson*, ed. Stephen D. Ricks, Donald W. Parry, and Andrew H. Hedges (Provo, UT: Foundation for Ancient Research and Mormon Studies, 2000), 310–11.

6. "On the Trail to the Golden Gate," *Baltimore Southern Methodist*, November 4, 1915, Temple Square Mission Historical Record, 43.

7. "Winter Does Not Stop Them. Each Season Brings Tourists to Temple Block," *Deseret News*, February 8, 1936.

8. Levi Edgar Young to President A. W. Ivins, February 16, 1929, folder 10, Bureau of Information Correspondence, 1923–29, CHL.

9. See, for example, Temple Square Mission Historical Record, 75.

10. Benjamin Goddard, "Bureau of Information and Church Literature," *Young Woman's Journal* 8, no. 11 (November 1902): 483–86.

11. Temple Square Mission Historical Record, 122–23.

12. Joseph J. Cannon, "Temple Square," *Temple Square Topics* 3, no. 9 (November 1939): 1.

13. "Letters and Tracts Serve as Successful Missionary Medium," *Deseret News*, March 3, 1934.

14. Pearl M. Fritz to Bureau of Information, February 15, 1936, box 2, folder 4, Bureau of Information Correspondence, 1936–43.

15. Pearl M. Fritz to Joseph S. Peery, March 10, 1936, box 2, folder 4, Bureau of Information Correspondence, 1936–43.

16. Pearl M. Fritz and Shallow Water to Joseph S. Peery, March 24, 1936, box 2, folder 4, Bureau of Information Correspondence, 1936–43.

17. Orson Rega Card, "The Temple Square Mission: A Foreign Mission at Home," *Improvement Era* 36 (July 1933): 517, 520.

202 NOTES TO PAGES 113–119

18. "Over 110,000 Tourists from All Parts of World Taste Hospitality of Temple Block during August," *Deseret News*, September 7, 1936.
19. Card, "Temple Square Mission," 517, 520; Portia Austin, "Observation by Worker at Temple Square Mission," *Deseret News*, April 18, 1936.
20. Richard L. Evans, in *One-Hundred Nineteenth Semi-Annual General Conference of the Church of Jesus Christ of Latter-day Saints* (Salt Lake City: The Church of Jesus Christ of Latter-day Saints, 1948), 64–65.
21. Ronald O. Barney and W. Randall Dixon, "Church Headquarters," in *Mapping Mormonism: An Atlas of Latter-day Saint History*, 2nd ed., ed. Brandon S. Plewe, S. Kent Brown, Donald Q. Cannon, and Richard H. Jackson (Provo, UT: BYU Press, 2014), 114–17.
22. "Temple Square Center Planned," *Deseret News and Salt Lake Telegram*, June 28, 1960.
23. Matthew Richardson, "Bertel Thorvaldsen's Christus: A Latter-day Saint Icon of Christian Evidence," in *Art and Spirituality: The Visual Culture of Christian Faith*, ed. Herman du Toit and Doris R. Dant (Provo, UT: BYU Studies, 2008), 189–201.
24. "Sparkle, Splendor on Temple Square," *Deseret News and Salt Lake Telegram*, December 8, 1965.
25. "Historic S. L. Sites Declared Landmarks," *Deseret News*, January 28, 1964.
26. Edward O. Anderson, "Salt Lake Temple," *Improvement Era* 66, no. 11 (November 1963): 1008; "Excavations Expose Depths of Temple Footings," *Church News* (Salt Lake City), March 30, 1963, 6.
27. Henry A. Smith, "S. L. Temple Additions Dedicated," *Deseret News*, May 21, 1963.
28. R. Douglas Brackenridge, "'About the Worst Man in Utah': William R. Campbell and the Crusade against Brigham H. Roberts, 1898–1900," *Journal of Mormon History* 39, no. 1 (Winter 2013): 68–157.
29. B. Carmon Hardy, *Solemn Covenant: The Mormon Polygamous Passage* (Urbana: University of Illinois Press, 1992), 206–309.
30. Kathleen Flake, *The Politics of American Religious Identity: The Seating of Senator Reed Smoot, Mormon Apostle* (Chapel Hill: The University of North Carolina Press, 2005), 2–11.
31. "Official Statement by President Joseph F. Smith," *Deseret Evening News* (Salt Lake City), April 6, 1904.
32. Michael Harold Paulos, ed., *The Mormon Church on Trial: Transcripts of the Reed Smoot Hearings* (Salt Lake City: Signature Books, 2008), 86–88, 160–161, 229–32.
33. Flake, *Politics of American Religious Identity*, 82–83.
34. Anthon H. Lund, journal, October 26, 1905, CHL; George F. Richards, journal, April 8, 1906, CHL.
35. George F. Richards, journal, July 21, 1909, CHL; "Joe Musser Has Now Taken No. 3," *Salt Lake Tribune*, August 8, 1909, 1; "New Polygamy Is Not Under the Ban," *Salt Lake Tribune*, August 15, 1909, 1.
36. Brian C. Hales, *Modern Polygamy and Mormon Fundamentalism* (Salt Lake City: Greg Kofford Books, 2006), 108.
37. Charles W. Penrose, journal, February 22, March 1, 28, 1911, CHL.
38. Penrose, journal, May 10, 11, 1911.
39. Burton J. Hendrick, "The Mormon Revival of Polygamy," *McClure's Magazine* 36, nos. 3–4 (January–February 1911): 245, 258, 461, 464; Kenneth L. Cannon II, "'And Now It Is the Mormons': The Magazine Crusade against the Mormon Church, 1910–1911," *Dialogue: A Journal of Mormon Thought* 46, no. 1 (Spring 2013): 1–63.
40. Alfred Henry Lewis, "The Viper on the Hearth," *Cosmopolitan Magazine* 50, no. 4 (March 1911): 439; Thomas G. Alexander, *Mormonism in Transition: A History of the Latter-day Saints, 1890–1930* (Urbana: University of Illinois Press, 1986), 70–72.
41. Lewis, "Viper on the Hearth," 445.
42. Alfred Henry Lewis, "The Viper's Trail of Gold," *Cosmopolitan Magazine* 50, no. 6 (May 1911): 823.
43. Lewis, "Viper's Trail of Gold," 831.
44. Kent Walgren, "Inside the Salt Lake Temple: Gisbert Bossard's 1911 Photographs," *Dialogue: A Journal of Mormon Thought* 29, no. 3 (Fall 1996): 1–43; Nelson B. Wadsworth, *Set in Stone, Fixed in Glass: The Great Mormon Temple and Its Photographers* (Salt Lake City: Signature Books, 1992), 355–78.
45. "Reveals the Conspiracy That Gained the Photographs," *Salt Lake Tribune*, September 18, 1911; Walgren, "Inside the Salt Lake Temple," 2.
46. Gary James Bergera, "'I'm Here for the Cash': Max Florence and the Great Mormon Temple," *Utah Historical Quarterly* 47, no. 1 (Winter 1979): 54–63.

NOTES TO PAGES 119–129   203

47. "Gilbert L. Bossard, Convert, Is Named as One Who Photographed Interior of Salt Lake Temple," *Salt Lake Tribune*, September 17, 1911; "Reveals the Conspiracy That Gained the Photographs."
48. "Photographs Secretly Taken of Mormon Temple's Interior; Sent for Sale to Church Chief," *Salt Lake Tribune*, September 16, 1911.
49. "Max Florence Sees Riches in Temple Views," *Salt Lake Tribune*, September 18, 1911.
50. "Max Florence Sees Riches in Temple Views."
51. "Church to Issue Book on Temples," *Deseret Evening News*, September 21, 1911; "Mormons to Issue Views," *New-York Tribune*, September 22, 1911.
52. James E. Talmage, journal, September 21–30, 1911, L. Tom Perry Special Collections, Brigham Young University, Provo, UT; Wadsworth, *Set in Stone, Fixed in Glass*, 366–69.
53. Walgren, "Inside the Salt Lake Temple," 7–9.
54. "Florence's Lecture a Dismal Failure," *Deseret Evening News*, November 13, 1911; Walgren, "Inside the Salt Lake Temple," 10–11.
55. Wadsworth, *Set in Stone, Fixed in Glass*, 371.
56. "Reveals the Conspiracy That Gained the Photographs."
57. "Max Florence Sees Riches in Temple Views."
58. "Talmage Book Ready," *Deseret Evening News*, September 28, 1912.
59. James E. Talmage, *The House of the Lord: A Study of Holy Sanctuaries Ancient and Modern* (Salt Lake City: The Deseret News, 1912), 294–95.
60. Talmage, *The House of the Lord*, 17.
61. Bradley Kime, "Exhibiting Theology: James E. Talmage and Mormon Public Relations, 1915–20," *Journal of Mormon History* 40, no. 1 (Winter 2014): 208–38.
62. Kime, "Exhibiting Theology," 219.
63. James E. Talmage, *The Vitality of Mormonism: An Address* (Salt Lake City: Deseret News, 1917), 8; Kime, "Exhibiting Theology," 220.

Chapter 7

1. "The American Religion: The Mormon Centenary and Utah," *Time*, April 7, 1930, 26–28, 30.
2. *The Message of the Ages: A Sacred Pageant Commemorating the One Hundredth Anniversary of the Organization of the Church of Jesus Christ of Latter-day Saints* (Salt Lake City: Heber J. Grant, 1930), 32.
3. Wilford Woodruff, George Q. Cannon, and Joseph F. Smith, "An Address to the Officers and Members of the Church of Jesus Christ of Latter-day Saints," March 18, 1893, [1], CHL.
4. Joseph F. Smith, in *Seventy-First Annual Conference of the Church of Jesus Christ of Latter-day Saints* (Salt Lake City: Deseret News, 1901), 69; Gary L. Boatright Jr., "'We Shall Have Temples Built': Joseph F. Smith and a New Era of Temple Building," in *Joseph F. Smith: Reflections on the Man and His Times*, ed. Craig K. Manscill, Brian D. Reeves, Guy L. Dorius, and J. B. Haws (Provo, UT: Religious Studies Center, Brigham Young University, 2013), 306.
5. Boatright, "'We Shall Have Temples Built,'" 303–19.
6. Boatright, "'We Shall Have Temples Built,'" 303–19.
7. The St. George Temple continued to set the precedent for temple worship even after the Salt Lake Temple's dedication for a time. When a procedural question about posthumous sealings was brought to President Wilford Woodruff and Joseph F. Smith in July 1893, they determined that what had been done in the Endowment House and the St. George Temple "should prevail in all the Temples," including the Salt Lake Temple. Marriner W. Merrill, journal, July 12, 1893, CHL.
8. Devery S. Anderson, *The Development of LDS Temple Worship, 1846–2000: A Documentary History* (Salt Lake City: Signature Books, 2011), 159.
9. Anthon H. Lund, journal, January 10, February 28, 1911, CHL.
10. For more on George F. Richards as temple president, see Dale C. Mouritsen, "A Symbol of New Directions: George Franklin Richards and the Mormon Church, 1861–1950" (PhD diss., Brigham Young University, 1982), 198–215.
11. Anderson, *Development of LDS Temple Worship*, 211–12.
12. Anderson, *Development of LDS Temple Worship*, 196.
13. Anderson, *Development of LDS Temple Worship*, 208–9.
14. Anderson, *Development of LDS Temple Worship*, 208–9.
15. Anderson, *Development of LDS Temple Worship*, 211.
16. Mouritsen, "Symbol of New Directions," 213–15.

204 NOTES TO PAGES 129–139

17. Brigham Young, "The Temple Corner Stones—The Apostleship," in *Journal of Discourses*, 26 vols. (Liverpool: F. D. Richards, 1855–86), 1:134–35.
18. James E. Talmage, *The House of the Lord: A Study of Holy Sanctuaries Ancient and Modern* (Salt Lake City: The Church of Jesus Christ of Latter-day Saints, 1912).
19. Talmage, *House of the Lord*, 181–94.
20. Talmage, *House of the Lord*, 194–200. The Main Assembly Room filled the entire fourth floor of the structure; on both ends of the room were terraced platforms with pulpits, just like in the Kirtland, Nauvoo, and St. George temples.
21. W. Keith Warner, "Council of the First Presidency and the Quorum of the Twelve Apostles," in *Encyclopedia of Mormonism*, ed. Daniel H. Ludlow (New York: Macmillan, 1992), 1:327.
22. N. Eldon Tanner, "The Administration of the Church," *Ensign*, November 1979, 47–48.
23. "The Solemn Assembly," *Deseret Evening News* (Salt Lake City), July 3, 1899; Lund, journal, July 2, 1899.
24. Francis M. Gibbons, *George Albert Smith: Kind and Caring Christian, Prophet of God* (Salt Lake City: Deseret Book, 1990), 272–73; see also Harold B. Lee, in *One Hundred Twenty-First Semi-annual Conference of the Church of Jesus Christ of Latter-day Saints* (Salt Lake City: The Church of Jesus Christ of Latter-day Saints, 1950), 131–32.
25. Joseph F. Smith, in *Eighty-Ninth Semi-Annual Conference of the Church of Jesus Christ of Latter-day Saints* (Salt Lake City: Deseret News, 1918), 2; Joseph Fielding Smith, *Life of Joseph F. Smith: Sixth President of The Church of Jesus Christ of Latter-day Saints* (Salt Lake City: Deseret Book, 1969), 466.
26. James E. Talmage, journal, October 31, 1918, L. Tom Perry Special Collections, Harold B. Lee Library, Brigham Young University, Provo, UT; see also Lund, journal, October 31, 1918.
27. "The Sustaining of Church Officers," *Ensign*, May 1976, 19.
28. "Additions to D&C Approved," *Church News*, June 2, 1979, 3.
29. Eduardo Balderas, "Northward to Mesa," *Ensign*, September 1972, 30–33.
30. Sheri Dew, *Go Forward with Faith: The Biography of Gordon B. Hinckley* (Salt Lake City: Deseret Book, 1996), 176–78.
31. J. B. Haws, *The Mormon Image in the American Mind: Fifty Years of Public Perception* (New York: Oxford University Press, 2013), 31.
32. L. L. Rado to Harold W. Burton, September 28, 1962, folder 4, New York World's Fair Committee Subject Files, 1961–65, CHL.
33. L. L. Rado to Harold W. Burton, October 9, 1962, folder 4, New York World's Fair Committee Subject Files.
34. GSM to L. L. Rado, November 13, 1962, folder 4, New York World's Fair Committee Subject Files.
35. David W. Evans to Irene Staples, October 16, 1975, in "The Mormon Pavilion at the New York World's Fair, 1964–65," Irene Edwards Staples Scrapbook, CHL.
36. George Capeis to David W. Evans, November 20, 1962, folder 4, New York World's Fair Committee Subject Files.
37. Nathaniel Smith Kogan, "The Mormon Pavilion: Mainstreaming the Saints at the New York World's Fair, 1964–65," *Journal of Mormon History* 35, no. 4 (Fall 2009): 37–43.
38. Kogan, "Mormon Pavilion," 45–50.
39. Joshua M. Matson, "Where the World, Babel, and Zion Meet: Redefining the Mormon People at the 1964–65 Mormon Pavilion," *Journal of Mormon History* 44, no. 3 (July 2018): 111.

Chapter 8

1. E. Dale LeBaron, "Anthony U. Obinna," in *Encyclopedia of Latter-day Saint History*, ed. Arnold K. Garr, Donald Q. Cannon, and Richard O. Cowan (Salt Lake City: Deseret Book, 2000), 862–63.
2. Anthony Uzodimma Obinna, "Voice from Nigeria," *Ensign*, December 1980, 30.
3. See Russell W. Stevenson, "The Celestial City: 'Mormonism' and American Identity in Post-Independence Nigeria," *African Studies Review* 63, no. 2 (June 2020): 304–330.
4. Obinna, "Voice from Nigeria," 30; see also Fidelia Obinna, interview by Anthonia C. Nwachukwu, March 8, 2010, transcript, 1–3, CHL; Rendell N. Mabey and Gordon T. Allred, *Brother to Brother: The Story of the Latter-day Saint Missionaries Who Took the Gospel to Black Africa* (Salt Lake City: Bookcraft, 1984), 34–37.
5. Obinna, "Voice from Nigeria," 30.
6. Obinna, "Voice from Nigeria," 30.

NOTES TO PAGES 140–145   205

7. Gregory L. Prince and Wm. Robert Wright, *David O. McKay and the Rise of Modern Mormonism* (Salt Lake City: University of Utah Press, 2005), 81–94.

8. W. Paul Reeve, *Religion of a Different Color: Race and the Mormon Struggle for Whiteness* (Salt Lake City: Oxford University Press, 2015).

9. J. B. Haws, *The Mormon Image in the American Mind: Fifty Years of Public Perception* (New York: Oxford University Press, 2013), 18.

10. Richard S. Van Wagoner, *The Complete Discourses of Brigham Young*, vol. 1 (Salt Lake City: Smith-Pettit Foundation, 2009), 468; Reeve, *Religion of a Different Color*, 155.

11. Quincy D. Newell, *Your Sister in the Gospel: The Life of Jane Manning James, a Nineteenth-Century Black Mormon* (New York: Oxford University Press, 2019), 105.

12. Newell, *Your Sister in the Gospel*, 106–7; Reeve, *Religion of a Different Color*, 202; Newell, "Jane Manning James."

13. Newell, *Your Sister in the Gospel*, 113–14.

14. Jonathan A. Stapley, "Adoptive Sealing Ritual in Mormonism," *Journal of Mormon History* 37, no. 3 (Summer 2011): 107–12.

15. Newell, *Your Sister in the Gospel*, 115; Reeve, *Religion of a Different Color*, 202.

16. George Q. Cannon, journal, August 22, 1895, CHL.

17. Council minutes, January 2, 1902, George A. Smith Family Papers, Special Collections, J. Willard Marriott Library, University of Utah, Salt Lake City; Reeve, *Religion of a Different Color*, 207.

18. Jeremy Talmage and Clinton D. Christensen, "Black, White, or Brown? Racial Perceptions and the Priesthood Policy in Latin America," *Journal of Mormon History* 44, no. 1 (January 2018): 119–45.

19. Max Perry Mueller, "The Pageantry of Protest in Temple Square," in *Out of Obscurity: Mormonism since 1945*, ed. Patrick Q. Mason and John G. Turner (New York: Oxford University Press, 2016), 125, 132–37; Armand L. Mauss, *All Abraham's Children: Changing Mormon Conceptions of Race and Lineage* (Urbana: University of Illinois Press, 2003), 232–35.

20. Prince and Wright, *David O. McKay and the Rise of Modern Mormonism*, 69–70; *One Hundred Thirty-Third Semi-Annual General Conference of The Church of Jesus Christ of Latter-day Saints* (Salt Lake City: The Church of Jesus Christ of Latter-day Saints, 1963), 91.

21. Newell G. Bringhurst, *Saints, Slaves, and Blacks: The Changing Place of Black People within Mormonism* (Westport, CT: Greenwood Press, 1981), 181.

22. Johnie M. Driver, quoted in Matthew L. Harris, "Martin Luther King, Civil Rights, and Perceptions of a 'Communist Conspiracy,'" in *Thunder from the Right: Ezra Taft Benson in Mormonism and Politics*, ed. Matthew L. Harris (Urbana: University of Illinois Press, 2019), 133.

23. Haws, *Mormon Image in the American Mind*, 47–71.

24. "Blast Damages S. L. Temple—Believed Work of Vandals," *Deseret News* (Salt Lake City), November 14, 1962; Jim G. Baldwin, "Blast Damages Temple in S. L.," *Salt Lake Tribune*, November 15, 1962; "Temple Blast Continues as Mystery," *Salt Lake Tribune*, November 16, 1962; "Detonation of Plastic Explosive Damages Front Door of Salt Lake Temple," *Church News* (Salt Lake City), November 17, 1962.

25. Prince and Wright, *David O. McKay and the Rise of Modern Mormonism*, 72.

26. Harris, "Martin Luther King," 138.

27. Armand L. Mauss, *The Angel and the Beehive: The Mormon Struggle with Assimilation* (Urbana: University of Illinois Press, 1994), 211–12. Current First Presidency member Dallin H. Oaks, who was president of Brigham Young University during the 1970s, recently reflected on the effects of the race-based restriction: "I observed the pain and frustration experienced by those who suffered these restrictions and those who criticized them and sought for reasons. I studied the reasons then being given and could not feel confirmation of the truth of any of them. . . . I determined to be loyal to our prophetic leaders and to pray—as promised from the beginning of these restrictions—that the day would come when all would enjoy the blessings of priesthood and temple." "President Oaks' Full Remarks from the LDS Church's 'Be One' Celebration," *Church News*, June 1, 2018.

28. Edward L. Kimball, "Spencer W. Kimball and the Revelation on the Priesthood," *BYU Studies* 47, no. 2 (2008): 46–57.

29. *One Hundred Forty-Eighth Semi-Annual Conference of the Church of Jesus Christ of Latter-day Saints* (Salt Lake City: The Church of Jesus Christ of Latter-day Saints, 1978), 22; Doctrine and Covenants, Official Declaration 2.

30. Kimball, "Spencer W. Kimball and the Revelation on the Priesthood," 67–76.

206 NOTES TO PAGES 145–154

31. Kimball, "Spencer W. Kimball and the Revelation on the Priesthood," 69.
32. Anthony U. Obinna, Francis I. Obinna, and Raymond I. Obinna to the First Presidency, December 1, 1978, Edwin Q. Cannon Papers, CHL, quoted in Obinna, "Voice from Nigeria," 30.
33. Haws, *The Mormon Image in the American Mind*, 79–80.
34. Quoted in Haws, *The Mormon Image in the American Mind*, 79–80; Heber G. Wolsey, interview, Salt Lake City, 1979, CHL.
35. "Marketing the Mormon Image: An Interview with Wendell J. Ashton," *Dialogue: A Journal of Mormon Thought* 10, no. 3 (Spring 1977): 15; Haws, *The Mormon Image in the American Mind*, 79.
36. For more on Benson's association with far-right politics, see Robert A. Goldberg, "From New Deal to New Right," in Harris, *Thunder from the Right*, 68–96.
37. Edward L. Kimball, *Lengthen Your Stride: The Presidency of Spencer W. Kimball* (Salt Lake City: Deseret Book, 2005), 177–178; Haws, *The Mormon Image in the American Mind*, 88–89.
38. First Presidency of The Church of Jesus Christ of Latter-day Saints, "Reaffirmation of the First Presidency's Position on ERA," August 24, 1978, CHL.
39. Haws, *The Mormon Image in the American Mind*, 88.
40. Ben Ling, "Signs Back ERA at LDS Meet," *Salt Lake Tribune*, April 5, 1981.
41. Kelli N. Morrill, "From Housewives to Protesters: The Story of Mormons for the Equal Rights Amendment" (master's thesis, Utah State University, 2018), 26.
42. Deana Lloyd and Bob Sallander, "3 ERA Supporters Refuse to Accept Church Prophet as 'Political Leader,' " *Daily Universe* (Provo, UT), October 6, 1980.
43. "Signs Back ERA at LDS Meet."
44. "Statues' Replicas Are Made," *Church News*, March 31, 1979.
45. "The Role of Womanhood to Be Depicted in Relief Society Monument," *Ensign*, March 1976, 79; Janet Brigham, "News of the Church: Nauvoo Monument to Women," *Ensign*, September 1978, 75.

Chapter 9

1. Russell M. Nelson, "Spencer W. Kimball: Man of Faith," *Ensign*, December 1985, 40.
2. Spencer W. Kimball, journal, April 9, 1972, CHL.
3. Susan Sessions Rugh, *Are We There Yet? The Golden Age of American Family Vacations* (Lawrence: University of Kansas Press, 2008), 5.
4. "Extensive Renovation Begins on S.L. Temple," *Deseret News and Salt Lake Telegram*, August 18, 1962; "LDS Church Now Engaged in Record Building Program," *Daily Herald* (Provo, UT), October 4, 1962.
5. "Temple Dates Closing June 29," *Deseret News and Salt Lake Telegram*, March 8, 1962.
6. "Extensive Renovation Begins on S.L. Temple."
7. "Digging Uncovers S.L. Temple Footings," *Deseret News and Salt Lake Telegram*, September 6, 1962.
8. Henry A. Smith, "Pres. McKay Officiates at Special Rites in Salt Lake Temple," *Deseret News and Salt Lake Telegram*, May 25, 1963.
9. "Notice of S.L. Temple Opening," *Deseret News and Salt Lake Telegram*, May 18, 1963; Smith, "Pres. McKay Officiates at Special Rites in Salt Lake Temple."
10. New landscaping was installed around the square once excavation and below-grade construction was completed in 1965. "A New Fall Dress," *Deseret News* (Salt Lake City), September 25, 1965.
11. David W. Evans, quoted in Brent L. Top, "The Mormon Pavilion at the 1964–1965 New York World's Fair," in *An Eye of Faith: Essays in Honor of Richard O. Cowan*, ed. Kenneth L. Alford and Richard E. Bennett (Provo, UT: Religious Studies Center, Brigham Young University, 2015), 341–42.
12. Glen M. Leonard, "Antiquities, Curiosities, and Latter-day Saint Museums," in *The Disciple as Witness: Essays on Latter-day Saint History and Doctrine in Honor of Richard Lloyd Anderson*, ed. Stephen D. Ricks, Donald W. Parry, and Andrew H. Hedges (Salt Lake City: Deseret Book, 2002), 313.
13. Hal Knight, "Library, Museum to Be Built," *Church News*, August 16, 1980, 3, 6.
14. "LDS Leader Dedicated New Visitors Center," *Salt Lake Tribune*, June 2, 1978.
15. Francis M. Gibbons, "Dedicatory Services, Visitors Center South, Temple Square, Salt Lake City, Utah, June 1, 1978," 11, CHL.

NOTES TO PAGES 155–160   207

16. Jill W. Knapp, "The Pilgrimage Phenomenon: An Analysis of the Motivations of Visitors to Temple Square" (master's thesis, Brigham Young University, 1989), 52–53, 55–67; see also Sherrie Lee Martin Wood, "A Geographic Investigation into the Purpose and Motivation of Nonresident Tourist Visits to Temple Square" (master's thesis, University of Utah, 1980). According to Knapp's 1988 survey, the vast majority (69 percent) of guests to Temple Square had visited before, and of those, 39 percent had been there at least six times previously. Most of the first-time guests identified as nonreligionists, Catholics, and Protestants. When asked what they liked most about Temple Square, they responded as follows: appearance (37 percent), feeling/atmosphere (13 percent), Tabernacle and choir (11 percent), guides and tours (6 percent), visitors' centers (2 percent), and friendly people (1 percent). Knapp, "Pilgrimage Phenomenon," 69–86.

17. Don C. Woodward, "Multi-Million Dollar Project—ZCMI Plans Downtown Mall in Dramatic New Expansion," *Deseret News*, May 27, 1969; "Plans for ZCMI Mall Will Be Ready April 15," *Deseret News*, March 9, 1971; "ZCMI Center Open for Business," *Deseret News*, July 17, 1975.

18. G. Homer Durham, *N. Eldon Tanner: His Life and Service* (Salt Lake City: Deseret Book, 1982), 208–9.

19. Woodward, "Multi-Million Dollar Project."

20. Lisa Scharoun, *America at the Mall: The Cultural Roll of a Retail Utopia* (Jefferson, NC: McFarland, 2012), 49.

21. "How to Revitalize a Core Area: S. L. Plan," *Deseret News*, May 28, 1969.

22. Scharoun, *America at the Mall*, 46–55; Ira G. Zepp, *The New Religious Image of Urban America: The Shopping Mall as Ceremonial Center* (Westminster, MD: Christian Classics, 1986).

23. Gregory L. Prince and Wm. Robert Wright, *David O. McKay and the Rise of Modern Mormonism* (Salt Lake City: University of Utah Press, 2005), 269.

24. Prince and Wright, *David O. McKay and the Rise of Modern Mormonism*, 270.

25. Keith W. Wilcox, *A Personal Testimony concerning the Washington Temple* (Salt Lake City: n.p.), [2]–[8], CHL; "New Temple Design," *Evening Star* (Washington, DC), April 14, 1968.

26. "2,500 Attend Dedication Rites for Site of LDS Temple in East," *Salt Lake Tribune*, December 8, 1968.

27. Richard O. Cowan, "Washington D.C. Temple," in *Encyclopedia of Latter-day Saint History*, ed. Arnold K. Garr, Donald Q. Cannon, and Richard O. Cowan (Salt Lake City: Deseret Book, 2000), 1315; see also Richard O. Cowan, *Temples to Dot the Earth* (Salt Lake City: Bookcraft, 1989), 174–78.

28. Spencer W. Kimball, "We Feel an Urgency," *Ensign*, August 1980, 2.

29. Richard O. Cowan, *The Church in the Twentieth Century* (Salt Lake City: Bookcraft, 1985), 369–71; "Temples of the Church," in *Deseret News 2013 Church Almanac* (Salt Lake City: Deseret News, 2013), 217–18.

30. Samuel Ross Palfreyman, "The Landscape of Modern Mormonism: Understanding The Church of Jesus Christ of Latter-day Saints through Its Twentieth-Century Architecture" (PhD diss., Boston University, 2020), 77.

31. Mark L. Grover, "The Mormon Priesthood Revelation and the Sao Paulo, Brazil Temple," *Dialogue: A Journal of Mormon Thought* 23 (Spring 1990): 51.

32. Kimball, "We Feel an Urgency," 2.

33. Cowan, *Church in the Twentieth Century*, 372.

34. "Temples of the Church," 217–18.

35. "100 Million Endowments Performed for the Dead," *Ensign*, November 1988, 111.

36. Kahlile B. Mehr, "How Much of the Human Family Has Had Its Temple Work Done?," *Ensign*, March 1997, 73.

37. See Joseph Fielding Smith, *Doctrines of Salvation*, comp. Bruce R. McConkie (Salt Lake City: Bookcraft, 1955), 2:167–68, 251–52.

38. Heather A. Maile, interview, Carlingford, New South Wales, Australia, March 1, 2018, CHL.

39. Queenie P. K. Chew, interview, Singapore, September 20, 1996, CHL.

40. Some members received direct help from Latter-day Saints to visit the Salt Lake Temple. Frank Talley, a wealthy American businessman who resided in Puerto Rico, used his personal airplane to fly converts to Salt Lake City in the 1970s and 1980s to receive temple ordinances and to experience general conference for the first time. See Clinton D. Christensen, "Senior Missionaries in the Caribbean: Opening the Islands of the Sea, 1978–90," in *Go Ye into All the World: The Growth and Development of Mormon Missionary Work*, ed. Reid L. Neilson and Fred E. Woods (Provo, UT: Religious Studies Center, 2012), 425–44; Miguel A. Alvarado and Iris Emma Pazo interview, Puerto Rico, March 1, 2015, CHL.

208 NOTES TO PAGES 161–170

41. Marion D. Hanks, "Salt Lake Temple," in *Encyclopedia of Mormonism*, ed. Daniel H. Ludlow (New York: Macmillan, 1992), 3:1254; see also "Salt Lake Temple," *Ensign*, January 1978, 80.
42. See, for example, Walter H. and Lida L. Pierce, interview, Nauvoo, IL, August 15, 2016, CHL; Gilbert Blue, interview, Rock Hill, SC, March 2, 2014.
43. Brandon S. Plewe, S. Kent Brown, Donald Q. Cannon, and Richard H. Jackson, eds., *Mapping Mormonism: An Atlas of Latter-day Saint History* (Provo, UT: BYU Press, 2014), 174.
44. *Wonders of the World: A Guide to the Masterworks of Civilization* (Chicago: Rand McNally, 1991), 6, 164–65.
45. "Salt Lake Temple One of World's Wonders," *Ensign*, June 1993, 79.
46. Hanks, "Salt Lake Temple," 3:1252–54; see also "Salt Lake Temple," *Ensign*, 80.
47. Loren C. Dunn, "The Temple Is the 'Heart of Sacred Work,'" *Church News*, February 6, 1993, 3, 12.
48. "Salt Lake Temple Prepared for Anniversary," *Ensign*, October 1991, 78; "A Temple Renewed," *Ensign*, March 1993, 42–43.
49. Thomas S. Monson, "The Temple of the Lord," *Ensign*, May 1993, 4.
50. Boyd K. Packer, "The Temple, the Priesthood," *Ensign*, May 1993, 18–20.
51. Julie A. Dockstader, "The Mountain of the Lord: Film Dramatizes Struggle of Saints to Build Temples," *Church News*, March 20, 1993, 8–9.
52. *One Hundred Sixty-Third Annual General Conference of the Church of Jesus Christ of Latter-day Saints* (Salt Lake City: The Church of Jesus Christ of Latter-day Saints, 1993), 89.
53. *One Hundred Sixty-Third Annual General Conference of the Church of Jesus Christ of Latter-day Saints*, 92–93.
54. "The Spirit of God," in *Hymns of The Church of Jesus Christ of Latter-day Saints* (Salt Lake City: The Church of Jesus Christ of Latter-day Saints, 1985), no. 2.

Chapter 10

1. Sheri L. Dew, *Go Forward with Faith: The Biography of Gordon B. Hinckley* (Salt Lake City: Deseret Book, 1996), 537–38.
2. Latter-day Saint leaders often refer to the collective church as "a peculiar people," borrowing from the biblical usage of the term: "But ye are a chosen generation, a royal priesthood, an holy nation, a peculiar people" (1 Peter 2:9).
3. Howard W. Hunter, "Exceeding Great and Precious Promises," *Ensign*, November 1994, 8.
4. J. B. Haws, *The Mormon Image in the American Mind: Fifty Years of Public Perception* (New York: Oxford University Press, 2013), 263.
5. Kenneth L. Woodward, "A Mormon Moment," *Newsweek*, September 10, 2001, 44.
6. Ana Figueroa, "Salt Lake's Big Jump," *Newsweek*, September 10, 2001, 52.
7. Julie Cart, "Mormons to Let the Games Reign," *Los Angeles Times*, January 13, 2002.
8. J. B. Haws, "Why the 'Mormon Olympics' Didn't Happen," in *An Eye of Faith: Essays in Honor of Richard O. Cowan*, ed. Kenneth L. Alford and Richard E. Bennett (Provo, UT: Religious Studies Center, Brigham Young University, 2015), 365–87; *Welcome* [Friends to All Nations] (Salt Lake City: The Church of Jesus Christ of Latter-day Saints, 2001).
9. Hank Stuever, "Unmentionable No Longer: What Do Mormons Wear? A Polite Smile, If Asked about 'the Garment,'" *Washington Post*, February 26, 2002.
10. Peggy Fletcher Stack, "The 'Mormon' Olympics That Weren't," *Salt Lake Tribune*, February 24, 2012.
11. Stuever, "Unmentionable No Longer"; Haws, *Mormon Image in the American Mind*, 174.
12. Jan Shipps, "Spinning Gold: Mormonism and the Olympic Games," *Dialogue: A Journal of Mormon Thought* 36, no. 1 (Spring 2003): 137.
13. Stuever, "Unmentionable No Longer."
14. Cart, "Mormons to Let the Games Reign."
15. *Official Report of the XIX Olympic Winter Games: Salt Lake City 2002* (Salt Lake City: SLOC, 2002), 104; Cart, "Mormons to Let the Games Reign."
16. Gordon B. Hinckley, "The Church Goes Forward," *Ensign*, May 2002, 6.
17. Robert D. Hales, "Out of Darkness into His Marvelous Light," *Ensign*, May 2002, 69. Apostle Henry B. Eyring made similar comments to the media. See Tim Dahlberg, "Sparking an Old Flame," *Chicago Sun-Times*, January 27, 2002.
18. Max Perry Mueller, "The Pageantry of Protest in Temple Square," in *Out of Obscurity: Mormonism since 1945*, ed. Patrick Q. Mason and John G. Turner (New York: Oxford University Press, 2016), 125.

NOTES TO PAGES 170–176 **209**

19. *Realizing a Vision: The New Church Plaza* (Salt Lake City: The Church of Jesus Christ of Latter-day Saints, 2002), 1.
20. *Realizing a Vision*, 1.
21. *Realizing a Vision*, 2.
22. *Realizing a Vision*, 2.
23. *Realizing a Vision*, 3.
24. ACLU Utah, "ACLU Returns to Court in Controversy over Free Speech in Salt Lake City's 'Main Street Plaza,'" December 5, 2005, https://www.aclu.org/press-releases.
25. ACLU Utah, "First Unitarian Church v. Salt Lake City Corporation (2003)," July 28, 2003, https://www.acluutah.org.
26. ACLU Utah, "First Unitarian Church v. Salt Lake City Corporation (2003)"; Richard Piatt, "LDS Church Takes Control of Main Street Plaza," KSL.com, July 28, 2003, https://www.ksl.com/arti cle/89752/lds-church-takes-control-of-main-st-plaza; Josh Loftin and Brady Snyder, "Main St. Plaza Deal Done," *Deseret News* (Salt Lake City), July 29, 2003.
27. ACLU Utah, "ACLU Returns to Court in Controversy over Free Speech."
28. Rosemary Winters, "LDS Church Posts Tougher Signs on Plaza," *Salt Lake Tribune*, September 28, 2009.
29. Mueller, "Pageantry of Protest in Temple Square," 140.
30. Joseph Walker, "LDS Church Responds to Priesthood Meeting Request by Activists," *Deseret News*, September 24, 2013; Whitney Evans and Carole Mikita, "Debate over LDS Women's Roles Spotlighted in Protest," KSL.com, October 5, 2013, https://www.ksl.com/article/27133 883/debate-over-lds-womens-roles-spotlighted-in-protest.
31. Whitney Evans, "Women Seeking Priesthood March Again to Temple Square," *Deseret News*, April 5, 2014.
32. Mueller, "Pageantry of Protest in Temple Square," 142–43.
33. Dell Van Orden, "Inspiration Came for Smaller Temples on Trip to Mexico," *Church News* (Salt Lake City), August 1, 1998; see also R. Scott Lloyd, "Temples Have Proliferated in 20 Years since Smaller Design Announced," *Church News*, March 22, 2017.
34. Scott Taylor, "Construction of Mormon Temples Boomed in Past 30 Years," *Deseret News*, May 28, 2010; Gordon B. Hinckley, "New Temples to Provide 'Crowning Blessings' of the Gospel," general conference address, Salt Lake City, April 1998, https://www.churchofjesuschrist.org/ study/general-conference/1998/04/new-temples-to-provide-crowning-blessings-of-the-gospel.
35. Shaun D. Stahle, "Boston Temple Will Be Ready for Dedication—as No. 100," *Church News*, September 25, 2000; Shaun D. Stahle, "Picture-Perfect Temple Dedication in Boston: Striking Edifice Is Ready for Ordinances; But Still No Steeple," *Deseret News*, October 2, 2000.
36. Hunter, "Exceeding Great and Precious Promises."
37. Gordon B. Hinckley, "Of Missions, Temples, and Stewardship," general conference address, Salt Lake City, October 1995, https://www.churchofjesuschrist.org/study/general-conference/ 1995/10/of-missions-temples-and-stewardship.
38. Russell M. Nelson, "Personal Preparation for Temple Blessings," general conferences address, Salt Lake City, April 2001, https://www.churchofjesuschrist.org/study/general-conference/ 2001/04/personal-preparation-for-temple-blessings; 1 Nephi 14:4.
39. Margaret D. Nadauld, "Hold High the Torch," general conference address, Salt Lake City, April 2002, https://www.churchofjesuschrist.org/study/general-conference/2002/04/ hold-high-the-torch.
40. "Making Progress," *New Era* 32, no. 1 (January 2002): 18.
41. "Set Your Sights," *New Era* 32, no. 5 (May 2002): 19; "Dream Date," *New Era* 34, no. 10 (October 2004): 19; "Best Friends Forever," *New Era* 40, no. 3 (March 2008): 17.
42. In at least one documented instance, the Salt Lake Temple was actually mistaken for a Disney castle. See Herb Scribner, "This 'Beauty and the Beast' Phone Case Went Viral for Having the Salt Lake Temple on It," *Deseret News*, August 17, 2018.
43. Dieter F. Uchtdorf, "Your Happily Ever After," general conference address, Salt Lake City, April 2010, https://www.lds.org/general-conference/2010/04.
44. Uchtdorf, "Your Happily Ever After"; see also Salt Lake Temple photo canvas wrap and "Princess Castle Temple Quote Salt Lake City Utah LDS Temple Custom Canvas Wrap," Etsy, www.etsy.com.
45. *Deseret News 2012 Church Almanac* (Salt Lake City: Deseret News, 2012), 205; Pew Research Center, "America's Changing Religious Landscape," Religion and Public Life, May 12, 2015, 21, 39, 50, https://www.pewforum.org/2015/05/12/americas-changing-religious-landscape/.

210 NOTES TO PAGES 176–182

46. Laurie Goodstein, "Some Mormons Search the Web and Find Doubt," *New York Times*, July 20, 2013; Peggy Fletcher Stack, "In This New Era of Doubt, Will a Stronger Mormon Faith Emerge," *Salt Lake Tribune*, March 11, 2016.
47. NPR, "Transcript: Mitt Romney's Faith Speech," December 6, 2007, https://www.npr.org/templates/story/story.php?storyId=16969460; Matthew L. Bowman, *The Mormon People: The Making of an American Faith* (New York: Random House, 2012), 226–28.
48. Noah Feldman, "What Is It about Mormonism," *New York Times Magazine*, January 6, 2008.
49. Feldman, "What Is It about Mormonism."
50. J. Spencer Fluhman, "Secrets and the Making of Mormon Moments," in *Faith in the New Millennium: The Future of Religion and American Politics*, ed. Matthew Avery Sutton and Darren Dochuk (New York: Oxford University Press, 2016), 221–24.
51. "Romney's Mormon Faith Takes Center Stage," *Wall Street Journal*, August 29, 2012; ABC News, "Mitt Romney, Jon Huntsman 2012: Mormon Church in Spotlight," August 3, 2011, https://www.youtube.com/watch?v=GGb-mR8wajE.
52. PBS, "The Mormons," *Frontline*, directed by Helen Whitney, 2007, transcript, https://www.pbs.org/mormons/etc/script.html; video, https://www.pbs.org/video/frontline-the-mormons-part-one/.
53. Kenneth L. Woodward, "The Presidency's Mormon Moment," *New York Times*, April 9, 2007.
54. Ben Winslow, "LDS Church Critical of Media Reports on FLDS," *Deseret News*, April 12, 2008.
55. CNN, "Polygamist Prophet Preaches from Jail," July 27, 2011, video, https://www.youtube.com/watch?v=qL4cQcXgbuQ; Carrie A. Moore, "Media Get a Big 'F' for Stories on FLDS," *Deseret News*, May 12, 2006.
56. Matt Bowman, "The Temple and 'Big Love': Mormonism and American Culture," *Patheos*, June 22, 2009, https://www.patheos.com/resources/additional-resources/2009/06/the-temple-and-big-love-06222009.aspx.
57. "A Mormon Responds to Proposition 8," *Vanity Fair*, November 17, 2008; PBS, "Mormons and Proposition 8," *Religion and Ethics Newsweekly*, May 22, 2009, https://www.pbs.org/wnet/religionandethics/2009/05/22/may-22-2009-mormons-and-proposition-8/3019/; Sarah Pulliam Bailey, "Mormon Church to Allow Baptisms, Blessings for Children of LGBT Parents, Reversing 2015 Policy," *Washington Post*, April 4, 2019.
58. John G. Turner, "Why Race Is Still a Problem for Mormons," *New York Times*, August 18, 2012; ABC News, "Inside the Mormon Church," August 22, 2012, video, https://www.youtube.com/watch?v=ytYpcUmQPRk; Peter Henderson, "Insight: Mormon Church Made Wealthy by Donations," Reuters, August 12, 2012, https://www.reuters.com/article/us-usa-politics-mormons/insight-mormon-church-made-wealthy-by-donations-idUSBRE87B05W20120812.
59. Kurtis Lee, "Mormon Church Ramps Up Opposition to Medical Marijuana Effort in Utah, Speaking Out Publicly," *Los Angeles Times*, August 23, 2018.
60. Scott Taylor, "Replica Exhibit Lets Visitors Explore Salt Lake Temple," *Church News*, May 28, 2010.
61. The Church of Jesus Christ of Latter-day Saints, "Scaled Model Provides Salt Lake Temple Open House Experience," Newsroom, May 28, 2010, https://newsroom.churchofjesuschrist.org/article/scaled-model-provides-salt-lake-temple-open-house-experience.
62. The Church of Jesus Christ of Latter-day Saints, "Temple Garments," Newsroom, accessed November 11, 2019, https://newsroom.churchofjesuschrist.org/article/temple-garments.
63. Church of Jesus Christ Temples, "About," accessed November 11, 2019, https://churchofjesuschristtemples.org/about/.
64. The Church of Jesus Christ of Latter-day Saints, "Are Mormons Christian," Gospel Topics Essays, accessed November 11, 2019, https://www.churchofjesuschrist.org/study/manual/gospel-topics-essays/christians; John G. Turner, *The Mormon Jesus: A Biography* (Cambridge, MA: Harvard University Press, 2016), 292–93.
65. Russell M. Nelson, "Opening the Heavens for Help," *Liahona* 44, no. 5 (May 2020): 72–74.
66. John G. Turner, *The Mormon Jesus: A Biography* (Cambridge, MA: Belknap Press of Harvard University Press, 2016), 288–93.
67. Stephen H. Webb, "Mormonism Obsessed with Christ," *First Things* (blog), February 2012, https://www.firstthings.com/article/2012/02/mormonism-obsessed-with-christ.
68. Armand L. Mauss, *The Angel and the Beehive: The Mormon Struggle with Assimilation* (Urbana: University of Illinois Press, 1994), 3–4.
69. Bowman, *The Mormon People*, xix; Jan Shipps, *Mormonism: The Story of a New Religious Tradition* (Urbana: University of Illinois Press, 1985), 38, 127.

NOTES TO PAGES 182–185   211

70. Turner, *The Mormon Jesus*, 17–18, 215.
71. Russell M. Nelson, "Becoming Exemplary Latter-day Saints," general conference address, Salt Lake City, October 2018, https://www.churchofjesuschrist.org/study/general-conference/2018/10/becoming-exemplary-latter-day-saints.
72. Russell M. Nelson, "Closing Remarks," general conference address, Salt Lake City, April 2019, https://www.churchofjesuschrist.org/study/general-conference/2019/04/57nelson.
73. Nelson, "Closing Remarks."
74. Tad Walch, "Salt Lake Temple to Close for Four Years as Temple Square Undergoes Seismic Change," *Deseret News*, April 18, 2019; Sarah Jane Weaver, "President Nelson Details Plans for Salt Lake Temple during Its 4-Year Closure for Renovation," *Church News*, April 19, 2019.
75. Weaver, "President Nelson Details Plans for Salt Lake Temple."
76. Weaver, "President Nelson Details Plans for Salt Lake Temple."
77. "Baptism for the Dead," *Times and Seasons* (Nauvoo, IL) 3, no. 12 (April 15, 1842): 761.

Bibliography

"100 Million Endowments Performed for the Dead." *Ensign*, November 1988.

ABC News. "Inside the Mormon Church," August 22, 2012. Video. https://www.youtube.com/watch?v=ytYpcUmQPRk.

ABC News. "Mitt Romney, Jon Huntsman 2012: Mormon Church in Spotlight," August 3, 2011. Video. https://www.youtube.com/watch?v=GGb-mR8wajE.

ACLU Utah. "ACLU Returns to Court in Controversy over Free Speech in Salt Lake City's 'Main Street Plaza.'" December 5, 2005. https://www.aclu.org/press-releases.

ACLU Utah. "First Unitarian Church v. Salt Lake City Corporation (2003)." July 28, 2003. https://www.acluutah.org.

Adams, Charles P., and Gustive O. Larson. "A Study of the LDS Church Historian's Office, 1830–1900." *Utah Historical Quarterly* 40, no. 4 (Fall 1972): 370–89.

Alexander, Thomas G. *Mormonism in Transition: A History of the Latter-day Saints, 1890–1930.* Urbana: University of Illinois, 1996.

Alexander, Thomas G. "The Odyssey of a Latter-day Prophet: Wilford Woodruff and the Manifesto of 1890." *Journal of Mormon History* 17 (1991): 169–206.

Alexander, Thomas G. *Things in Heaven and Earth: The Life and Times of Wilford Woodruff, a Mormon Prophet.* Salt Lake City: Signature Books, 1991.

Alford, Kenneth L. "'We Have Now the Territory on Wheels': Direct and Collateral Costs of the 1858 Move South." *Journal of Mormon History* 45, no. 2 (April 2019): 92–114.

Alford, Kenneth L., and Richard E. Bennett, eds. *An Eye of Faith: Essays in Honor of Richard O. Cowan.* Provo, UT: Religious Studies Center, Brigham Young University, 2015.

Allen, James B. *Trials of Discipleship: The Story of William Clayton, a Mormon.* Urbana: University of Illinois Press, 1987.

Allen, James B., Jessie L. Embry, and Kahlile B. Mehr. *Hearts Turned to the Fathers: A History of the Genealogical Society of Utah, 1894–1994.* Provo, UT: Brigham Young University, 1995.

Alvarado, Miguel A., and Iris Emma Pazo. Interview. Puerto Rico, March 1, 2015. CHL.

Anderson, Devery S. *The Development of LDS Temple Worship, 1846–2000: A Documentary History.* Salt Lake City: Signature Books, 2011.

Anderson, Edward H. "The Bureau of Information." *Improvement Era* 25, no. 2 (December 1921): 131–39.

Anderson, Edward O. "Salt Lake Temple." *Improvement Era* 66, no. 11 (November 1963): 1008.

Anderson, James H. "The Salt Lake Temple." *The Contributor* 14, no. 6 (April 1893): 243–320.

Anderson, Paul L. "Truman O. Angell: Architect and Saint." In *Supporting Saints: Life Stories of Nineteenth-Century Mormons*, edited by Donald Q. Cannon and David J. Whittaker, 133–73. Provo, UT: Religious Studies Center, Brigham Young University, 1985.

Andrew, Laurel B. *The Early Temples of the Mormons: The Architecture of the Millennial Kingdom in the American West.* Albany: State University of New York Press, 1978.

Angell, Truman O. "Autobiography." In *Our Pioneer Heritage*, 20 vols., compiled by Kate B. Carter, Vol. 10, 194–222. Salt Lake City: Daughters of the Utah Pioneers, 1937–77.

Angell, Truman O. Journal. Truman O. Angell Journals and Record Book, 1851–81. CHL.

Annals of the Southern Utah Mission, 1903–1906. CHL.

Arrington, J. Earl. "William Weeks, Architect of the Nauvoo Temple." *BYU Studies* 19, no. 3 (1979): 337–60.

214 BIBLIOGRAPHY

Arrington, Leonard J. *Great Basin Kingdom: An Economic History of the Latter-day Saints, 1830–1900.* Salt Lake City: University of Utah Press, 2005.

Balderas, Eduardo. "Northward to Mesa." *Ensign,* September 1972.

"Baptism for the Dead." *Times and Seasons* (Nauvoo, IL) 3, no. 12 (April 15, 1842): 759–61.

Barlow, Philip L. *Mormons and the Bible: The Place of the Latter-day Saints in American Religion.* New York: Oxford University Press, 2013.

Barlow, Philip L. "To Mend a Fractured Reality: Joseph Smith's Project." *Journal of Mormon History* 38, no. 3 (Summer 2012): 28–50.

Barlow, Philip L. "Toward a Mormon Sense of Time." *Journal of Mormon Studies* 33, no. 1 (Spring 2007): 1–37.

Barney, Ronald O. *Mormon Vanguard Brigade of 1847: Norton Jacob's Record.* Logan: Utah State University Press, 2005.

Barney, Ronald O., and W. Randall Dixon. "Church Headquarters." In *Mapping Mormonism: An Atlas of Latter-day Saint History,* 2nd ed., edited by Brandon S. Plewe, S. Kent Brown, Donald Q. Cannon, and Richard H. Jackson, 114–17. Provo, UT: BYU Press, 2014.

Barrell, H. C., and Laron Pratt. Letter to Wilford Woodruff and counselors, May 1, 1892. First Presidency (Wilford Woodruff) Correspondence, 1887–1898. CHL.

Baugh, Alexander L. "'For This Ordinance Belongeth to My House': The Practice of Baptisms for the Dead outside the Nauvoo Temple." *Mormon Historical Studies* 3, no. 1 (Spring 2002): 47–58.

Bennett, Richard E. "'Has the Lord Turned Bankrupt?' The Attempted Sale of the Nauvoo Temple, 1846–1850." *Journal of the Illinois State Historical Society* 95, no. 3 (Autumn 2002): 235–63.

Bennett, Richard E. "'Line upon Line, Precept upon Precept': Reflections on the 1877 Commencement of the Performance of Endowments and Sealings for the Dead." *BYU Studies* 44, no. 3 (2005): 38–77.

Bennett, Richard E. *Mormons at the Missouri: Winter Quarters, 1846–1852.* Norman: University of Oklahoma Press, 1987.

Bennett, Richard E. *Temples Rising: A Heritage of Sacrifice.* Salt Lake City: Deseret Book, 2019.

Bennett, Richard E. "'The Upper Room': The Nature and Development of Latter-day Saint Temple Work." *Journal of Mormon History* 41, no. 2 (April 2015): 1–34.

Bennett, Richard E. "'We Are a Kingdom to Ourselves': The Council of Fifty Minutes and the Mormon Exodus West." In *Council of Fifty,* 153–66.

Bennett, Richard E. *We'll Find the Place: The Mormon Exodus, 1846–1848.* Salt Lake City: Deseret Book, 1997.

Bennett, Richard E. "'Which Is the Wisest Course?' The Transformation in Mormon Temple Consciousness, 1870–1898." *BYU Studies* 52, no. 2 (2013): 5–43.

Bergera, Gary James. "'I'm Here for the Cash': Max Florence and the Great Mormon Temple." *Utah Historical Quarterly* 47, no. 1 (Winter 1979): 54–63.

"Best Friends Forever," *New Era* 40, no. 3 (March 2008): 17.

Bishop, M. Guy, and Richard Neitzel Holzapfel. "The 'St. Peter's of the New World': The Salt Lake Temple, Tourism, and a New Image for Utah." *Utah Historical Quarterly* 61, no. 2 (Spring 1993): 136–49.

Black, Susan Easton. "How Large Was the Population of Nauvoo?" *BYU Studies* 35, no. 2 (1995): 91–94.

Blue, Gilbert. Interview. Rock Hill, SC, March 2, 2014. CHL.

Boatright, Gary L., Jr. "'We Shall Have Temples Built': Joseph F. Smith and a New Era of Temple Building." In *Joseph F. Smith: Reflections on the Man and His Times,* edited by Craig K. Manscill, Brian D. Reeves, Guy L. Dorius, and J. B. Haws, 303–19. Provo, UT: Religious Studies Center, Brigham Young University, 2013.

The Book of Mormon: Another Testament of Jesus Christ. Salt Lake City: The Church of Jesus Christ of Latter-day Saints, 2013.

BIBLIOGRAPHY 215

Bowman, Matt. "The Temple and 'Big Love': Mormonism and American Culture." *Patheos*, June 22, 2009. https://www.patheos.com/resources/additional-resources/2009/06/the-temple-and-big-love-06222009.aspx.

Bowman, Matthew L. *The Mormon People: The Making of an American Faith*. New York: Random House, 2012.

Brackenridge, R. Douglas. "'About the Worst Man in Utah': William R. Campbell and the Crusade against Brigham H. Roberts, 1898–1900." *Journal of Mormon History* 39, no. 1 (Winter 2013): 68–157.

Bradley, Martha Elizabeth, and Lowell M. Durham Jr. "John Hafen and the Art Missionaries." *Journal of Mormon History* 12 (1985): 91–105.

Brigham, Janet. "News of the Church: Nauvoo Monument to Women." *Ensign*, September 1978.

Brigham Young Office Files, 1832–78. CHL.

Brigham Young Office Files Transcriptions, 1974–78. CHL.

Bringhurst, Newell G. *Saints, Slaves, and Blacks: The Changing Place of Black People within Mormonism*. Westport, CT: Greenwood Press, 1981.

Brown, Lisle G., comp. *Nauvoo Sealings, Adoptions, and Anointings: A Comprehensive Register of Persons Receiving LDS Temple Ordinances, 1841–46*. Salt Lake City: Smith-Petit Foundation, 2006.

Brown, Lisle G. "'Temple Pro Tempore': The Salt Lake City Endowment House." *Journal of Mormon History* 34, no. 4 (Fall 2008): 1–68.

Brown, Samuel B. "Early Mormon Adoption Theology and the Mechanics of Salvation." *Journal of Mormon History* 37, no. 3 (Summer 2011): 3–52.

Bullock, Thomas. Thomas Bullock Journals, 1843–49, CHL.

Bureau of Information Correspondence, 1923–29. CHL.

Bureau of Information Correspondence, 1936–43. CHL.

Bush, Lester E., Jr. "Mormonism's Negro Doctrine: An Historical Overview." *Dialogue: A Journal of Mormon Thought* 8, no. 13 (Spring 197): 11–68.

Campbell, Craig S. *Images of the New Jerusalem: Latter Day Saint Faction Interpretations of Independence, Missouri*. Knoxville: University of Tennessee Press, 2004.

Cannon, George Q. Journals, 1855–64, 1872–1901. CHL.

Cannon, Joseph J. "Temple Square." *Temple Square Topics: Official Organ of Temple Square Mission* 3, no. 9 (November 1939): 1–2.

Cannon, Kenneth L., II. "'And Now It Is the Mormons': The Magazine Crusade against the Mormon Church, 1910–1911." *Dialogue: A Journal of Mormon Thought* 46, no. 1 (Spring 2013): 1–63.

Card, Orson Rega. "The Temple Square Mission: A Foreign Mission at Home." *Improvement Era* 36 (July 1933): 517, 520.

"Celebration of the Anniversary." *Times and Seasons* 2 (April 15, 1841): 375–77.

Chew, Queenie P. K. Interview. Singapore, September 20, 1996. CHL.

Chidester, David, and Edward T. Linenthal, eds. *American Sacred Space*. Bloomington: Indiana University Press, 1995.

Christensen, Clinton D. "Senior Missionaries in the Caribbean: Opening the Islands of the Sea, 1978–90." In *Go Ye into All the World: The Growth and Development of Mormon Missionary Work*, edited by Reid L. Nielson and Fred E. Woods, 425–44. Provo, UT: Religious Studies Center, 2012.

Church History Department Pitman Shorthand Transcriptions, 2013–17. CHL.

The Church of Jesus Christ of Latter-day Saints. "Are Mormons Christian," Gospel Topics Essays. Accessed January 20, 2020. https://www.churchofjesuschrist.org/study/manual/gospel-topics-essays/christians.

The Church of Jesus Christ of Latter-day Saints. "Excerpts from Three Addresses by President Wilford Woodruff regarding the Manifesto." Official Declaration 1. Accessed January 20, 2020. https://www.churchofjesuschrist.org/study/scriptures/dc-testament/od/1.

216 BIBLIOGRAPHY

The Church of Jesus Christ of Latter-day Saints. "Plural Marriage and Families in Early Utah." Gospel Topics Essays. Accessed January 20, 2020. https://www.churchofjesuschrist.org/study/manual/gospel-topics-essays/plural-marriage-and-families-in-early-utah.

The Church of Jesus Christ of Latter-day Saints. "Scaled Model Provides Salt Lake Temple Open House Experience." Newsroom, May 28, 2010. https://newsroom.churchofjesuschrist.org/article/scaled-model-provides-salt-lake-temple-open-house-experience.

The Church of Jesus Christ of Latter-day Saints. "Temple Garments." Newsroom. Accessed January 20, 2020. https://newsroom.churchofjesuschrist.org/article/temple-garments.

Church of Jesus Christ Temples. "About." Accessed November 11, 2019. https://churchofjesuschristtemples.org/about/.

Clayton, William. "An Interesting Journal." *Juvenile Instructor* 21, no. 10 (May 15, 1886): 157–58.

CNN. "Polygamist Prophet Preaches from Jail." July 27, 2011. Video. https://www.youtube.com/watch?v=qL4cQcXgbuQ.

Cornwall, Marie, Camela Courtright, and Laga Van Beek. "How Common the Principle? Women as Plural Wives in 1860." *Dialogue: A Journal of Mormon Thought* 26 (Summer 1993): 139–53.

Cowan, Richard O. *The Church in the Twentieth Century*. Salt Lake City: Bookcraft, 1985.

Cowan, Richard O. "The Design, Construction, and Role of the Salt Lake Temple." In Esplin and Alford, *Salt Lake City: The Place Which God Prepared*, 47–67.

Cowan, Richard O. *Temples to Dot the Earth*. Salt Lake City: Bookcraft, 1989.

Cowan, Richard O. "Washington D.C. Temple." In Garr, Cannon, and Cowan, *Encyclopedia of Latter-day Saint History*, 1315.

Dallin, Cyrus E. Letter to Gaylen S. Young, July 30, 1938. CHL.

Davidson, Karen Lynn, and others, eds. *Histories*. Vol. 2: *Assigned Historical Writings, 1831–1847*. Volume 2 of the Histories series of *The Joseph Smith Papers*, edited by Dean C. Jessee, Ronald K. Esplin, and Richard Lyman Bushman. Salt Lake City: Church Historian's Press, 2012.

Daynes, Kathryn M. *More Wives Than One: Transformation of the Mormon Marriage System, 1840–1910*. Urbana: University of Illinois Press, 2001.

Daynes, Kathryn M. "Striving to Live the Principle in Utah's First Temple City: A Snapshot of Polygamy in St. George, Utah, in June 1880." *BYU Studies Quarterly* 51, no. 4 (2012): 69–95.

Derr, Jill Mulvay, Carol Cornwall Madsen, Kate Holbrook, and Matthew J. Grow, eds. *The First Fifty Years of Relief Society: Key Documents in Latter-day Saint Women's History*. Salt Lake City: Church Historian's Press, 2016.

Deseret News 2013 Church Almanac. Salt Lake City: Deseret News, 2013.

Dew, Sheri L. *Go Forward with Faith: The Biography of Gordon B. Hinckley*. Salt Lake City: Deseret Book, 1996.

Dinger, John S. "'A Mean Conspirator' or 'The Noblest of Men': William Marks's Expulsion from Nauvoo." *John Whitmer Historical Association Journal* 34, no. 2 (Fall–Winter 2014): 12–38.

Dirkmaat, Gerrit J., and others, eds. *Documents*. Vol. 3: *February 1833–March 1834*. Volume 3 of the Documents series of *The Joseph Smith Papers*, edited by Ronald K. Esplin and Matthew J. Grow. Salt Lake City: Church Historian's Press, 2014.

The Doctrine and Covenants of the Church of Jesus Christ of Latter-day Saints: Containing Revelations Given to Joseph Smith, the Prophet, with Some Additions by His Successors in the Presidency of the Church. Salt Lake City: The Church of Jesus Christ of Latter-day Saints, 2013.

"Dream Date." *New Era* 34, no. 10 (October 2004): 19.

Ehat, Andrew F. "Joseph Smith's Introduction of Temple Ordinances and the 1844 Mormon Succession Question." Master's thesis, Brigham Young University, 1982.

Eighty-Ninth Semi-Annual Conference of the Church of Jesus Christ of Latter-day Saints. Salt Lake City: Deseret News, 1918.

BIBLIOGRAPHY 217

"An Epistle of the First Presidency of the Church of Jesus Christ of Latter-day Saints, Read at the Semi-Annual Conference, Held at Coalville, Summit County, Utah, October, 1886." Digital Collections, Harold B. Lee Library, Brigham Young University, Provo, UT. https://contentdm.lib.byu.edu/digital/collection/NCMP1820-1846/id/22669.

Esplin, Ronald K. "Joseph, Brigham, and the Twelve: A Succession of Continuity." *BYU Studies* 21, no. 3 (Summer 1981): 301–41.

Esplin, Ronald K. "'A Place Prepared': Joseph, Brigham and the Quest for Promised Refuge in the West." *Journal of Mormon History* 9 (1982): 85–111.

Esplin, Scott C., and Kenneth L. Alford, eds. *Salt Lake City: The Place Which God Prepared.* Provo, UT: Religious Studies Center, Brigham Young University, 2011.

Evans, David W. Letter to Irene Staples, October 16, 1975. In "The Mormon Pavilion at the New York World's Fair, 1964–65." Irene Edwards Staples Scrapbook. CHL.

Evans, Whitney, and Carole Mikita. "Debate over LDS Women's Roles Spotlighted in Protest." KSL.com, October 5, 2013. https://www.ksl.com/article/27133883/debate-over-lds-womens-roles-spotlighted-in-protest.

Feldman, Noah. "What Is It about Mormonism." *New York Times Magazine*, January 6, 2008. https://www.nytimes.com/2008/01/06/magazine/06mormonism-t.html.

"Feramorz L. Young." *The Contributor* 3 (November 1881): 39–42.

Figueroa, Ana. "Salt Lake's Big Jump." *Newsweek*, September 10, 2001.

Firmage, Edwin Brown, and Richard Collin Mangrum. *Zion in the Courts: A Legal History of the Church of Jesus Christ of Latter-day Saints, 1830–1900.* Urbana: University of Illinois Press, 1988.

First Presidency of The Church of Jesus Christ of Latter-day Saints, "Reaffirmation of the First Presidency's Position on ERA," August 24, 1978. CHL.

First Presidency (John Taylor) Correspondence, 1877–87. CHL.

First Presidency (Wilford Woodruff) General Correspondence Files, 1887–98. CHL.

Flake, Kathleen. "'Not to Be Riten': The Mormon Temple Rite as Oral Canon." *Journal of Ritual Studies* 9, no. 2 (Summer 1995): 1–21.

Flake, Kathleen. *The Politics of American Religious Identity: The Seating of Senator Reed Smoot, Mormon Apostle.* Chapel Hill: University of North Carolina Press, 2004.

Fluhman, J. Spencer. *"A Peculiar People": Anti-Mormonism and the Making of Religion in Nineteenth-Century America.* Chapel Hill: University of North Carolina Press, 2012.

Fluhman, J. Spencer. "Secrets and the Making of Mormon Moments." In *Faith in the New Millennium: The Future of Religion and American Politics*, edited by Matthew Avery Sutton and Darren Dochuk, 217–33. New York: Oxford University Press, 2016.

Friedland, Roger, and Richard Hecht. "The Bodies of Nations: A Comparative Study of Religious Violence in Jerusalem and Ayodhya." *History of Religions* 38, no. 2 (November 1998): 101–49.

Garr, Arnold K., Donald Q. Cannon, and Richard O. Cowan, eds. *Encyclopedia of Latter-day Saint History.* Salt Lake City: Deseret Book, 2000.

George A. Smith Family Papers. Special Collections, J. Willard Marriott Library, University of Utah, Salt Lake City.

George A. Smith Papers, 1834–77, CHL.

Gibbons, Francis M. "Dedicatory Services, Visitors Center South, Temple Square, Salt Lake City, Utah, June 1, 1978." CHL.

Gibbons, Francis M. *George Albert Smith: Kind and Caring Christian, Prophet of God.* Salt Lake City: Deseret Book, 1990.

Givens, Terryl L. *By the Hand of Mormon: The American Scripture That Launched a New World Religion.* New York: Oxford University Press, 2002.

Givens, Terryl, and Brian M. Hauglid. *The Pearl of Greatest Price: Mormonism's Most Controversial Scripture.* New York: Oxford University Press, 2019.

Goddard, Benjamin. "Bureau of Information and Church Literature." *Young Woman's Journal* 8, no. 11 (November 1902): 483–86.

218 BIBLIOGRAPHY

Goldberg, Robert A. "From New Deal to New Right." In *Thunder from the Right: Ezra Taft Benson in Mormonism and Politics*, edited by Matthew L. Harris, 68–96. Urbana: University of Illinois Press, 2019.

Gordon, Sarah Barringer. *The Mormon Question: Polygamy and Constitutional Conflict in Nineteenth-Century America*. Chapel Hill: University of North Carolina Press, 2002.

Granite Ward manuscript history and historical reports, 1877–1984. CHL.

Grow, Matthew J. *"Liberty to the Downtrodden": Thomas L. Kane, Romantic Reformer*. New Haven, CT: Yale University Press, 2009.

Grow, Matthew J., and R. Eric Smith, eds. *The Council of Fifty: What the Records Reveal about Mormon History*. Salt lake City: Deseret Book, 2017.

Grow, Matthew J., and others, eds. *Council of Fifty, Minutes, March 1844–January 1846*. Volume 1 of the Administrative Records series of *The Joseph Smith Papers*, edited by Ronald K. Esplin, Matthew J. Grow, and Matthew C. Godfrey. Salt Lake City: Church Historian's Press, 2016.

Hales, Robert D. "Out of Darkness into His Marvelous Light." *Ensign*, May 2002.

Hamilton, C. Mark. *Nineteenth Century Mormon Architecture and City Planning*. New York: Oxford University Press, 1995.

Hamilton, C. Mark. *The Salt Lake Temple: A Monument to a People*. Salt Lake City: University Services, 1983.

Hamilton, C. Mark. "A Symbolic Statement of Mormon Doctrine." In *The Mormon People: Their Character and Traditions*, edited by Thomas G. Alexander, 103–27. Provo, UT: Brigham Young University Press, 1980.

Hammond, Francis A. Journals, 1852–57, 1864–67, 1883–93. CHL.

Hanks, Marion D. "Salt Lake Temple." In Ludlow, *Encyclopedia of Mormonism*, 3:1254.

Hardy, B. Carmon. *Solemn Covenant: The Mormon Polygamous Passage*. Urbana: University of Illinois Press, 1992.

Harper, Steven C. *First Vision: Memory and Mormon Origins*. New York: Oxford University Press, 2019.

Harper, Steven C. "Freemasonry and the Latter-day Saint Temple Endowment Ceremony." In *A Reason for Faith: Navigating LDS Doctrine and Church History*, edited by Laura Harris Hales, 143–57. Provo, UT: Religious Studies Center, Brigham Young University, 2016.

Harris, Matthew L. "Martin Luther King, Civil Rights, and Perceptions of a 'Communist Conspiracy.' " In *Thunder from the Right: Ezra Taft Benson in Mormonism and Politics*, edited by Matthew L. Harris, 124–57. Urbana: University of Illinois Press, 2019.

Hartley, William G. "The Priesthood Reorganization of 1877: Brigham Young's Last Achievement." *BYU Studies* 20, no. 1 (1980): 3–36.

Hatch, John P. "From Prayer to Visitation: Reexamining Lorenzo Snow's Vision of Jesus Christ in the Salt Lake Temple." *Journal of Mormon History* 42, no. 3 (July 2016): 155–82.

Haws, J. B. *The Mormon Image in the American Mind: Fifty Years of Public Perception*. New York: Oxford University Press, 2013.

Haws, J. B. "Why the 'Mormon Olympics' Didn't Happen." In Alford and Bennett, *An Eye of Faith: Essays in Honor of Richard O. Cowan*, 365–87.

Hedges, Andrew H., and others, eds. *Journals*. Vol. 2: *December 1841–April 1843*. Volume 2 of the Journals series of *The Joseph Smith Papers*, edited by Dean C. Jessee, Ronald K. Esplin, and Richard Lyman Bushman. Salt Lake City: Church Historian's Press, 2011.

Henderson, Peter. "Insight: Mormon Church Made Wealthy by Donations." Reuters, August 12, 2012. https://www.reuters.com/article/us-usa-politics-mormons/insight-mormon-chu rch-made-wealthy-by-donations-idUSBRE87B05W20120812.

Hendrick, Burton J. "The Mormon Revival of Polygamy." *McClure's Magazine* 36, nos. 3–4 (January–February 1911): 245–61, 449–64.

Hill, Marvin S. *Quest for Refuge: The Mormon Flight from American Pluralism*. Salt Lake City: Signature Books, 1989.

Hinckley, Gordon B. "The Church Goes Forward." *Ensign*, May 2002.

BIBLIOGRAPHY 219

Hinckley, Gordon B. "New Temples to Provide 'Crowning Blessings' of the Gospel." General conference address. Salt Lake City, April 1998. https://www.churchofjesuschrist.org/study/general-conference/1998/04/new-temples-to-provide-crowning-blessings-of-the-gospel.

Hinckley, Gordon B. "Of Missions, Temples, and Stewardship." General conference address. Salt Lake City, October 1995. https://www.churchofjesuschrist.org/study/general-conference/1995/10/of-missions-temples-and-stewardship.

Historian's Office General Church Minutes, 1839–77. CHL.

Historian's Office History of the Church, 1839–ca. 1882. CHL.

Historian's Office Report of Speeches, 1845–85. CHL.

Historical Department. Journal History of the Church. 1896–. CHL.

Historical Department. Office Journal, 1844–2012. 102 vols. CHL.

"History, 1838–1856, volume C-1 [November 2, 1838–July 31, 1842]." The Joseph Smith Papers. https://www.josephsmithpapers.org/paper-summary/history-1838-1856-volume-c-1-2-november-1838-31-july-1842/.

The Holy Bible, Containing the Old and New Testaments Translated Out of the Original Tongues: And with the Former Translations Diligently Compared and Revised, by His Majesty's Special Command. Authorized King James Version with Explanatory Notes and Cross References to the Standard Works of the Church of Jesus Christ of Latter-day Saints. Salt Lake City: The Church of Jesus Christ of Latter-day Saints, 1979.

Holzapfel, Richard Neitzel. *Every Stone a Sermon: The Magnificent Story of the Construction and Dedication of the Salt Lake Temple.* Salt Lake City: Bookcraft, 1992.

Horne, Mary Isabella, and others. "To the Presidents and Members of the Relief Society of Salt Lake Stake of Zion, Greeting!" *Woman's Exponent* 6, no. 16 (January 15, 1878): 123.

Howlett, David J. *Kirtland Temple: The Biography of a Shared Mormon Sacred Space.* Urbana: University of Illinois Press, 2014.

Hunter, Howard W. "Exceeding Great and Precious Promises." *Ensign*, November 1994.

Hymns of The Church of Jesus Christ of Latter-day Saints. Salt Lake City: The Church of Jesus Christ of Latter-day Saints, 1985. `

Jackman, Levi. "A Short Sketch of the Life of Levi Jackman." CHL.

Jacob, Norton. Reminiscence and Journal, May 1844–January 1852. CHL.

Jenson, Andrew. Autobiography and Journals, 1864–1941. CHL.

Jessee, Dean C., and others, eds. *Journals.* Vol. 1: *1832–1839.* Volume 1 of the Journals series of *The Joseph Smith Papers*, edited by Dean C. Jessee, Ronald K. Esplin, and Richard Lyman Bushman. Salt Lake City: Church Historian's Press, 2008.

Joseph F. Smith Papers, 1854–1918. CHL.

Journal of Discourses. 26 vols. Liverpool: F. D. Richards, 1855–86.

Kane, Thomas L. *The Mormons: A Discourse Delivered before the Historical Society of Pennsylvania: March 26, 1850.* Philadelphia: King & Baird, 1850.

Kilde, Jeanne Halgren. *Sacred Power, Sacred Space: An Introduction to Christian Architecture and Worship.* New York: Oxford University Press, 2008.

Kilde, Jeanne Halgren. *When Church Became Theatre: The Transformation of Evangelical Architecture and Worship in Nineteenth-Century America.* New York: Oxford University Press, 2005.

Kimball, Edward L. "Spencer W. Kimball and the Revelation on the Priesthood." *BYU Studies* 47, no. 2 (2008): 46–57.

Kimball, Spencer W. Journals, 1905–81. CHL

Kimball, Spencer W. "We Feel an Urgency." *Ensign*, August 1980.

Kime, Bradley. "Exhibiting Theology: James E. Talmage and Mormon Public Relations, 1915–20." *Journal of Mormon History* 40, no. 1 (Winter 2014): 208–38.

Knapp, Jill W. "The Pilgrimage Phenomenon: An Analysis of the Motivations of Visitors to Temple Square." Master's thesis, Brigham Young University, 1989.

Kogan, Nathaniel Smith. "The Mormon Pavilion: Mainstreaming the Saints at the New York World's Fair, 1964–65." *Journal of Mormon History* 35, no. 4 (Fall 2009): 1–52.

220 BIBLIOGRAPHY

Kuehn, Elizabeth A., and others, eds., *Documents*. Vol. 10: *May–August 1842*. Volume 10 of the Documents series of *The Joseph Smith Papers*, edited by Matthew C. Godfrey, R. Eric Smith, Matthew J. Grow, and Ronald K. Esplin. Salt Lake City: Church Historian's Press, 2020.

Kuhre, William Dobbie. "Recollections of Temple Quarry, Little Cottonwood Canyon, and Old Granite." CHL.

Larson, Gustive O. *The "Americanization" of Utah for Statehood*. San Marino, CA: Huntington Library, 1971.

LeBaron, E. Dale. "Anthony U. Obinna." In Garr, Cannon, and Cowan, *Encyclopedia of Latter-day Saint History*, 862–63.

Lee, John D. Journals, May 1844–November 1853. CHL.

Leonard, Glen M. "Antiquities, Curiosities, and Latter-day Saint Museums." In *The Disciple as Witness: Essays in Honor of Richard Lloyd Anderson*, edited by Stephen D. Ricks, Donald W. Parry, and Andrew H. Hedges, 291–325. Provo, UT: Foundation for Ancient Research and Mormon Studies, 2000.

Lewis, Alfred Henry. "The Viper on the Hearth." *Cosmopolitan Magazine* 50, no. 4 (March 1911): 439–50.

Lewis, Alfred Henry. "The Viper's Trail of Gold." *Cosmopolitan Magazine* 50, no. 6 (May 1911): 823–33.

Livingston, James Campbell. "Sketch of the Life of James Campbell Livingston." James C. Livingston autobiographical sketch, undated. CHL.

Ludlow, Daniel, ed. *Encyclopedia of Mormonism*. 4 vols. New York: Macmillan, 1992.

Lund, Anthon H. Journals, 1860–1921. CHL.

Mabey, Rendell N., and Gordon T. Allred. *Brother to Brother: The Story of the Latter-day Saint Missionaries Who Took the Gospel to Black Africa*. Salt Lake City: Bookcraft, 1984.

MacKinnon, William P. *At Sword's Point, Part 1: A Documentary History of the Utah War to 1858*. Norman, OK: Arthur H. Clark, 2008.

MacKinnon, William P. *At Sword's Point, Part 2: A Documentary History of the Utah War, 1858–1859*. Norman, OK: Arthur H. Clark, 2016.

MacKinnon, William P. "Utah War: Impact and Legacy." *Journal of Mormon History* 29, no. 2 (Fall 2003): 186–248.

Madsen, Susan Arrington. "Lorenzo Snow and the Sacred Vision." *Friend* 23, no. 8 (August 1993): 14.

Maile, Heather A. Interview. Carlingford, New South Wales, Australia, March 1, 2018. CHL.

"Making Progress." *New Era* 32, no. 1 (January 2002): 16–18.

"Marketing the Mormon Image: An Interview with Wendell J. Ashton." *Dialogue: A Journal of Mormon Thought* 10, no. 3 (Spring 1977): 15–20.

Mason, Patrick Q. "God and the People: Theodemocracy in Nineteenth-Century Mormonism." *Journal of Church and State* 53, no. 3 (Summer 2011): 349–75.

Matson, Joshua M. "Where the World, Babel, and Zion Meet: Redefining the Mormon People at the 1964–65 Mormon Pavilion." *Journal of Mormon History* 44, no. 3 (July 2018): 89–111.

Mauss, Armand L. *All Abraham's Children: Changing Mormon Conceptions of Race and Lineage*. Urbana: University of Illinois Press, 2003.

Mauss, Armand L. *The Angel and the Beehive: The Mormon Struggle with Assimilation*. Urbana: University of Illinois Press, 1994.

McCallister, D. M. *A Description of the Great Temple, Salt Lake City, and a Statement concerning the Purposes for Which It Has Been Built*. Salt Lake City: Bureau of Information and Church Literature, 1904.

Mehr, Kahlile B. "How Much of the Human Family Has Had Its Temple Work Done?" *Ensign*, March 1997.

Merrill, Marriner W. Journal and Reminiscences, 1888–94. CHL.

The Message of the Ages: A Sacred Pageant Commemorating the One Hundredth Anniversary of the Organization of the Church of Jesus Christ of Latter-day Saints. Salt Lake City: Heber J. Grant, 1930.

BIBLIOGRAPHY 221

"Ministry of Lorenzo Snow: A Vision of the Lord." Churchofjesuschrist.org, May 2012. Video, https://www.churchofjesuschrist.org/media/video/2012-05-0504-ministry-of-lorenzo-snow-a-vision-of-the-lord?lang=eng.

"Minute Book 1." The Joseph Smith Papers. https://www.josephsmithpapers.org/paper-summary/minute-book-1/.

"Minutes of a Conference of The Church of Jesus Christ of Latter-day Saints, Held in Nauvoo, Ill., Commencing Oct. 1st, 1841." *Times and Seasons* (Nauvoo, IL) 2 (October 15, 1841): 577–78.

Monson, Thomas S. "The Temple of the Lord." *Ensign*, May 1993.

"A Mormon Responds to Proposition 8." *Vanity Fair*, November 17, 2008. https://www.vanityfair.com/news/2008/11/a-mormon-responds-to-proposition-8.

Morrill, Kelli N. "From Housewives to Protesters: The Story of Mormons for the Equal Rights Amendment." Master's thesis, Utah State University, 2018.

Mouritsen, Dale C. "A Symbol of New Directions: George Franklin Richards and the Mormon Church, 1861–1950." PhD diss., Brigham Young University, 1982.

Mueller, Max Perry. "The Pageantry of Protest in Temple Square." In *Out of Obscurity: Mormonism since 1945*, edited by Patrick Q. Mason and John G. Turner, 123–43. New York: Oxford University Press, 2016.

Nadauld, Margaret D. "Hold High the Torch." General conference address. Salt Lake City, April 2002. https://www.churchofjesuschrist.org/study/general-conference/2002/04/hold-high-the-torch.

Neilson, Reid L., and R. Mark Melville, eds. *The Saints Abroad: Missionaries Who Answered Brigham Young's 1852 Call to the Nations of the World*. Provo, UT: Religious Studies Center, Brigham Young University, 2019.

Neilson, Reid L., and Nathan N. Waite, eds. *Settling the Valley, Proclaiming the Gospel: The General Epistles of the Mormon First Presidency*. New York: Oxford University Press, 2017.

Nelson, Louis P., ed. *American Sanctuary: Understanding Sacred Spaces*. Bloomington: Indiana University Press, 2006.

Nelson, Russell M. "Becoming Exemplary Latter-day Saints." General conference address. Salt Lake City, October 2018. https://www.churchofjesuschrist.org/study/general-conference/2018/10/becoming-exemplary-latter-day-saints.

Nelson, Russell M. "Closing Remarks." General conference address. Salt Lake City, April 2019. https://www.churchofjesuschrist.org/study/general-conference/2019/04/57nelson.

Nelson, Russell M. "Personal Preparation for Temple Blessings." General conferences address. Salt Lake City, April 2001. https://www.churchofjesuschrist.org/study/general-conference/2001/04/personal-preparation-for-temple-blessings.

Nelson, Russell M. "Spencer W. Kimball: Man of Faith." *Ensign*, December 1985, 39–41.

Newell, Quincy D. *Your Sister in the Gospel: The Life of Jane Manning James, A Nineteenth-Century Black Mormon*. New York: Oxford University Press, 2019.

New York World's Fair Committee Subject Files, 1961–65. CHL.

Nicholson, John. "Temple Manifestations." *The Contributor* 14, no. 2 (December 1894): 116–18.

NPR. "Transcript: Mitt Romney's Faith Speech." December 6, 2007. https://www.npr.org/templates/story/story.php?storyId=16969460.

Obinna, Anthony Uzodimma. "Voice from Nigeria." *Ensign*, December 1980.

Obinna, Fidelia. Interview by Anthonia C. Nwachukwu. March 8, 2010. Transcript. CHL.

Official Report of the XIX Olympic Winter Games: Salt Lake City 2002. Salt Lake City: SLOC, 2002.

"Old Testament Revision 1." The Joseph Smith Papers. https://www.josephsmithpapers.org/paper-summary/old-testament-revision-1/1.

Olmstead, Jacob W. "From Pentecost to Administration: A Reappraisal of the History of the Hosanna Shout." *Mormon Historical Studies* 2, no. 2 (Fall 2001): 7–37.

222 BIBLIOGRAPHY

Olmstead, Jacob W., Josh Probert, and Elwin Robison. "Myths and Realities of the Salt Lake Temple Foundation." *Journal of Mormon History* 48, no. 4 (October 2022): 32–65.

One Hundred Forty-Eighth Semi-Annual Conference of the Church of Jesus Christ of Latter-day Saints. Salt Lake City: The Church of Jesus Christ of Latter-day Saints, 1978.

One-Hundred Nineteenth Semi-Annual General Conference of the Church of Jesus Christ of Latter-day Saints. Salt Lake City: The Church of Jesus Christ of Latter-day Saints, 1948.

One Hundred Sixty-Third Annual General Conference of the Church of Jesus Christ of Latter-day Saints. Salt Lake City: The Church of Jesus Christ of Latter-day Saints, 1993.

One Hundred Thirty-Third Semi-Annual General Conference of the Church of Jesus Christ of Latter-day Saints. Salt Lake City: The Church of Jesus Christ of Latter-day Saints, 1963.

One Hundred Twenty-First Semi-Annual Conference of the Church of Jesus Christ of Latter-day Saints. Salt Lake City: The Church of Jesus Christ of Latter-day Saints, October 1950.

Packer, Boyd K. "The Temple, the Priesthood." *Ensign*, May 1993.

Park, Benjamin E. "The Council of Fifty and the Perils of Democratic Governance." In *Council of Fifty*, 43–54.

Park, Benjamin E. *Kingdom of Nauvoo: The Rise and Fall of a Religious Empire on the American Frontier.* New York: Liveright, 2020.

Paulos, Michael Harold, ed. *The Mormon Church on Trial: Transcripts of the Reed Smoot Hearings.* Salt Lake City: Signature Books, 2008.

PBS. "The Mormons." *Frontline*, directed by Helen Whitney. 2007. Transcript, https://www.pbs.org/mormons/etc/script.html. Video, https://www.pbs.org/video/frontline-the-mormons-part-one/.

PBS. "Mormons and Proposition 8." *Religion and Ethics Newsweekly*, May 22, 2009. https://www.pbs.org/wnet/religionandethics/2009/05/22/may-22-2009-mormons-and-proposition-8/3019/.

The Pearl of Great Price: A Selection from the Revelations, Translations, and Narrations of Joseph Smith, First Prophet, Seer, and Revelator to the Church of Jesus Christ of Latter-day Saints. Salt Lake City: The Church of Jesus Christ of Latter-day Saints, 2013.

Penrose, Charles W. Journals, 1854–1911, CHL.

Peterson, Paul H. "The Mormon Reformation of 1856–1857: The Rhetoric and the Reality." *Journal of Mormon History* 15 (1989): 59–87.

Pew Research Center. "America's Changing Religious Landscape." Religion and Public Life, May 12, 2015. https://www.pewforum.org/2015/05/12/americas-changing-religious-landscape/.

Piatt, Richard. "LDS Church Takes Control of Main Street Plaza." KSL.com, July 28, 2003. https://www.ksl.com/ article/89752/lds-church-takes-control-of-main-st-plaza.

Pierce, Walter H., and Lida L. Pierce. Interview. Nauvoo, IL, August 15, 2016. CHL.

Pleasant Grove Branch Relief Society Minutes and Records, 1868–1901. CHL.

Poll, Richard D. "The Move South." *BYU Studies* 29, no. 4 (1989): 65–88.

Prince, Gregory L., and Wm. Robert Wright, *David O. McKay and the Rise of Modern Mormonism.* Salt Lake City: University of Utah Press, 2005.

Public Works Account Books, 1848–87. CHL.

Raynor, Wallace A. *Everlasting Spires: The Story of the Salt Lake Temple.* Salt Lake City: Deseret Book, 1965.

Raynor, Wallace A. "History of the Construction of the Salt Lake Temple." Master's thesis, Brigham Young University, 1961.

Realizing a Vision: The New Church Plaza. Salt Lake City: The Church of Jesus Christ of Latter-day Saints, 2002.

Reeve, W. Paul. *Religion of a Different Color: Race and the Mormon Struggle for Whiteness.* Salt Lake City: Oxford University Press, 2015.

Richards, Franklin D. Journal. Richards Family Collection, 1837–1961. CHL.

BIBLIOGRAPHY   223

Richards, George F. Journals, 1880–1909. CHL.

Richardson, Matthew. "Bertel Thorvaldsen's Christus: A Latter-day Saint Icon of Christian Evidence." In *Art and Spirituality: The Visual Culture of Christian Faith*, edited by Herman du Toit and Doris R. Dant, 189–201. Provo, UT: BYU Studies, 2008.

Roberts, B. H. *The Life of John Taylor, Third President of The Church of Jesus Christ of Latter-day Saints*. Salt Lake City: George Q. Cannon and Sons, 1892.

Robison, Elwin C. *The First Mormon Temple: Design, Construction, and Context of the Kirtland Temple*. Provo, UT: Brigham Young University, 1997.

Robison, Elwin C. *Gathering as One: The History of the Mormon Tabernacle in Salt Lake City*. Provo, UT: Brigham Young University Press, 2013.

Rogers, Brent M. *Unpopular Sovereignty: Mormons and the Federal Management of Early Utah Territory*. Lincoln: University of Nebraska Press, 2017.

Rogers, Brent M., and others, eds. *Documents*. Vol. 5: *October 1835–January 1838*. Volume 5 of the Documents series of *The Joseph Smith Papers*, edited by Ronald K. Esplin, Matthew J. Grow, and Matthew C. Godfrey. Salt Lake City: Church Historian's Press, 2017.

"The Role of Womanhood to Be Depicted in Relief Society Monument." *Ensign*, March 1976.

Romney, Miles. Journal, ca. March 1850–May 1855. CHL.

Rugh, Susan Sessions. *Are We There Yet? The Golden Age of American Family Vacations*. Lawrence: University of Kansas Press, 2008.

Salt Lake Stake General Minutes, 1869–1977. CHL.

"Salt Lake Temple." *Ensign*, January 1978.

Salt Lake Temple Architectural Drawings, 1853–93. CHL.

"Salt Lake Temple One of World's Wonders." *Ensign*, June 1993.

"Salt Lake Temple Prepared for Anniversary." *Ensign*, October 1991.

Scharoun, Lisa. *America at the Mall: The Cultural Roll of a Retail Utopia*. Jefferson, NC: McFarland, 2012.

Secrist, Ann Eliza. Letter to Jacob F. Secrist, May 30, 1853. Jacob F. Secrist Collection, 1841–74. CHL.

"Set Your Sights." *New Era* 32, no. 5 (May 2002): 19.

Seventy-First Annual Conference of the Church of Jesus Christ of Latter-day Saints. Salt Lake City: Deseret News, 1901.

Shipps, Jan. *Mormonism: The Story of a New Religious Tradition*. Urbana: University of Illinois Press, 1985.

Shipps, Jan. "The Principle Revoked: A Closer Look at the Demise of Plural Marriage." *Journal of Mormon History* 11 (1984): 65–77.

Shipps, Jan. "Spinning Gold: Mormonism and the Olympic Games." *Dialogue: A Journal of Mormon Thought* 36, no. 1 (Spring 2003): 133–49.

Smith, George D., ed. *An Intimate Chronicle: The Journals of William Clayton*. Salt Lake City: Signature Books, 1991.

Smith, Joseph Fielding. *Doctrines of Salvation*. Compiled by Bruce R. McConkie. Salt Lake City: Bookcraft, 1955.

Smith, Joseph Fielding. *Life of Joseph F. Smith: Sixth President of The Church of Jesus Christ of Latter-day Saints*. Salt Lake City: Deseret Book, 1969.

Snow, LeRoi C. "An Experience of My Father's." *Improvement Era* 35, no. 11 (September 1933): 677, 679.

Staker, Mark L. *Hearken, O Ye People: The Historical Setting of Joseph Smith's Ohio Revelations*. Salt Lake City: Greg Kofford Books, 2010.

Stapley, Jonathan A. "Adoptive Sealing Ritual in Mormonism." *Journal of Mormon History* 37, no. 3 (Summer 2011): 53–117.

Stapley, Jonathan A. *The Power of Godliness: Mormon Liturgy and Cosmology*. New York: Oxford University Press, 2018.

224 BIBLIOGRAPHY

Stapley, Jonathan A., and Kristine L. Wright. "'They Shall Be Made Whole': A History of Baptism for Health." *Journal of Mormon History* 34, no. 4 (Fall 2008): 69–112.

Stuever, Hank. "Unmentionable No Longer: What Do Mormons Wear? A Polite Smile, If Asked about 'the Garment.'" *Washington Post*, February 26, 2002.

Stuy, Brian H., ed. *Collected Discourses Delivered by President Wilford Woodruff, His Two Counselors, the Twelve Apostles, and Others.* 5 vols. Burbank, CA: Brian H. Stuy, 1987–92.

Stuy, Brian H. "'Come, Let Us Go Up to the Mountain of the Lord': The Salt Lake Temple Dedication." *Dialogue: A Journal of Mormon Thought* 31, no. 3 (Fall 1998): 101–22.

"The Sustaining of Church Officers." *Ensign*, May 1976.

Talmage, James E. *The House of the Lord: A Study of Holy Sanctuaries Ancient and Modern.* Salt Lake City: The Church of Jesus Christ of Latter-day Saints, 1912.

Talmage, James E. Journals. 30 vols. James E. Talmage Papers. L. Tom Perry Special Collections, Harold B. Lee Library, Brigham Young University, Provo, UT.

Talmage, James E. *The Vitality of Mormonism: An Address.* Salt Lake City: Deseret News, 1917.

Talmage, Jeremy, and Clinton D. Christensen. "Black White, or Brown? Racial Perceptions and the Priesthood Policy in Latin America." *Journal of Mormon History* 44, no. 1 (January 2018): 119–45.

Tanner, N. Eldon. "The Administration of the Church." *Ensign*, November 1979.

"A Temple Renewed." *Ensign*, March 1993.

Temples of the Church of Jesus Christ of Latter-day Saints. "Temple Locations." Statistics. Accessed January 20, 2020. https://churchofjesuschristtemples.org/statistics/locations/.

Temple Souvenir Album, April 1892. Salt Lake City: Magazine Printing Company, 1892.

Temple Square Mission Historical Record, 1902–42. CHL.

Tobler, Ryan G. "'Saviors on Mount Zion': Mormon Sacramentalism, Mortality, and the Baptism for the Dead." *Journal of Mormon History* 39, no. 4 (Fall 2013): 182–238.

Top, Brent L. "The Mormon Pavilion at the 1964–1965 New York World's Fair." In Alford and Bennett, *An Eye of Faith: Essays in Honor of Richard Cowan,* 321–47.

"Trial of Elder Rigdon." *Times and Seasons* 5 (September 15, 1844): 647–48.

Truman O. Angell Architectural Drawings, 1851–67. CHL.

Tullidge, Edward W. *The History of Salt Lake City and Its Founders.* Salt Lake City: E. W. Tullidge, 1886.

Turner, John G. *Brigham Young: Pioneer Prophet.* Cambridge, MA: Harvard University Press, 2012.

Turner, John G. *The Mormon Jesus: A Biography.* Cambridge, MA: Harvard University Press, 2016.

Uchtdorf, Dieter F. "Your Happily Ever After." General conference address. Salt Lake City, April 2010. https://www.lds.org/general-conference/2010/04.

Van Wagoner, Richard S. *Mormon Polygamy: A History.* Salt Lake City: Signature Books, 1989.

Wadsworth, Nelson B. *Set in Stone, Fixed in Glass: The Great Mormon Temple and Its Photographers.* Salt Lake City: Signature Books, 1992.

Walgren, Kent. "Inside the Salt Lake Temple: Gisbert Bossard's 1911 Photographs." *Dialogue: A Journal of Mormon Thought* 29, no. 3 (Fall 1996): 1–43.

Walker, Ronald W. *Wayward Saints: The Godbeites and Brigham Young.* Urbana: University of Illinois Press, 1998.

Walker, Ronald W., Richard E. Turley Jr., and Glen M. Leonard. *Massacre at Mountain Meadows.* New York: Oxford University Press, 2008.

Warner, W. Keith. "Council of the First Presidency and the Quorum of the Twelve Apostles." In Ludlow, *Encyclopedia of Mormonism,* 1:327.

Wayment, Thomas A. "Intertextuality and the Purpose of Joseph Smith's New Translation of the Bible." In *Foundational Texts of Mormonism: Examining Major Early Sources,* edited by Mark Ashurst-McGee, Robin Jensen, and Sharalyn D. Howcroft, 74–100. New York: Oxford University Press, 2018.

Webb, Stephen H. "Mormonism Obsessed with Christ." *First Things* (blog), February, 2012. https://www.firstthings.com/article/2012/02/mormonism-obsessed-with-christ.

BIBLIOGRAPHY   225

Welcome [Friends to All Nations]. Salt Lake City: The Church of Jesus Christ of Latter-day Saints, 2001.

West, Franklin L. *Life of Franklin D. Richards.* Salt Lake City: Deseret News, 1924.

Westwood, P. Bradford. "The Early Life and Career of Joseph Don Carlos Young (1855–1938): A Study of Utah's First Institutionally Trained Architect to 1884." Master's thesis, University of Pennsylvania, 1994.

Widtsoe, John A. Letter to Noah S. Pond, October 30, 1946. Noah S. Pond Correspondence, 1939, 1946. CHL.

Wilcox, Keith W. *A Personal Testimony concerning the Washington Temple.* Salt Lake City, n.p., [2]–[8], CHL.

Wolsey, Heber G. Interview. Salt Lake City, 1979. CHL.

Wonders of the World: A Guide to the Masterworks of Civilization. Chicago: Rand McNally, 1991.

Wood, Sherrie Lee Martin. "A Geographic Investigation into the Purpose and Motivation of Nonresident Tourist Visits to Temple Square." Master's thesis, University of Utah, 1980.

Woodruff, Wilford. Journals and Papers, 1828–98. CHL.

Woodruff, Wilford. "Zion's Camp—Mormon Battalion—Pioneers." *Elders' Journal* 4, no. 6 (December 15, 1906): 122–30.

Woodruff, Wilford, George Q. Cannon, and Joseph F. Smith. "An Address to the Officers and Members of the Church of Jesus Christ of Latter-day Saints," March 18, 1893. CHL.

Woods, Fred E. "Perpetual Emigrating Fund." In Garr, Cannon, and Cowan, *Encyclopedia of Latter-day Saint History*, 910.

Woodward, Kenneth L. "A Mormon Moment." *Newsweek*, September 10, 2001.

Wright, Dennis A., and Rebekah E. Westrup. "Ensign Peak: A Historical Review." In Esplin and Alford, *Salt Lake City: The Place Which God Prepared*, 27–46.

Wright, Kristine. "'We Baked a Lot of Bread': Reconceptualizing Mormon Women and Ritual Objects." In *Women and Mormonism: Historical and Contemporary Perspectives*, edited by Kate Holbrook and Matthew Bowman, 82–100. Salt Lake City: University of Utah Press, 2016.

Young, Brigham. *A Series of Instructions and Remarks by President Brigham Young at a Special Council, Tabernacle, March 21, 1858.* Salt Lake City: n.p., 1858.

Young, Brigham. "The Temple Corner Stones—The Apostleship." In *Journal of Discourses*, 1:134–35.

Young, Eugene. "Inside the New Mormon Temple." *Harper's Weekly* 37 (May 27, 1893): 510.

Young, Joseph Don Carlos. Letter to Tiffany and Co., September 20, 1892. In Joseph Don Carlos Young Letterpress Copybook, 1888–93. CHL.

Young, Joseph, A. P. Rockwood, H. S. Eldredge, and John Van Cott to "Dear Brother," November 10, 1876. Hiram W. Mikesell Collection, 1836–93. CHL.

Young, Levi Edgar. "The Angel Moroni and Cyrus Dallin." *Improvement Era*, 56, no. 4 (April 1953): 234–35, 268.

Zepp, Ira G. *The New Religious Image of Urban America: The Shopping Mall as Ceremonial Center.* Westminster, MD: Christian Classics, 1986.

Zobell, Albert L., Jr. "Cyrus E. Dallin and the Angel Moroni Statue." *Improvement Era* 72, no. 4 (April 1968): 4–7.

Index

For the benefit of digital users, indexed terms that span two pages (e.g., 52–53) may, on occasion, appear on only one of those pages.

Administration Building, 127
adoptions
  ending of, 102–4
  Jane Manning James case, 141
  Nauvoo practice, 15–16
Africans. *See* Blacks
Alberta Temple
  design, 126
American Civil Liberties Union (ACLU), 171
Angell, Truman O. Jr
  conflicts over design, 77–79
  demoted, 81
  letters to John Taylor, 79–80
  makes design recommendations, 79–80
  takes over temple design, 77–78
Angell, Truman O. Sr
  conflicts over son, 78–79
  death, 81
  designates duties to son, 62
  designs St. George Temple, 61
  innovations of, 56–58
  mission to Europe, 40–41
  retirement, 49–50
  reveals temple design, 33–34, 77
  Salt Lake Temple architect, 25, 31, 32–33, 35,
    40, 47, 50–51, 52–53, 73, 74–75, 76–77, 80
Arizona Temple, 126–27
Armstrong, Frank, 62

Balderas, Eduardo, 134–35
Ballard, Melvin J.
  missionary instructions, 111–12
baptism for the dead
  Nauvoo origins, 13
  preached by Brigham Young, 61
  St. George Temple, 62
Benson, Ezra T., 33
Benson, Ezra Taft
  health of, 162
  political views, 146
Bible
  Isaiah's prophecy, 101, 169–70

Joseph Smith's revision of, 9
  prophecies related to LDS settlement, 22
Big Cottonwood Canal Company
  irrigation efforts, 40
Big Cottonwood Canyon
  temple stones quarried from, 40
Blacks
  ban on temple and priesthood participation,
    139–46
  interest in the church, 139–40
Book of Mormon
  changes to, 134
  Christ-centeredness of, 181
  distributed at World Fair, 138
  prophecies on America, 8–9
  tourist and, 108
Bossard, Gisbert
  temple photograph controversy, 119–21
Brannon, Samuel
  receives epistle, 23
Brazilian Temple
  and Black temple and priesthood ban,
    143–44
Brown, Elizabeth
  consoles Relief Society sisters, 65
Brown, Hugh B.,
  and Black temple and priesthood ban,
    142–43
Buchanan, James, 44–45
Bullock, Thomas
  reads talk at cornerstone ceremony, 28
  surveys temple block, 23

Camp Floyd, 45
Cannon, Angus M.
  plural marriage teachings, 69
Cannon, George Q.
  addresses antipolygamy efforts, 70–71
  and adoptive sealings, 103–4
  aids in temple design, 62
  criticized by Richards, 128–29
  missionary, 37

228 INDEX

Cannon, George Q (*cont.*)
  Salt Lake Temple dedication, 98, 102
  standardizes endowment ceremony, 127–28
  and temple procedures, 128
Central Pacific Railroad, 51–52
  construction of, 154
church finances, 155
Church History Museum, 153
Church Office Building, 148–49, 153–54, 179
civil rights movement, 143–44
Civil War, 47, 50, 67
Clark, J. Reuben
  called to First Presidency, 133–34
Clayton, William
  Nauvoo exodus of, 7
Compromise of 1850, 41–42
Council of Fifty, 4
Council House, 35, 39
Cowley, Matthias F.
  removed from Quorum of Twelve, 117–18
Cristus, 114, 137–38, 181

Dallin, Cyrus
  sculpts angel statue, 86
Doctrine and Covenants
  changes to, 134
Dyer, Frank, 70

Edmunds Tucker Act, 70
endowment
  ceremonial clothing publicized, 180–81
  ceremony standardized, 127–28
  film and, 135
  Nauvoo ceremony, 13–14, 15–16, 34–35
  proxy ordinance performed, 62, 158
  relationship to masonry, 13–14
  Salt Lake Temple statistics, 106
  translation of, 134–35
Endowment House
  demolition of, 71
  limits of, 60, 61, 104
  purpose of, 35–36
  statistics, 59
Ensign Peak, 21, 34–35
Equal Rights Amendment
  church stance on, 146–47
  protests over, 147–48
Evans, Richard L.
  Temple Square Mission, 114

Fairbanks, John, 82–83
Family History Library, 153, 158
First Presidency

  Equal Rights Amendment stance, 146
  temple meetings of, 130–33
Florence, Max
  temple photographs controversy, 119–21
Folsom, William H., 49–51, 79
freemasonry
  relationship to temple ordinances, 13–14,
    75–76

gathering, 37–38. *See also* immigrants
Genealogical Library. *See* Family History
    Library
Genealogical Society of Utah. *See also* Family
    History Library
  formation of, 104
Grant, Heber J.
  death of, 133–34
  Time magazine cover, 124–25
Gray, Darius
  and lifting of Black temple and priesthood ban

Hafen, John, 82–83
Hales, Robert G., 169–70
Hanks, Marion D., 160–61, 162
Hawaiian Temple, 125, 126–27, 159–60
Hinckley, Gordon B.
  conceives of smaller temples, 172–73
  encourages temple attendance, 174
  expands temple building, 173
  incorporates use of film for endowment, 135
  on lifting Black temple and priesthood ban,
    144
  media requests for, 165–66
  prophecy and the Olympics, 169
  60 Minutes interview, 165–66
  speaks at visitor's center dedication, 154
  temple centennial, 162–64
  travels to Mexico, 172–73
Hosanna Shout, 24, 97–98, 101–2
Hunter, Howard W.
  emphasizes temple worthiness, 173–74
  and role of temple, 166

immigrants
  influx of, 42, 49–50, 54
  railroad and, 51
  temple building and, 37
  temple ordinances performed for, 34–35
  tithing funds and, 38–39
Ivins, Antoine R., 134–35

James, Jane Manning
  seeks temple ordinances, 141–42

INDEX 229

Jeffs, Warren, 178
Johnson, Sonia
  ERA protests, 147–48
Johnston, Albert Sidney. *See* Utah War

Kane, Thomas L., 19, 44–45
Kelly, Kate, 172
Kimball, Heber C.
  attends cornerstone ceremony, 8
  called to First Presidency, 23–24
  returns to Winter Quarters, 23
  and temple stones, 31–32
Kimball, Spencer W.
  announces construction plans, 153
  Black temple and priesthood ban, 143–46
  health, 150
  Official Declaration 2, 134
  temple building under, 158
Kirtland Temple
  abandonment of, 12
  building of, 10–11
  dedication of, 163–64
  manifestations in, 12
  ordinances of, 11–12
  social aspects of, 13
  women and, 13, 90

Latter-day Saints
  activity rate among millennials, 176
  assimilation of, 108–9, 115–16, 124–25,
    153–54, 182
  centennial celebration, 124–25
  public image, 109–11, 115–19, 136–38, 153–
    54, 165–66
  relationship with Evangelicals, 176–77
  renewed emphasis on Christ, 181–82
  self-image, 98–99
  2002 Winter Olympics, 167–70, 176–77
Lawrence, Henry W., 70–71
Lee, Harold B.
  blesses Spencer W. Kimball, 150
Little Cottonwood Canyon
  labor at, 54
  quarries established at, 48–49, 52–54
  towns developed from, 53–54
Livingston, James Campbell
  supervises quarry, 55, 58–59
Logan Temple
  Angell conflict, 77–79
  baptismal font, 91
  site selected, 63–64
Lund, Anthon H.
  temple president, 105–6, 128

Lyman, Francis M.
  capstone ceremony, 86

Main Street Plaza
  controversies, 171–73
  plans for, 170–71
Manifesto. *See* plural marriage
Manti Temple
  site selected, 63–64
Marks, William, 29
marriage. *See* sealings
McAllister, John T., 79, 127–28
McKay, David O.
  Black protest and, 143
  called to First Presidency, 133–34
  church growth under, 140
  rededicates Salt Lake Temple, 115, 152
  temple building era of, 156–58
missionary work, 36–37
Monson, Thomas S.
  temple centennial, 162–63
Mormon Reformation, 42–43, 46
Mormon Tabernacle Choir, 136, 162,
    168
Mormons. *See* Latter-day Saints
Moroni
  Joseph Smith and, 87
  statue, 86–87
Morrill Anti-Bigamy Act, 67–68
Musser, Joseph W.
  excommunication, 117

Nadauld, Margaret D.
  on temple attendance, 174
National Association for the Advancement of
    Colored People (NAACP)
  demonstrations by, 142–43
Native Americans, 42
Nauvoo, Illinois
  Latter-day Saint exodus of, 7–8, 15–16, 17,
    18, 19–20
  settlement of, 12
Nauvoo Legion, 44–45
Nauvoo Temple
  Brigham Young and, 35–36
  building of, 12–13, 15–16, 39–40
  cornerstone ceremony at, 28–29
  design, 33–34
  destruction, 24
  ordinances in, 12, 13–14, 15–16, 28–29,
    104–5 (*see also* baptism for the dead;
    endowment; sealing)
  women and temple labor, 59, 90

230 INDEX

Nelson, Russell M.
  emphasizes proper name of church, 181
  encourages temple attendance, 174
  performs heart surgery on Spencer W.
    Kimball, 150
  and temple renovations, 182–84
New York World's Fair
  Mormon Pavilion, 136–37, 152–53
Nuttall, L. John, 127–28

Obinna, Anthony Uzodimma
  conversion, 139–40, 145–46, 148
Ordain Women, 172

Pearl of Great Price
  changes to, 134
  and temple symbolism, 75
People's Party, 70, 95–96
Perpetual Emigrating Fund, 37–38, 42. *See also*
  gathering; immigrants
persecution, 33, 66–69
plural marriage
  as ancient law, 100
  antipolygamy crusades, 67, 69–72
  B. H. Roberts and, 115–16
  curtailing of, 70–72
  dramatized, 179
  economic advantages of, 66–67
  Edmunds Tucker Act, 70
  encouraged, 69
  Manifesto of 1890, 71–72, 95, 99–100, 102,
    115–16
  and Mitt Romney campaigns, 177–78
  Mormon Reformation and, 42–43
  Morrill Anti-Bigamy Act, 67–68
  Nauvoo revelation on, 15
  opposition to, 43–44, 61, 65, 66, 67,
    69–70
  post-Manifesto, 116, 117
  raids against, 69–70
  and Reed Smoot case, 116–17
  teachings about, 66–67
  "underground," 70
politics
  controversy, 95–96
polygamy. *See* plural marriage
Pond, Allie
  visits grandfather in temple, 1–3
Pratt, Lorus, 82–83
Pratt, Orson
  delivers sermon at temple block, 22
  introduces new presidency, 24
  surveys land, 23

Pratt, Parley P.
  feels Joseph Smith's presence, 33–34
  and temples, 18
primary organization
  and temple building, 65–66
Promontory Summit. *See* Transcontinental
  Railroad
Public Communications Department
  and Homefront advertisements, 146
Public Works Department, 36, 39, 49, 55

Quorum of the Twelve
  temple meetings of, 130–33

railroads. *See* Transcontinental Railroad; Union
  Pacific Railroad; Utah Central Railroad
Raleigh, Alonzo H., 47
Red Brick Store
  ordinances performed in, 13–14, 34–35
Red Butte Canyon, 31–32, 39–40
Relief Society
  counseled amid federal prosecutions, 65
  defense of plural marriage, 66–67
  suffrage efforts, 65
  and temple labor, 59, 65–66
  Utah origins, 65
Reynolds, George
  conviction of, 67–68
Richards, Franklin D.
  Angell controversies, 78–79
  as church's public face, 70
  compiles Pearl of Great Price, 75
  on Salt Lake Temple, 98
Richards, George F.
  criticizes Cannon, 128–29
  revises ordinances and procedures,
    128–29
  Salt Lake Temple president, 106, 128
  succession procedures, 133–34
Richards, Willard
  attends cornerstone ceremony, 28
  called to First Presidency, 23–24
  reports temple groundbreaking, 25–26
Rigdon, Sidney
  Kirtland Temple dedication, 28
  succession claims of, 16, 17, 29–30
Roberts, B. H.
  election of, 115–16
Romney, George, 136, 142, 176–77
Romney, Miles, 25, 61
Romney, Mitt
  presidential runs, 166–67, 176–78
  2002 Winter Olympics, 167, 168–69

INDEX 231

St. George, Utah, 60–61, 62–63
St. George Temple
  baptismal font, 91
  Brigham Young speaks at, 61–62
  construction of, 61
  endowment ceremony standardized at,
    127–28
  partial dedication of, 61
  proposal for, 60
  setting for, 61
Salt Lake Temple. *See also* Temples; Temple
    Square
  accidents at site, 58
  angel statue, 86
  annex, 89
  antipolygamy activity at, 69–70
  architectural design, 31–33
  art, 176
  Big Love and, 179
  Black temple and priesthood ban and,
    140–42
  bombing of, 143
  brand imaging, 174–75, 179
  capstone ceremony, 81, 83–87
  centennial of, 162–64
  construction of, 39–40, 44–45, 50–51, 55–57,
    72
  construction curtailed, 40–41, 42, 47, 48–49,
    51–52
  cornerstone ceremony, 27–31, 37
  decorating interior, 89–93
  dedication, 95–102
  donations for, 88–89
  government confiscation of, 70
  groundbreaking ceremony, 25–27
  Holy of Holies, 1–2, 91–92, 129–30
  influence of, 129
  interior design, 82–83, 129–30
  and Isaiah's prophecy, 101
  laborers for, 37–38, 39, 51–52, 54–59
  meetings in, 130–33
  millennial role of, 50
  Mountain of the Lord's House, 162, 163
  open house, 93–94
  ordinance workers, 105
  patrons of, 107
  pilgrimages to, 159
  press coverage of, 93–95, 162
  priesthood blessings at, 150
  prominent leaders married at, 161
  protective role, 166
  proxy work performed at, 62
  rededication, 115, 152

renovations, 106–7, 114–15, 148–49, 151–52,
    182–83, 184–85
repairs to foundation, 47, 48
replica, 180
revelation and, 135–36
schedule, 106
site chosen, 8, 21–22, 25–26
stones, 31–32, 39–40, 48–49, 50–51, 55–57
succession deliberations, 133–34
as symbol, 6, 72–74, 75–76, 108–9, 125, 129–
    30, 148, 166–67, 169–70, 184
Temple Furnishing Committee, 89–90
temple presidents, 105–6
tourism and, 4–5, 108–11, 122, 151
2002 Winter Olympics, 167–68, 169–70,
    176–77
and US invasion, 45
wall around temple block, 39
Salt Lake Valley
  prophecies concerning, 22
  settling of, 20–21, 22, 23
sealings
  adoptive, 15, 102–4, 141
  annex and, 115
  early Utah practice, 35
  Endowment House statistics, 59–60
  initiation of, 4, 14–15
  intergenerational, 104
  Nauvoo marriage statistics, 15–16
  plural marriage and, 72
  St. George Temple and, 61, 62
Second Coming, 28, 33, 50, 158
self-reliance, 38–39
Sharp, John, 55
Sherwood, Henry G.
  surveys temple block, 23
Smith, Bathsheba W.
  temple matron, 105–6
Smith, Emma
  and Jane Manning James, 141
  succession and, 29–30
Smith, George A.
  on temple design, 33–34
  on temples, 18
Smith, George Albert
  succession to presidency, 133–34
Smith, John
  attends cornerstone ceremony, 28
Smith, Joseph
  appears in vision, 8
  Bible revision of, 9
  Council of Fifty, 4
  First Vision of, 1–2, 3, 91–93

232   INDEX

Smith, Joseph (*cont.*)
  freemasonry and, 75–76
  Moroni visits, 87
  murder of, 15–16
  plural marriage and, 15
  revelations of, 9, 10, 12–14, 27, 37–38
  and Salt Lake Temple site, 21–22
  temples built by, 4, 5–6, 7–8, 10–13
  Zion of, 3–4, 9–10
Smith, Joseph F.
  announces new temples, 126–27
  capstone ceremony, 84–86
  on Manifesto, 99–100
  missionary, 126
  post-Manifesto plural marriage, 116
  public image of, 117–19, 146, 148–49
  responds to Bossard photographs, 119
  stands as proxy, 141
  temple president, 105–6
  vision of, 134
Smith, Joseph Fielding
  presents father's vision to Council, 134
Smoot, Reed
  election and controversy, 116–17
Snow, Lorenzo
  meets granddaughter in temple, 1–2
  Salt Lake Temple dedication, 95
  succeeds to LDS presidency, 1–2, 105–6
  vision of, 1–3
Social Hall, 39
State of Deseret, 41–42. *See also* Utah
Strang, James
  succession claims of, 16
succession in presidency, 16, 133–34
Swiss Temple
  innovations and, 135

Tabernacle (new), 49–51, 111–12
Tabernacle (old), 27–28, 39
Talmage, James E.
  House of the Lord, 120, 121–22, 129–30
Tanner, N. Eldon
  describes temple meetings, 130–31
  Spencer W. Kimball health blessing, 150
Taylor, Frank Y., 79
Taylor, John
  death, 80
  in hiding, 76–77
  Jane Manning James and, 141
  responds to persecution, 68
  succeeds to church presidency, 76–77
Taylor, John W.
  removal from Quorum of Twelve, 117–18

Temple Square. *See also* Salt Lake Temple
  Assembly Hall, 111–12, 153–54
  Bureau of Information, 109–11
  Cristus, 114, 137–38
  and Latter-day Saint image, 110–11
  missionary work at, 109, 111–13
  National Historic Landmark, 114
  protests at, 147–48, 171–72
  renovations at, 152–54, 183–84
  tourism, 109–14, 122, 136, 140, 152–56
  2002 Winter Olympics, 167–69
  visitor's centers, 152–53, 154
Temples
  and antiquity, 17
  attendance encouraged, 69
  church centennial and, 125
  erected under Joseph Smith, 4
  growth and expansion, 156–59, 173
  opposition to, 64
  persecution follows plans for, 33
  planned for Zion in Missouri, 9–10
  revision of ordinances and procedures, 127–29
  rituals of, 4–5, 7–8, 11–12, 13–14, 15–16, 35,
    61, 72, 102–4, 181 (*see also* baptism for the
    dead; endowment; sealings)
  Second Coming and, 28, 33
  violence and, 17, 143
  women and, 13–14, 90
Thomas, T. P., 55–56
tithing
  General Tithing Office, 31–32, 38–39
  labor for, 57–58
  Mormon Reformation and, 42–43
  Nauvoo Temple and, 12–13
  public works and, 38, 58–59
  storehouses, 47, 51
  Temple building and, 36–37
Transcontinental Railroad
  construction of, 51–52
  effects of, 59
transportation
  for temple stone, 39–40
2002 Winter Olympics
  LDS presence at, 167–70, 176–77

Union Pacific Railroad, 51–52, 93
United Order, 62–64
Utah
  federal officials and, 43–44
  population, 70
  statehood, 115–16
  territorial government, 41–42
  US invasion of, 44–46, 47

INDEX   233

Utah Central Railroad, 52
Utah War, 44–46, 47

Ward, William
  interview, 81
  and Salt Lake Temple architecture, 31, 32–33,
    73–74, 75
Washington, DC Temple, 157, 159
Weeks, William, 25
Weggeland, Dan, 82–83
Wells, Daniel H., 36, 40, 42, 48, 55
Winter Quarters, 18–20, 23
women
  decorating temple interior, 90
  Relief Society, 59, 65–67
Woodruff, Wilford
  adoptive sealings, 103, 141
  on Brigham Young, 64
  capstone ceremony speech, 84
  death of, 1–2, 133–34
  and Latter-day Saint parallels with ancient
    Israel, 99
  and Manifesto, 70–72, 99–100
  on proxy temple work, 60
  revelation of, 101–2
  Salt Lake Temple dedication, 95
  Salt Lake Temple design, 80
  Salt Lake Temple site, 21
  on settling in the West, 20
  standardizes temple ordinance language, 62,
    127–28
  vision of, 68
  visits settlements, 68
  on worthiness, 98

Young, Brigham
  arrives in Salt Lake Valley, 20–21
  assigns missionaries, 36–37
  Black temple and priesthood ban, 140–41
  chooses Salt Lake Temple site, 8, 21–22
  cornerstone ceremony at temple site, 27–29
  death of, 64
  on economy, 59
  Ensign Peak and, 21
  groundbreaking at temple site, 25–27

on labor for temple, 51
leads saints to the west, 20–21
Nauvoo Temple and, 15–16
on "order of the priesthood," 30
oversees temple construction repairs, 48
predictions on temple completion, 50
press coverage of, 94–95
proposes Saint George Temple, 60
on purpose of temple, 3
and railroad contracts, 51, 52
reorganizes First Presidency, 23–24
returns to Winter Quarters, 23
revelation of, 19–20
self-reliance efforts, 38–39
speaks at St. George Temple, 61–62
spiritual rejuvenation efforts, 62–63
standardizes Temple ordinance language, 62
on succession, 16
teachings of, 30
on temple design, 31–32, 90–91
and temple symbolism, 73–74, 75, 76
territorial governor, 41–42, 44
and Union Pacific Railroad, 52
United Order of, 62–64
and US invasion, 44–46
vision of, 8, 21–22, 74–75
Young, Brigham Jr., 127–28
Young, Don Carlos
  capstone ceremony, 84–86
  designs Administration Building, 127
  designs temple annex, 89, 152
  designs temple interior, 82, 91–92
Young, George Q. Cannon
  on LDS portrayal of Christ, 114
Young, Zina D. H.
  stands as proxy, 141
  temple matron, 105–6

ZCMI Center, 155–56
Zion
  Joseph Smith and, 3–4, 9–10
  return to, 50
  as a society, 67
Zion's Cooperative Mercantile Institution
  (ZCMI), 89–90, 155